IMAGES
of America

THE SPRINGS
RESORT TOWNS OF SONOMA VALLEY

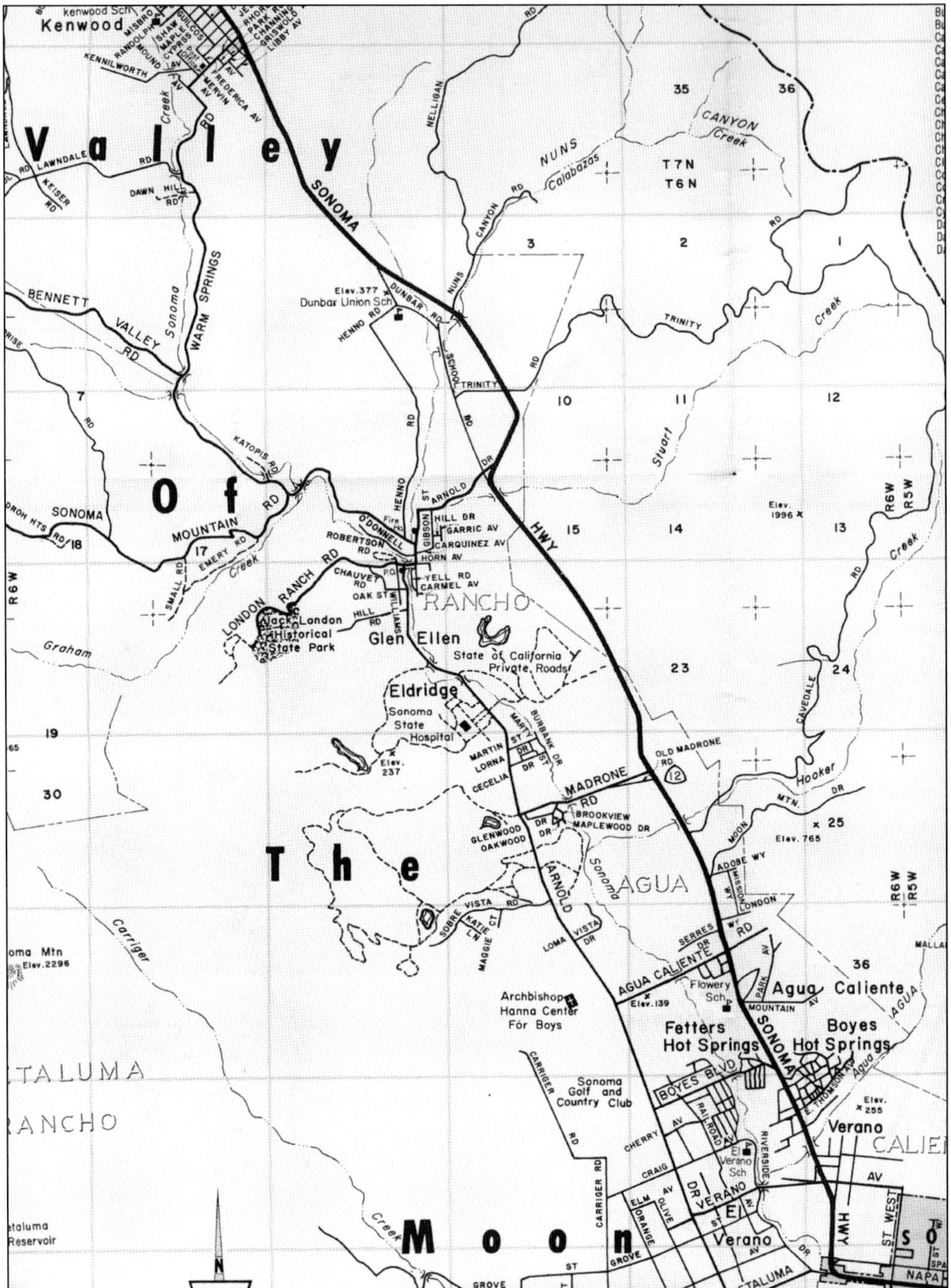

The Sonoma Valley Chamber of Commerce created this map in 1962. (Author's collection.)

On the Cover: The Baths at Boyes Hot Springs were roaring in the 1920s. Thousands of people visited on any given weekend during the summer, many of them arriving by automobile, even though the railroad was then the most convenient way to travel to the Sonoma Valley. (Author's collection.)

IMAGES
of America

THE SPRINGS
RESORT TOWNS OF SONOMA VALLEY

Michael Acker

ARCADIA
PUBLISHING

ISBN 978-1-4671-2430-0

Published by Arcadia Publishing
Charleston, South Carolina

Printed in the United States of America

Library of Congress Control Number: 2016950073

For all general information, please contact Arcadia Publishing:
Telephone 843-853-2070
Fax 843-853-0044
E-mail sales@arcadiapublishing.com
For customer service and orders:
Toll-Free 1-888-313-2665

Visit us on the Internet at www.arcadiapublishing.com

This book is dedicated to the memory of Diane Moll Smith, who, as director of the Depot Park Museum in Sonoma and as my friend, took me seriously, encouraged me, and marveled with me over the many fascinating details of the history of our valley.

It is also dedicated to the Sonoma Valley Historical Society—Diane Moll Smith's lifelong love and my essential resource.

Contents

Acknowledgments

In my early investigations of the history of the Springs, the help and encouragement of Diane Moll Smith, of the Depot Park Museum in Sonoma, was most important. Since Diane's sad passing, Sandi Hansen and Patricia Cullinan, both from the museum and the Sonoma Valley Historical Society, have continued to render invaluable assistance. I hope Robert Parmelee will allow me to consider him a mentor. His example and his help are wonderful. Historian Lynn Downey has lent me the benefit of her professional advice and knowledge of the Arcadia Publishing process, which was crucial in giving me the confidence to write this book.

Thanks are due to collectors Gordon Lindberg, James Berry, Marti Kramer, Jeff Gilbert, and Gary Heon. Katherine Rinehart of the Sonoma County Library has also been important to this project.

To the people of the Springs*, thank you for your passion about the place we call home, and thank you for your encouragement and approval.

Unless otherwise noted, all images are courtesy of the author's personal collection.

**Some controversy has arisen about the name. Some people feel it robs the towns of their individuality. It has been in use as a collective term since at least the 1930s. Whenever it is necessary for clarity, I always use the separate names. I live in the Springs (where, exactly? in Boyes Hot Springs), not Sonoma.*

Introduction

Sonoma Valley, also known as the Valley of the Moon, is located about 45 miles north and east of the Golden Gate Bridge. The original Miwok inhabitants of the area called their village Wukiliwa, which combines the Miwok words for fire and water. This name was adopted by Spanish and Mexican colonizers, who translated it as "Agua Caliente."

In 1836, Ignacio Pacheco, a sergeant in the Mexican army, was granted the Rancho Agua Caliente by the government of Mexico. He deemed it "unfit for agriculture" and traded it back for land in what became Marin County. He is believed to have been the first person to plant grapes there, and the part of Novato that is now called Ignacio was named after him.

European settlement of what has come to be known as the Springs area of Sonoma Valley began in earnest in July 1840, when Lazaro Piña was granted the 50,000-acre Rancho Agua Caliente. Piña built an adobe house finished with wood and was establishing his homestead when war broke out with the United States and he was drafted into the Mexican army.

After Piña died in the United States' invasion of Mexico in 1846, his heirs were not able to defend their title to the land in United States courts. In the years between 1860 and 1880, parts of the rancho were claimed by Joseph Hooker (who became a noted Union army general in the Civil War), Mariano G. Vallejo, M.K. Cady, and Thaddeus M. Leavenworth, among others.

In 1846, Vallejo deeded 1,000 acres of his portion of the rancho to Andrew Hoeppner, a music master, in exchange for piano lessons for Vallejo's children. Hoeppner became the first person to commercially develop the hot springs. In 1847, he advertised his Annenthal warm springs in the *Daily Alta California* (San Francisco) newspaper with the tagline "No More Rheumatism!"

Thaddeus M. Leavenworth came to California in 1847 with Stevenson's Regiment of New York Volunteers, raised to fight in the Mexican War. (The regiment's secondary purpose was to provide permanent settlers for California after the conquest.) During his tumultuous and controversial tenure as alcalde (the head executive under Mexican rule) of San Francisco from 1847 to 1849, he gained a reputation for less than honest dealings in real estate.

With Leavenworth's welcome in the City by the Bay worn out, he moved to Sonoma Valley, quite literally looking for greener pastures. Sometime in 1849, he acquired 320 acres of the Rancho Agua Caliente—a parcel that included the present-day Agua Caliente, Fetters Hot Springs, Boyes Hot Springs, and part of Maxwell Farm.

A few years later, the title to this parcel was disputed. The dispute went to the US Land Commission, which was set up by the federal government after the Mexican War to decide ownership of former Mexican land grants. Leavenworth's claim on the 320 acres of land—also claimed by Mariano G. Vallejo—was approved in 1860. According to local historian Robert Parmelee, "Apparently Leavenworth had better-appearing forged documents than his adversary."

In 1883, Capt. Henry E. Boyes, a retired British naval officer, arrived in Sonoma Valley with his wife, Antoinette. During their search for a genteel and healthful retreat, Leavenworth persuaded them to buy 110 boggy acres of his 320-acre tract, which happened to include a hot spring. Unfortunately, the naive Boyes had fallen prey to a scheme that Leavenworth had perfected in San Francisco; the title to the land Captain Boyes paid for was already held by someone else. Only after years in court did Boyes gain clear title to the land.

Wiser but undeterred, Boyes and his business partners set about trying to capitalize on his asset. Their first attempt, the Agua Rica Hot Sulphur Springs Association, was incorporated in 1895 but did not attract investors. In 1901, they tried again with the Boyes Hot Springs Corporation and were successful enough to build guest cottages, a clubhouse, a hotel, and a 75-foot-by-100-foot swimming pool (this became the Boyes Bath House).

The existence of the hot springs was apparently forgotten over time. An 1889 article in the *Sonoma Index-Tribune* states that, "It may not be generally known, but it is nevertheless a fact that there exists in the valley a hot mineral spring, the curative powers of which are remarkable. This spring, the waters of which are now running to waste, is located on Agua Rica Farm, two miles northwest of Sonoma, the property of Mr. and Mrs. Boyes." This statement is curious, as the Agua Caliente Springs was advertising in the paper at the time.

Boyes sold his interest in the resort in 1902 and built a grand house called El Mirador on a nearby knoll. Capt. Henry and Antoinette Boyes left the valley for San Diego in 1913. Boyes Hot Springs continued to prosper, and a post office was established there in 1911.

As early as 1909, real estate developers were platting residential subdivisions and selling building lots. By 1927, there were 22 subdivisions in the Springs, with names such as Boyes Hot Springs Park, Woodleaf Park, Fetters Springs Terrace, and Agua Caliente. In 1918, a small lot in Boyes Hot Springs Park Subdivision A was sold for $10 in gold; the deed contained covenants that prevented the new owner from establishing a gambling casino, saloon, or other "house of amusement."

The Boyes Bath House was enlarged under the management of Rudy G. Lichtenberg and Robert Parramore, and it remained the premier destination in Sonoma Valley for decades. Generations of Sonomans learned to swim in its huge pool.

Much of Boyes Hot Springs, including Boyes's resort, was destroyed in September 1923 by a disastrous fire that spread from the north. The next day, the *Sonoma Index-Tribune* headline read: "Boyes Hot Springs, Famous Summer Resort, Leveled by Flames." As an indication of the resiliency of the people, the subhead read: "Hot Springs Hotel Will Be Rebuilt." Among the buildings listed as destroyed were the cottages of J.W. Minges, the "mayor" of Boyes Hot Springs (which was not incorporated as a city), who said, "Boyes will rise from the ashes again! Fire cannot rob us of our mineral springs, our climate, and the whole-souled people who abide here, no siree!"

In 1927, a new hotel, which became the Sonoma Mission Inn, was built on the site of Boyes's original hotel. Its fortunes were up and down. It thrived through World War II, when it was under the control of the Navy and became a rest haven for members of the armed services. After the war, it became a residential hotel for a time, going through several owners. Today, the Fairmont Sonoma Mission Inn & Spa is a premier wine country resort.

The success of the Boyes Hot Springs resort, owned and operated by Henry and Antoinette Boyes, proved to be an example to others. In 1907, a couple from Pennsylvania by way of San Francisco—George and Emma Fetters—bought an old ranch a mile north of the Boyes property. The next year, they opened Fetters Hot Springs Resort. Soon after, they leased their resort to Morris Levy, who renamed it Eleda Hot Springs. The Fetters took over operation again in 1911.

The prominence of Agua Caliente Springs is captured by an 1889 article in the *Sonoma Index-Tribune* that read, in part:

> The famous health-giving springs, delightful location and basalt block interests of this progressive little village is destined at no distant day to make it a place of considerable importance. The town was laid out a little over a year ago by M.K. Cady, one of Sonoma Valley's most energetic and public-spirited men. The railroad runs through the place which boasts of an express office, post office, schoolhouse, hotel general merchandising store, butcher shop, and a blacksmiths shop. During the spring and summer months the Agua Caliente Springs Hotel is crowded with health and pleasure seekers who come to lave in its health restoring water and bask in never failing sunshine and balmy breezes. An Episcopal Church will be erected in Agua Caliente this summer.

The Agua Caliente Hotel, under the management of M.K. Cady, opened in the summer of 1885. In 1886, the *Index-Tribune* reported that "The Agua Caliente Hotel, Having been enlarged and refurbished, is now one of the most elegant and attractive summer and winter resorts on the coast." In 1887, the *Index-Tribune* informed readers that "The new swimming baths at the Agua Caliente Warm Springs are completed and now open to the public. They are the largest and best appointed mineral baths in the state. The water of these springs are of delightful temperature for bathing and their curative properties are highly endorsed by our leading physicians." This was well before Boyes commercialized his springs, though he and his wife were living in the valley at that time.

The "new" Agua Caliente Hotel—the stone edifice that exits today—was built in 1916. In August 1886, the Agua Caliente Post Office was established; it was the first post office between Sonoma and Glen Ellen. Mrs. C.F. Badger was appointed postmistress, and lockboxes cost 15¢ per month.

El Verano was established by George H. Maxwell and partners in 1887 as a real estate venture. Elaborate maps of the development were published, and well-known photographer Carlton Watkins was hired to make a series of photographs to promote the town. Maxwell soon went broke, however, and the area languished amidst a series of lawsuits brought by unhappy investors. El Verano, as a place name, is older than either Boyes Hot Springs or Fetters; both were once considered to be part of El Verano.

Despite Maxwell's financial difficulties, the natural beauty of the site remained a draw, and several of the area's most prominent resorts were established in El Verano, including Parente's, Paul's, El Verano Villa, and the Bellevue Hotel. El Verano also had an imposing railroad station that was demolished in the 1980s and replaced by the offices of the Valley of the Moon Water District.

The El Verano Post Office was founded in the 1890s and remains the heart of the community. The El Verano Inn, which began as Mullens Store in 1887, was recently lovingly restored and still functions as a tavern and music venue.

There would have been no resort era in Sonoma Valley without the railroads. The first railroads came into Sonoma Valley in the 1860s. Fifteen railroad companies were in business in the area during the 19th century, with some running narrow-gauge track and one—the Sonoma Valley Prismoidal Railway—using a unique monorail system.

By 1889, there were two railroads serving Sonoma Valley and the Springs and running on opposite sides of Sonoma Creek: the Santa Rosa & Carquinez on the east side and the San Francisco & North Pacific on the west side. Confusingly, the Santa Rosa & Carquinez went through the town of Verano, on the east side, while the San Francisco & North Pacific went through El Verano, just across the creek. The San Francisco & North Pacific became the Northwestern Pacific Railroad in 1907. The Santa Rosa & Carquinez was taken over by Southern Pacific in 1898.

For decades, the train was the most popular way for tourists to reach the resorts of the Springs, but in the 1920s, the railroads began to face competition from buses and automobiles. In 1921, the Northwestern Pacific Railroad was compelled to upgrade its fleet to meet customers' demands for speed and comfort.

In 1925, the Northwestern Pacific Railroad built a new depot in Boyes Hot Springs to replace the one lost in the fire of 1923. The *Sonoma Index-Tribune* reported that it was "of the uniform suburban type, rustic finish and cement floors. . . . The improvements are warmly welcomed by residents of the Springs who are taking great pride in the rebuilding of this popular section of Sonoma Valley." By 1930, stations on the Northwestern Pacific Railroad line began to be eliminated. The first to go was Glen Ellen. Boyes Hot Springs was threatened but managed to remain until 1942, when all the rails were torn up and used in the war effort.

In May 1937, the Golden Gate Bridge opened Marin County to development—and Sonoma Valley to the car-driving tourist. The towns of the Springs continued to thrive as resort destinations and as local business centers.

Mid-century growth and prosperity was in full swing by 1949, when Edith and Robert Lanning put in a new dance hall addition at their Resort Club located on the east side of the highway near Central Avenue. The new owners of the Fetters resort gave it a new look with a cocktail lounge with a circular bar. "Slim" Mayes built a new garage in Agua Caliente. The All-Girl Thrill Riders performed on the Fourth of July at the Boyes Ball Park. The Boyes Food Center opened. The Boyes Hot Springs Booster Club held a street dance at the Boyes Plaza. In February, the San Francisco Seals baseball team, featuring Lefty O'Doul, arrived for training.

By the 1950s, commerce had become more vital in the Springs. Mary Fazio opened her first Pizza Shack—in a true shack—in 1959. L.E. "Bud" Castner, a prominent real estate agent and investor, became a director of the Golden Gate Bridge District. Alexander "Zan" Stark operated the local *Valley of the Moon Daily Review* newspaper and made wonderful real-photo postcards. Pine Wagner continued her career as a pharmacist. The Gallo brothers were selling cars. The Boyes Bath House, then managed by Bill Johnson, remained a central attraction. The Valley of the Moon Water District formed in 1960.

A downturn began in 1969, the year the Boyes Bath House burned down. Plans to revive the resort never came to fruition. The Fetters Hotel was destroyed by fire in 1975, while Juanita Musson was a resident there; a few cabins were all that remained. The rest of the site was vacant into the 2000s.

In the 1970s, the Sonoma Mission Inn went up for sale for $100,000. The area's charming old summer homes, many of which had been converted for year-round use, were not selling.

In 1985, the Sonoma County Redevelopment Agency came to the Springs. The program, funded by property taxes, was meant to eradicate the blight in the area. The first order of business was to install sidewalks and streetlights. This effort came to a standstill until a group of community members banded together as the Verano-Springs Association in 1992 to pressure the government to act. In 2010, the first phase of the sidewalk project was completed, and—at long last—in 2016, the sidewalk and streetlight project was finished.

In 1996, area real estate values hit bottom, then rising prices in San Francisco and Silicon Valley drove many buyers north. One by one, new owners of the old homes of the Springs began to renovate and improve.

Sadly, historic buildings such as the Clementi Inn in Agua Caliente have been lost, but some have been saved and now house businesses.

Major new construction includes the Fetters Apartments on the former site of the Fetters Hot Springs Resort. The complex is being built by MidPen Housing and contains affordable housing and a community garden. The Fairmont Sonoma Mission Inn & Spa continues to be a prestigious destination. In 2016, there was even talk of a new Boyes Plaza, although the All-Girl Thrill Riders—who performed there in 1949 for the supposed centennial of the founding of Boyes Hot Springs—may not be available for the entertainment.

One

In Hot Water from the Beginning

California was colonized by Spain, then became part of Mexico, and in 1846, it was conquered by the United States under the concept of Manifest Destiny. California was a desirable prize for many reasons, even before gold was discovered in the area. Few may have known it at the time, but the hot springs of Sonoma Valley were among those prizes.

It is likely that the native inhabitants of the Valley of the Moon enjoyed the geothermal waters for centuries prior to the arrival of Europeans. During the Mexican period, there was some attempt to commercialize the hot springs, but it was not until later in the 19th century that the area became a fully developed resort destination.

The arrival of the railroads in the 1860s brought real estate developers and resort entrepreneurs to the area, followed by crowds of bathers and vacationers. During this period, the names Henry Boyes, George and Emma Fetters, Thaddeus M. Leavenworth, George Maxwell, and M.K. Cady came into the area's history alongside Mariano Vallejo and the rest of the Sonoma pantheon. The resorts accumulated in the dozens, from single cottages to grand hotels. Stores, taverns, and tradesmen proliferated to serve the visitors. Post offices were founded, and Wells Fargo served the area.

From the 1880s until well into the 20th century, the Sonoma Valley thrived. Resorts' main clientele consisted of middle-class families from San Francisco escaping the summer fog.

Fortunately, many postcards were published in this time. Along with a few photographs, these postcards offer students of history an enduring image of the resort life and environment in the early days of the Springs.

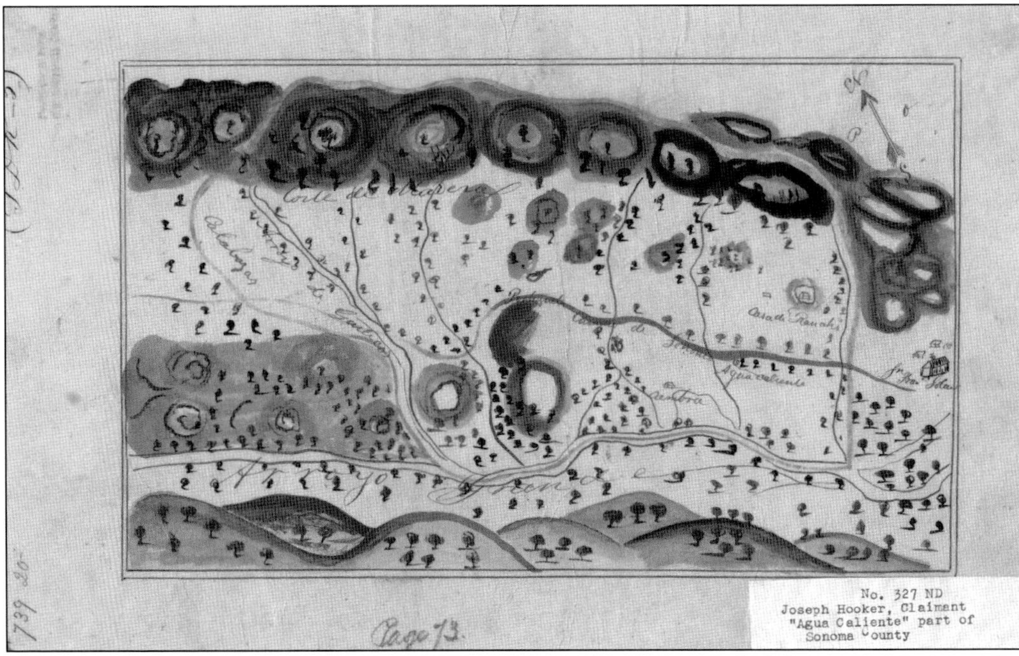

What is now called the Springs was, under Mexican rule, known as Rancho Agua Caliente. After the Mexican-American War of 1846–1848, California became a state in 1850, and land claims were thrown into dispute. *Diseños* (hand-drawn topographical maps) were used in court cases to decide ownership of tracts. This *diseño* featuring Agua Caliente was used to support the land claim of Joseph Hooker. (Courtesy of the Bancroft Library, University of California, Berkeley.)

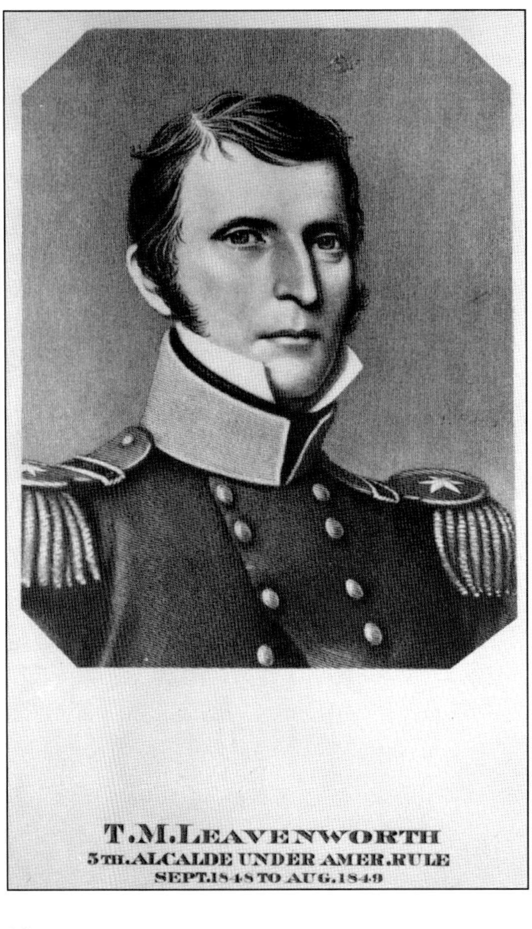

Thaddeus M. Leavenworth came to California in 1847 with Col. Jonathan Stevenson's 1st Regiment of New York Volunteers as regimental chaplain. After the end of the war with Mexico, he settled in San Francisco, soon becoming an alcalde—the chief civic officer under Mexican law. He decamped for Sonoma Valley in 1849.

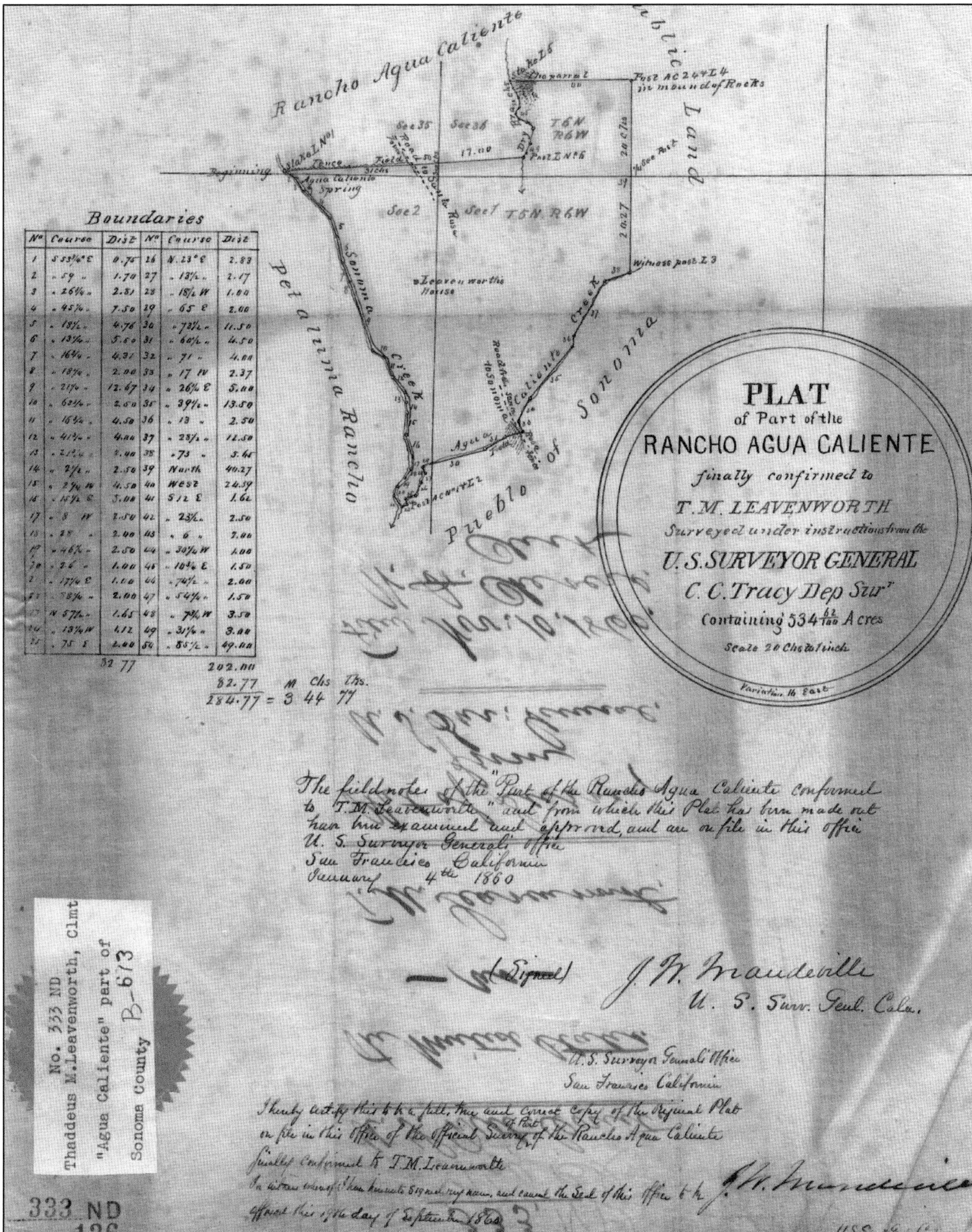

This is a "Plat of Part of the Rancho Agua Caliente finally confirmed to T.M. Leavenworth" in 1860, after decades in US district court. The plat is bounded on the west by Sonoma Creek and on the east by Agua Caliente Creek. It consisted of 534 acres. Thaddeus Leavenworth's land encompassed what is now Boyes Hot Springs, Agua Caliente, Fetters Hot Springs, El Verano, and Maxwell Park. He "sold" a portion of it to Henry Boyes in 1882, although the land was already owned by someone else. Boyes also spent years in court before his title cleared. This kind of land fraud was common in California in the years just after it became a state. (Courtesy of the Bancroft Library, University of California, Berkeley.)

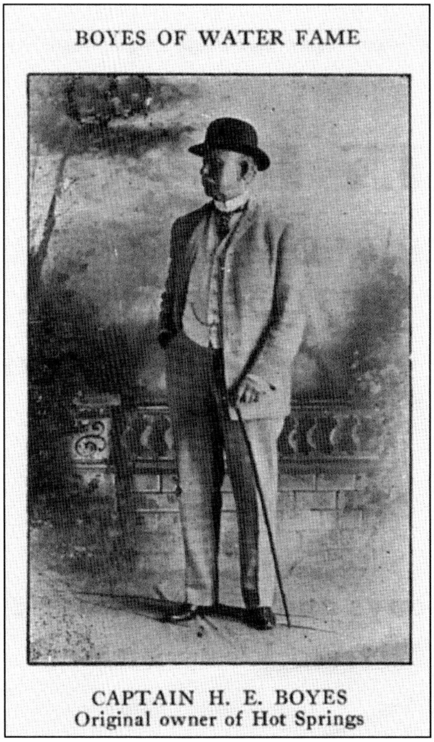

Capt. Henry E. Boyes was born in Hull, Yorkshire, England, on July 13, 1844. In 1858, he entered the Indian navy as a midshipman and was stationed at Bombay, remaining in India for about four years before serving on a troop ship and sailing to different ports around the world. He met his wife, Antoinette, while traveling in Switzerland, and they married in 1883. They came to California that same year. (Courtesy of the Sonoma Valley Historical Society.)

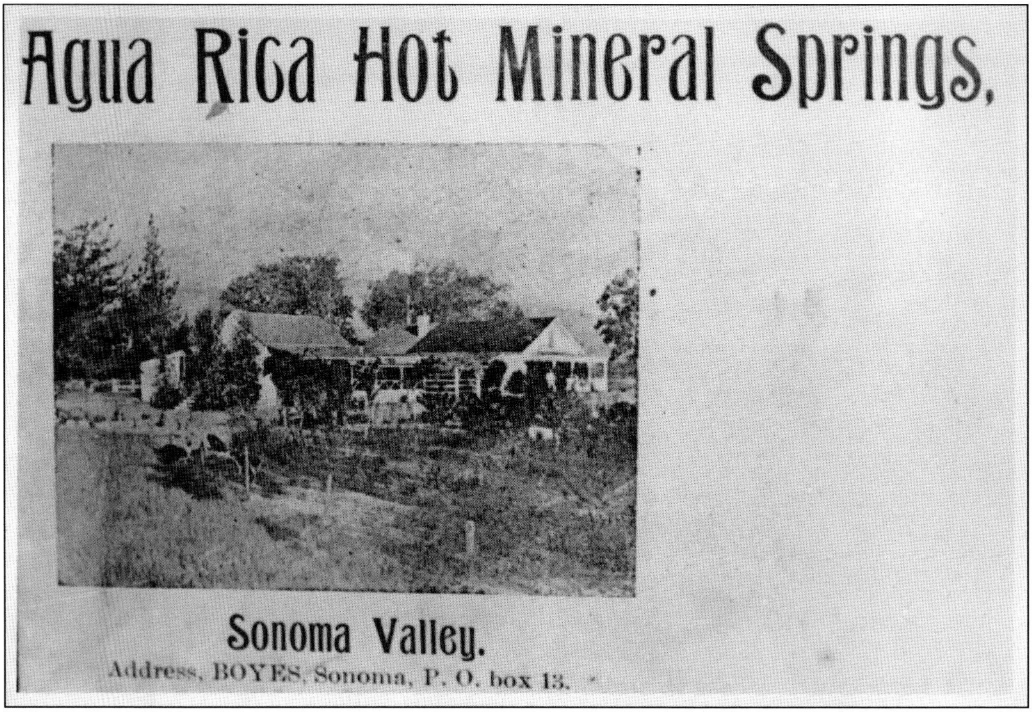

Henry Boyes incorporated his first Sonoma Valley resort, Agua Rica Hot Mineral Springs, in 1885. The land he bought from Thaddeus M. Leavenworth is shown on the official plat as having a house, which may be the one shown on this postcard. (Courtesy of Robert Parmelee.)

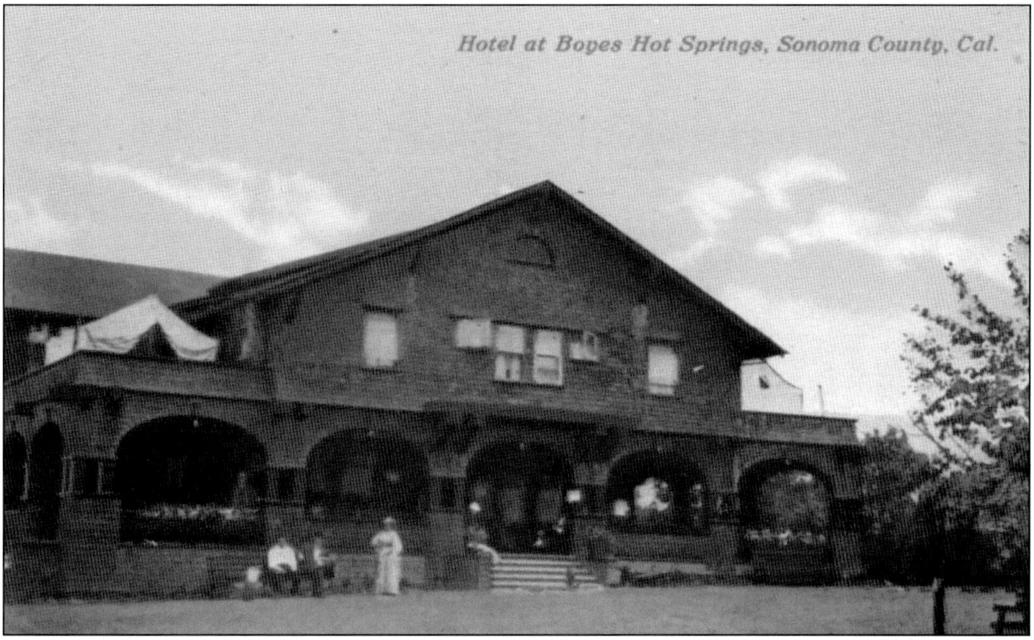

In 1902, the Boyes Hot Springs Corporation built its hotel adjacent to the hot springs on the land Henry E. Boyes purchased from Thaddeus M. Leavenworth. It became the center of the burgeoning resort communities of the Valley of the Moon.

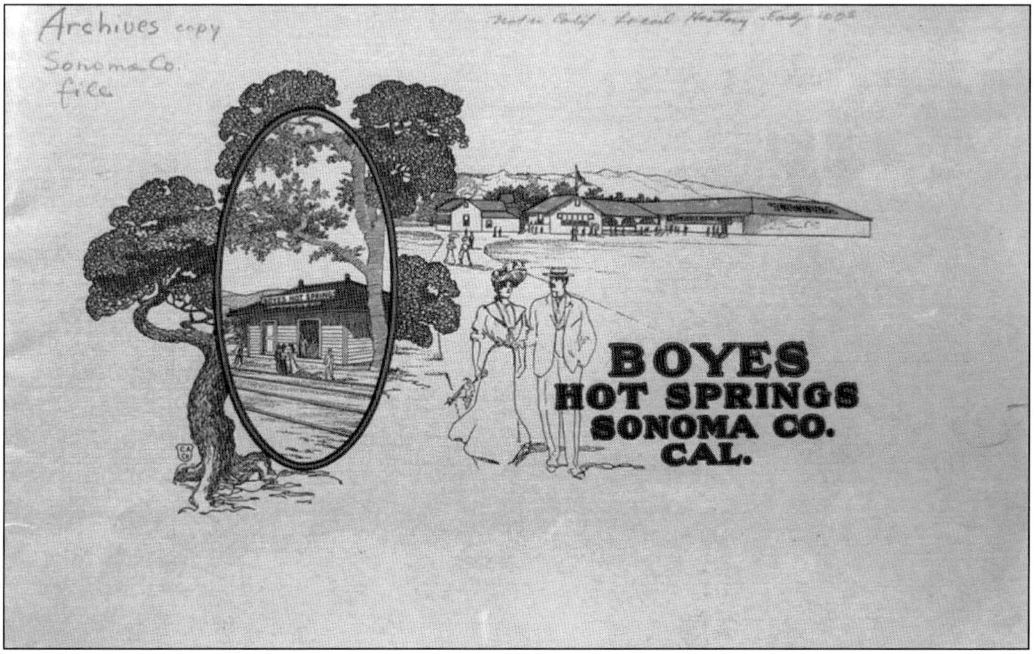

By the 1910s, the Boyes Hot Springs resort was issuing these elegant brochures. This cover page features the railroad depot framed by twisting oak trees and a somewhat fanciful drawing of the hotel and bathhouse in the background. Strolling vacationers are dressed in the latest fashions. An advertisement in the *San Francisco Call* in 1912 advised people to "send for booklet." (Courtesy of the Sonoma County Library.)

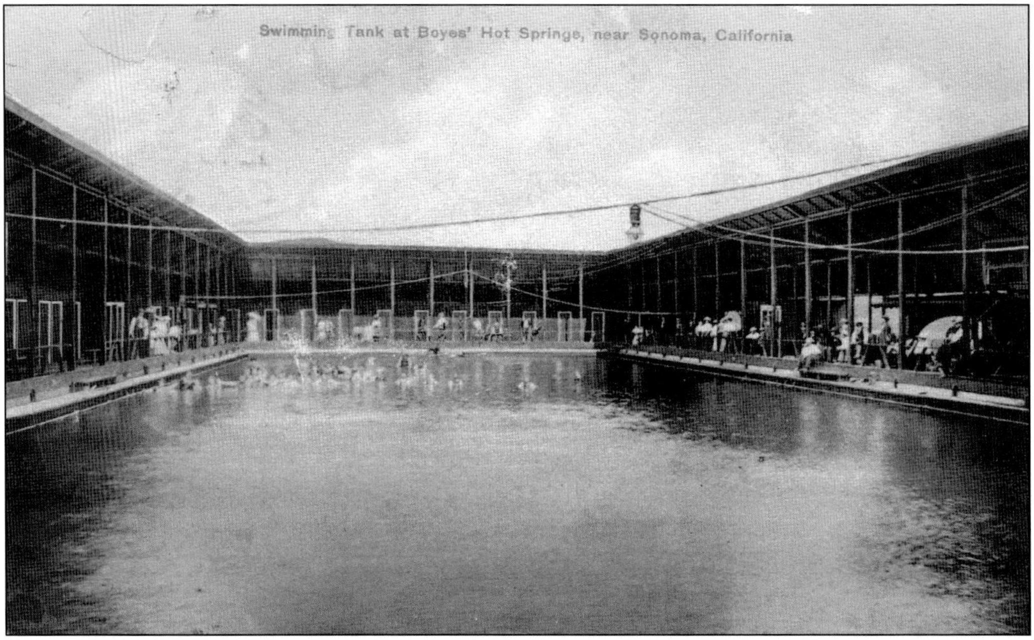

Taking the waters was what it was all about. The Boyes Hot Springs resort's large pool, shown on this 1910 postcard, measured 100 feet by 75 feet. It survived until the bathhouse burned down in 1969.

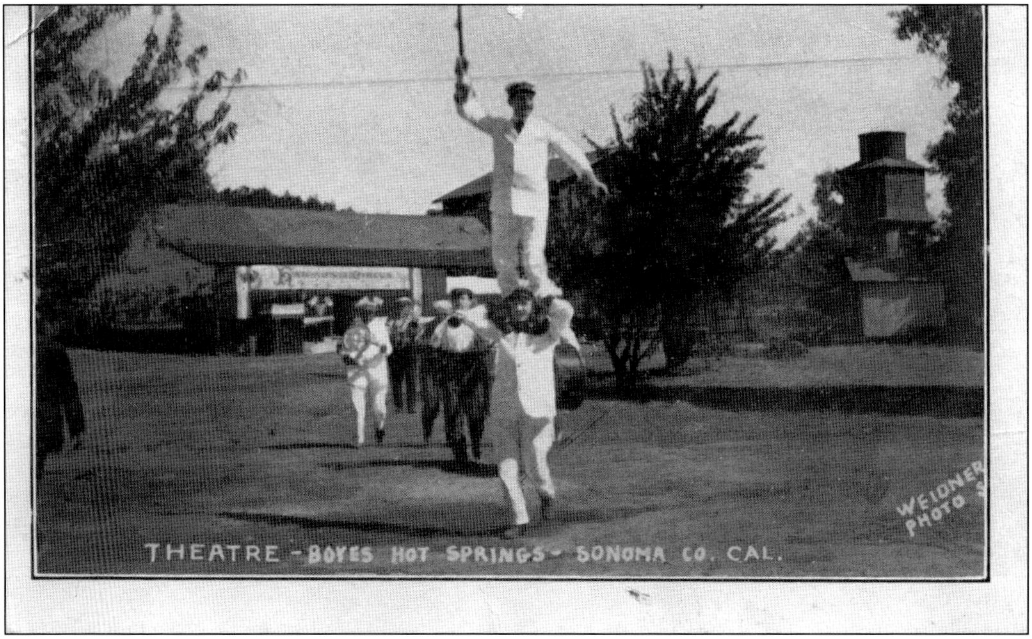

When "taking the waters," what does one do after getting one's fill? Dancing, plays, movies, and other entertainments were plentiful in the early days of Boyes Hot Springs.

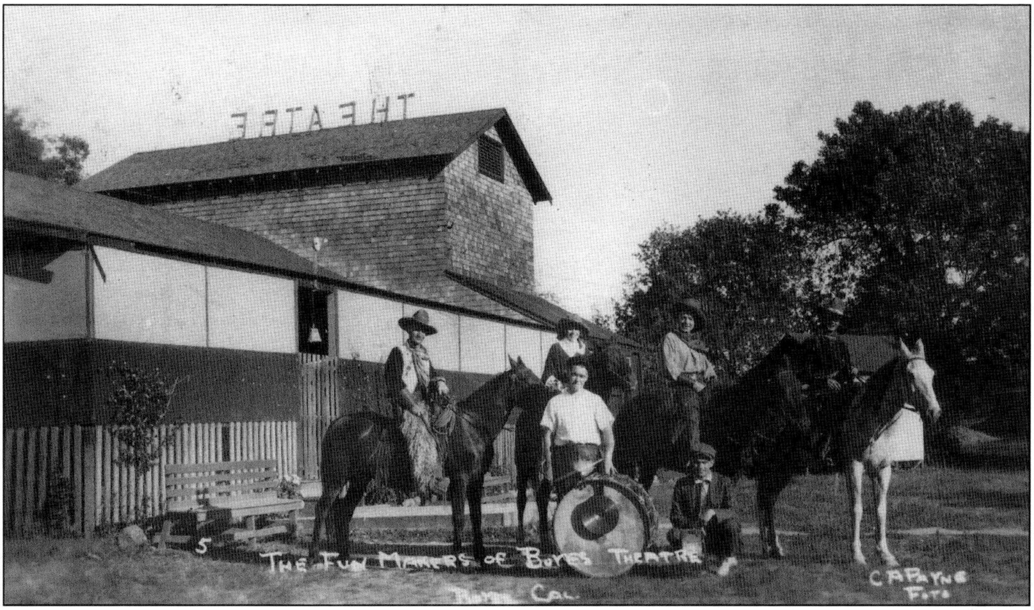

Après bath entertainment was provided by the Fun Makers. Were they horseback artists? The answer to this question is lost to history. Whatever they did, it clearly involved percussion. (Courtesy of the Sonoma Valley Historical Society.)

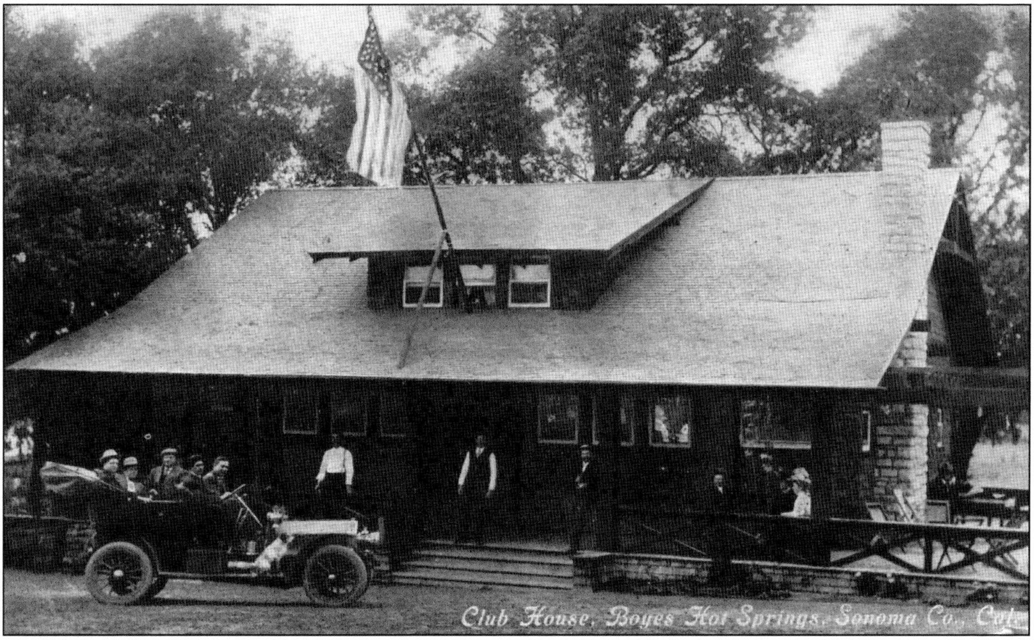

When this postcard was mailed in 1909, the Boyes Hot Springs Club House was well established. It was located in the vicinity of the railroad depot and "business district" of Boyes. It had a bar where visitors could sample the talents of "mixologists," a term in use at that time, and was a popular venue for public meetings and parties.

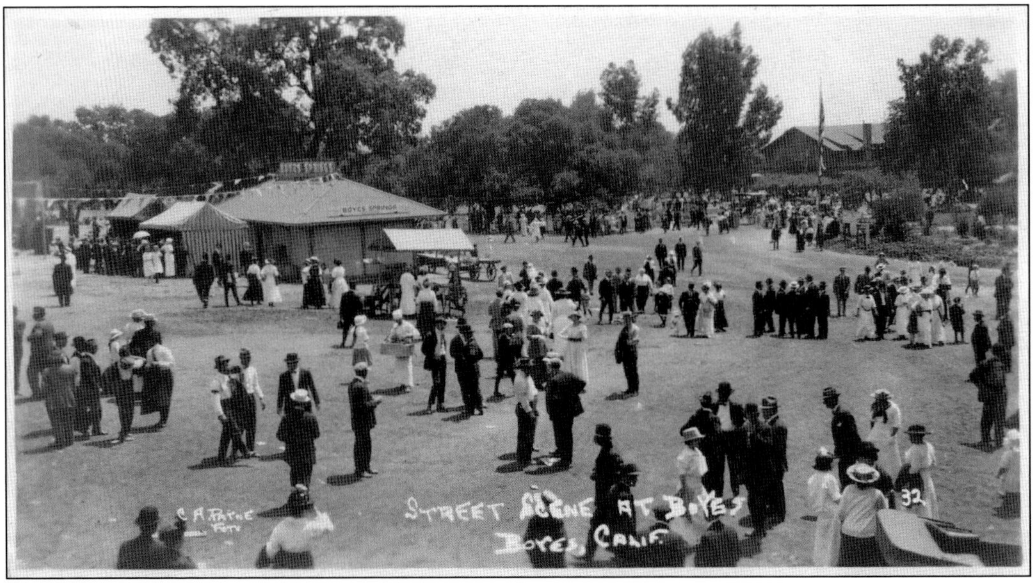

Although this photograph is labeled "Street Scene at Boyes," there is not a street in sight. This casual congregation of well-dressed "vacationists," as they were called, is shown strolling and standing in groups on the grassy expanse surrounding the depot. Tents—perhaps housing vendors of refreshments—with pennants flying overhead have been set up on the east side of the depot. A small sign near the flagpole reads "To the Baths."

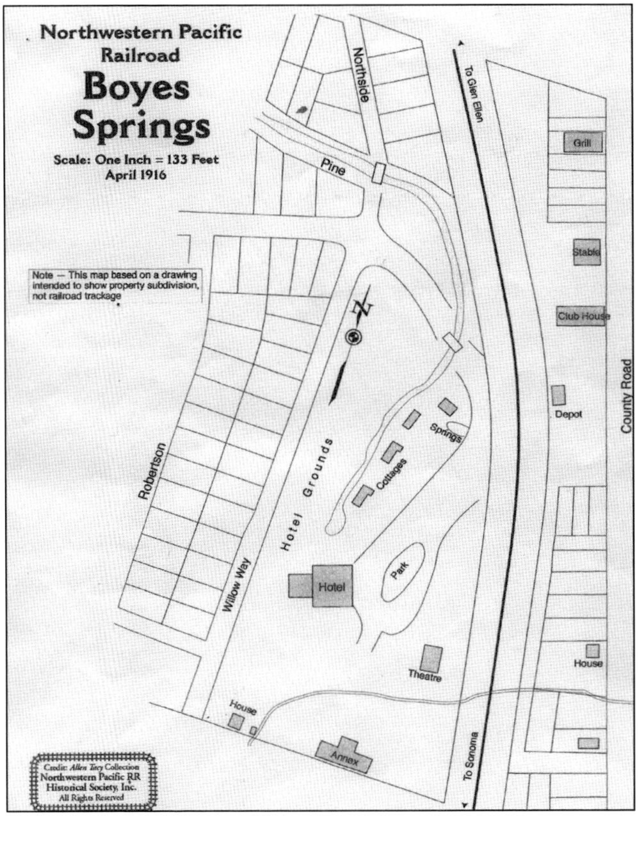

This map from 1916 shows the exact relationships of the prominent buildings of Boyes Hot Springs, noting the locations of the depot, hotel, theater, and clubhouse. At top right is Sam's Grill (see the top of page 52); that building still exists today. An interesting feature to note is the canal that ran from the hotel grounds down Pine Street. (Courtesy of the Northwestern Pacific Railroad Historical Society.)

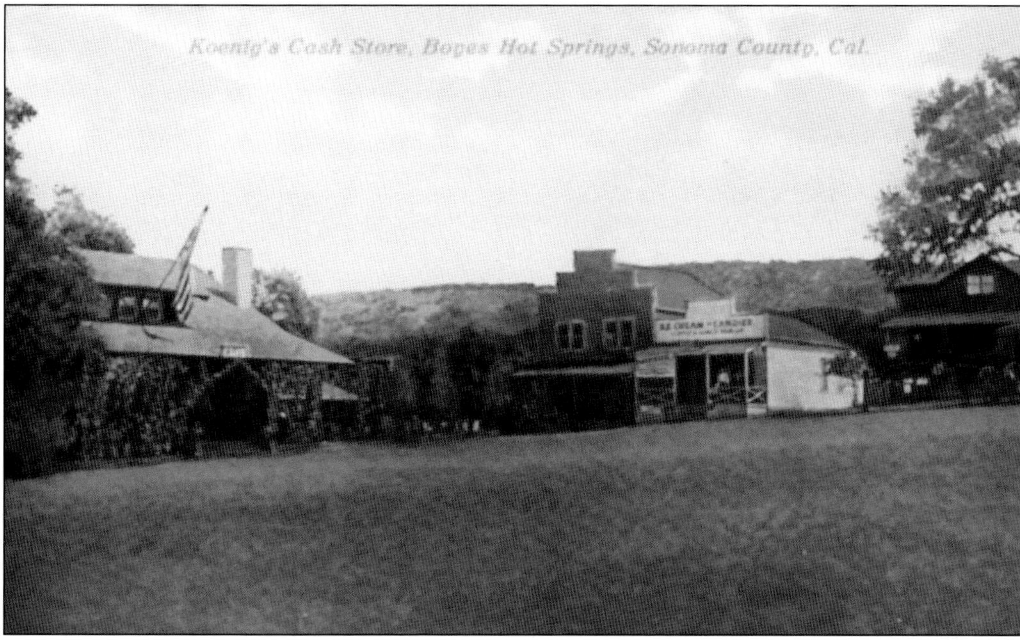

Koenig's Cash Store was a central feature of "downtown" Boyes Hot Springs around 1910. At far right is Graham's Cash Store, the first location of the Boyes Hot Springs post office. At left is the Boyes Hot Springs Club House. (Courtesy of Robert Parmelee.)

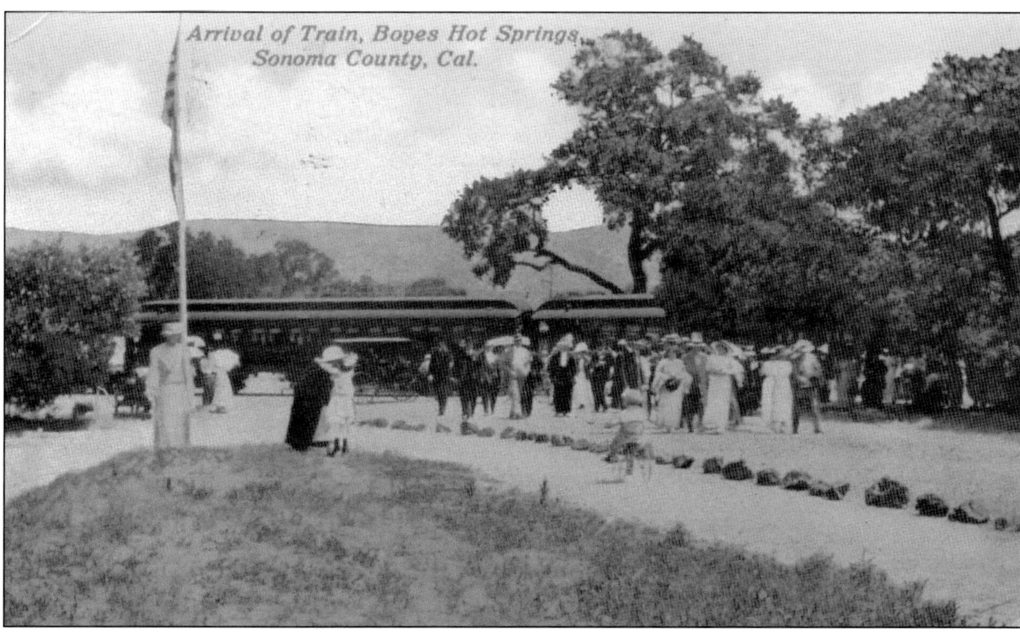

This card, sent in August 1915, was addressed to a Miss J. Evers at Potrero Avenue and Mariposa Street, San Francisco. The message on the back reads: "Will have to tell you all about it as I am too warm to write. Have written about 35 postals today. To everybody I ever knew, Regards. Reid." Much knowledge of the history of the Springs has been derived from "postals."

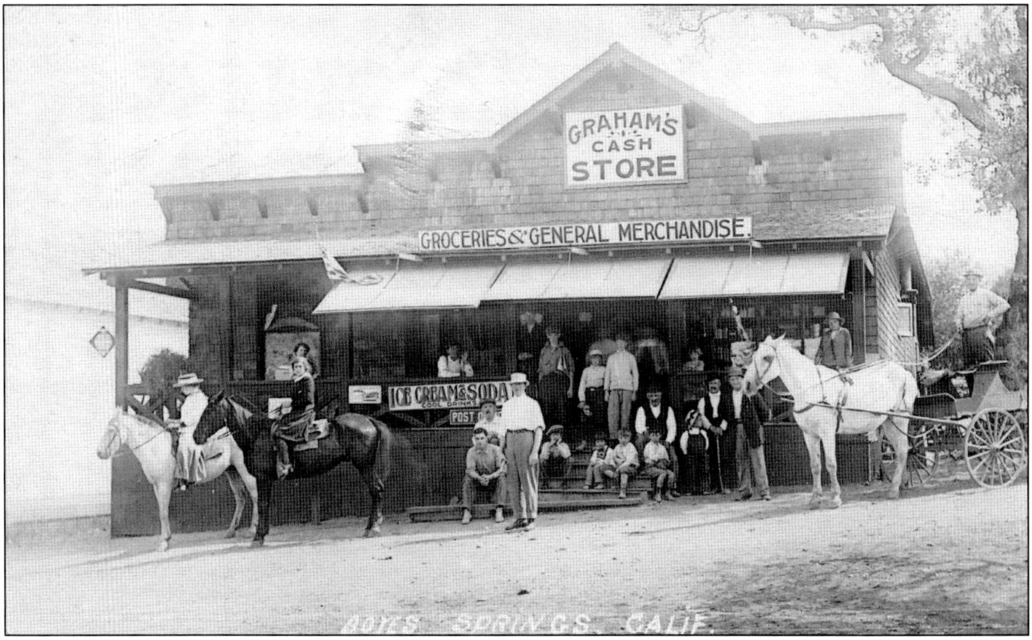

A.D. Graham bought the already-established store opposite Boyes Hot Springs in 1912. The Boyes Hot Springs post office had been opened there the previous year. Graham told the *Sonoma Index-Tribune*, "my motto will be cash, quick sales and small profits." (Courtesy of the California State Library.)

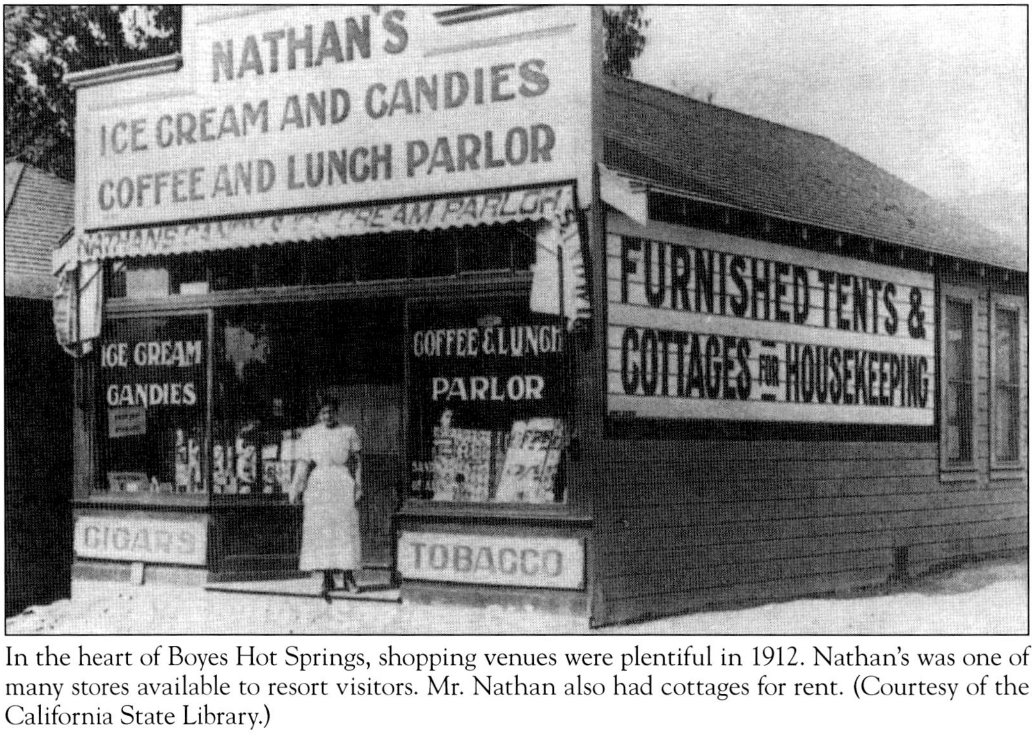

In the heart of Boyes Hot Springs, shopping venues were plentiful in 1912. Nathan's was one of many stores available to resort visitors. Mr. Nathan also had cottages for rent. (Courtesy of the California State Library.)

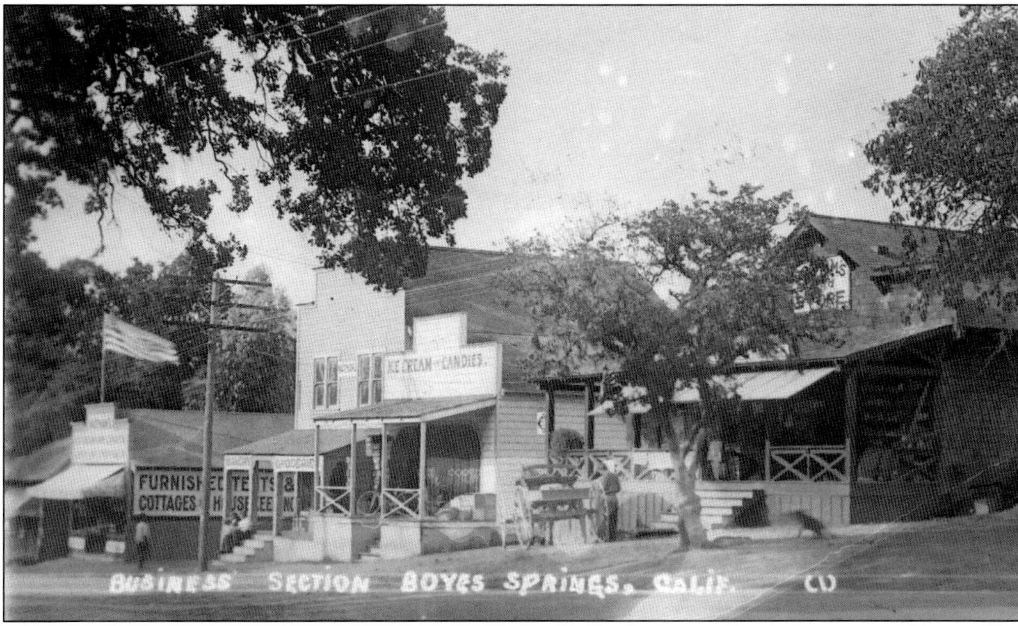

In 1912, the "business section" of Boyes Hot Springs consisted of this group of commercial buildings around the railroad depot, adjacent to the Boyes Hot Springs Club House. From left to right are Nathan's, an unidentified store, Koenig's Cash Store, and Graham's Cash Store. The street is Boyes Boulevard. (Courtesy of the California State Library.)

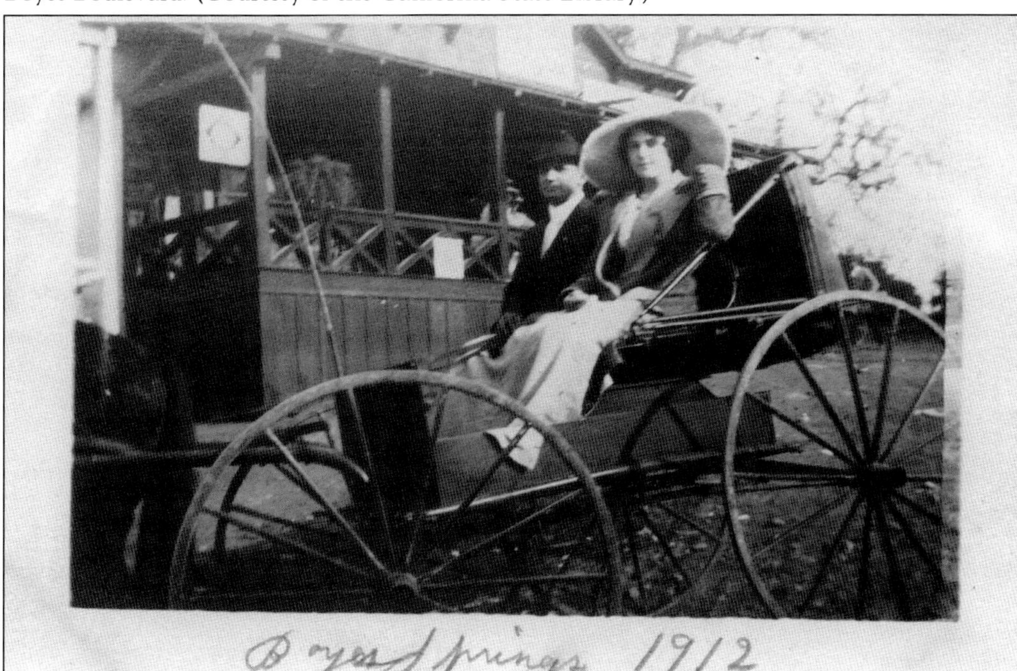

In 1912, the horse and buggy was still the most common means of transportation. An unidentified woman and gentleman sit in front of Graham's Cash Store, which was among a handful of establishments in Boyes Hot Springs around that year. Graham's Cash Store housed both the Wells Fargo Express office and the post office.

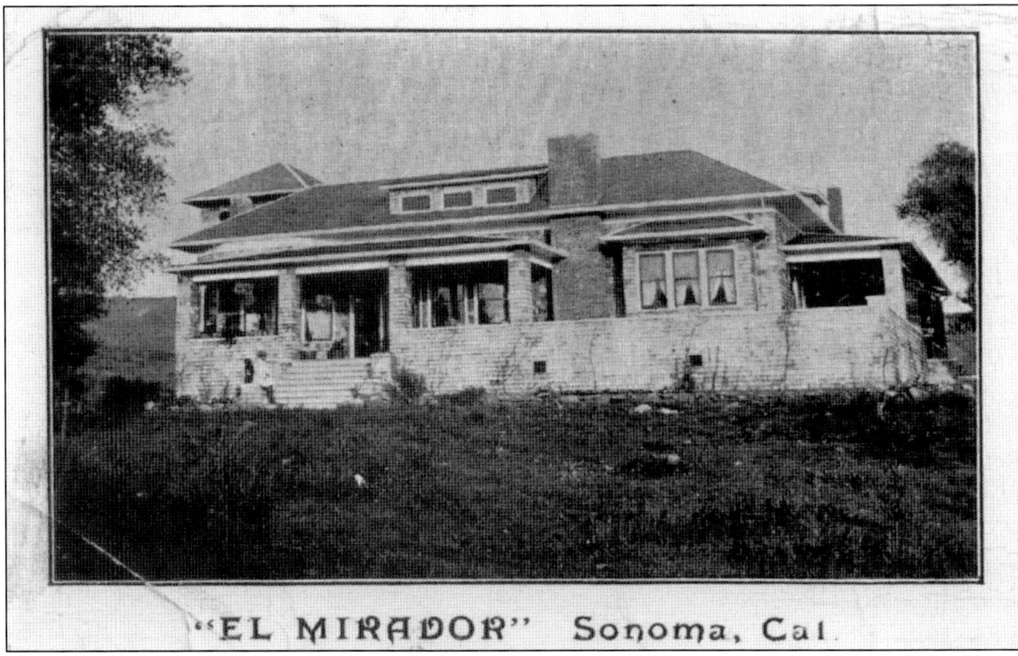

After the success of their Boyes Hot Springs resort, Henry and Antoinette Boyes built their gracious and modern home, El Mirador, across the highway on top of a low rise overlooking the Springs (hence the Spanish name, which means "viewpoint"). It was the scene of "many hospitable social affairs," according to the *Sonoma Index-Tribune*. Boyes and his wife left the valley for San Diego in 1913. El Mirador was destroyed by fire in 1917. (Courtesy of Robert Parmelee.)

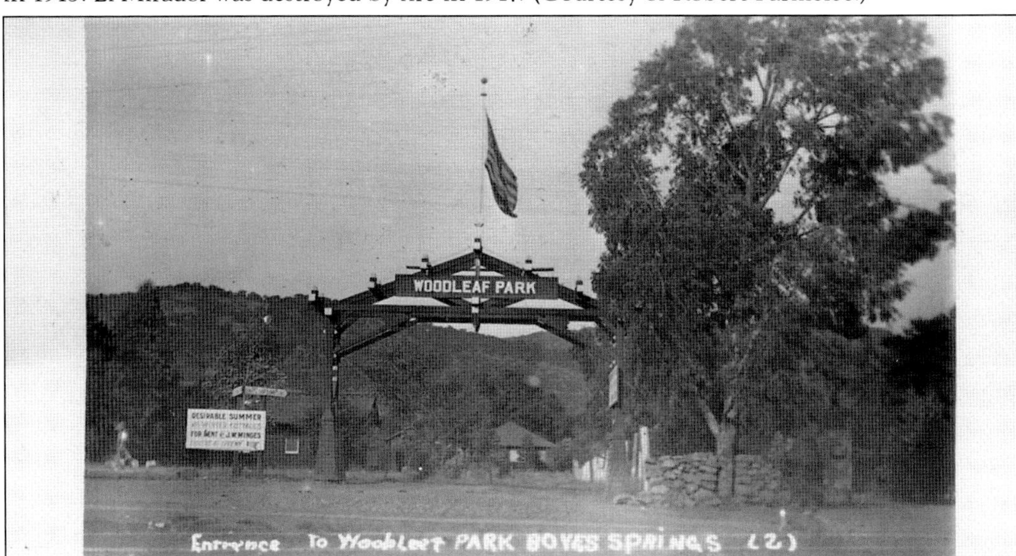

The sign in front of the archway advertises "Desirable Summer *and* Winter Cottages for Rent" by J.W. Minges. Minges was considered for many years to be the "mayor" of the unincorporated Boyes Hot Springs. In addition to renting cottages, he ran a restaurant and was president of the Boyes Springs Improvement Club and a great booster of the area. Woodleaf Park was one of many subdivisions platted between 1900 and World War I. This card is postmarked 1913. (Courtesy of Lloyd Cripps.)

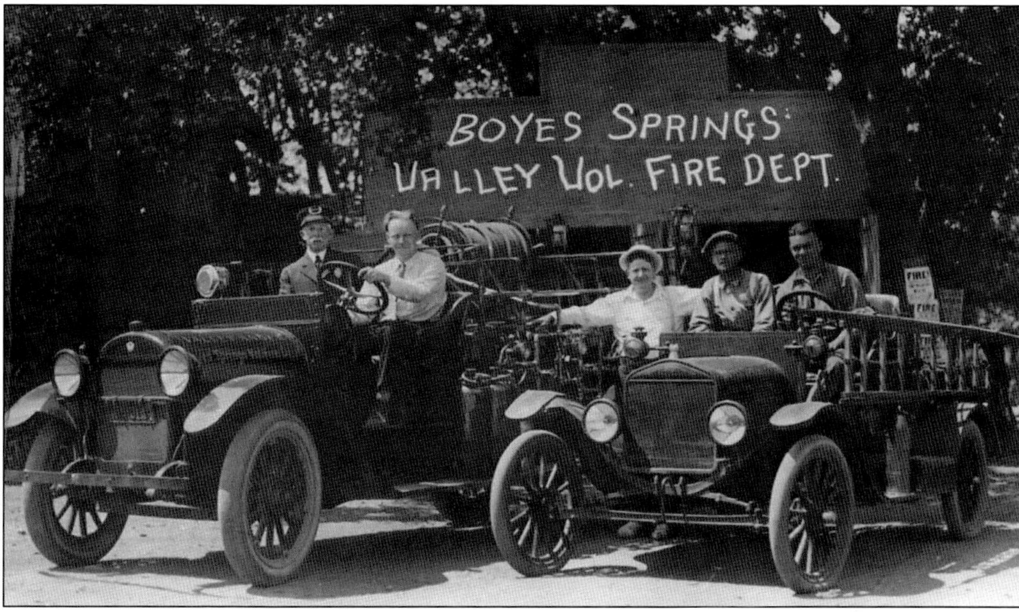

As in San Francisco and much of the West, fire was an ever-present danger in the Springs. Even before the conflagration of 1923, many fires caused major losses. Volunteers did all they could to fight fires, but they were often overwhelmed. The Boyes Springs Volunteer Fire Department was founded in 1916. The firefighters pose here with their engines around 1920. In 1936, the department's new fire station, built with WPA assistance, opened on the highway. (Courtesy of Robert Parmelee.)

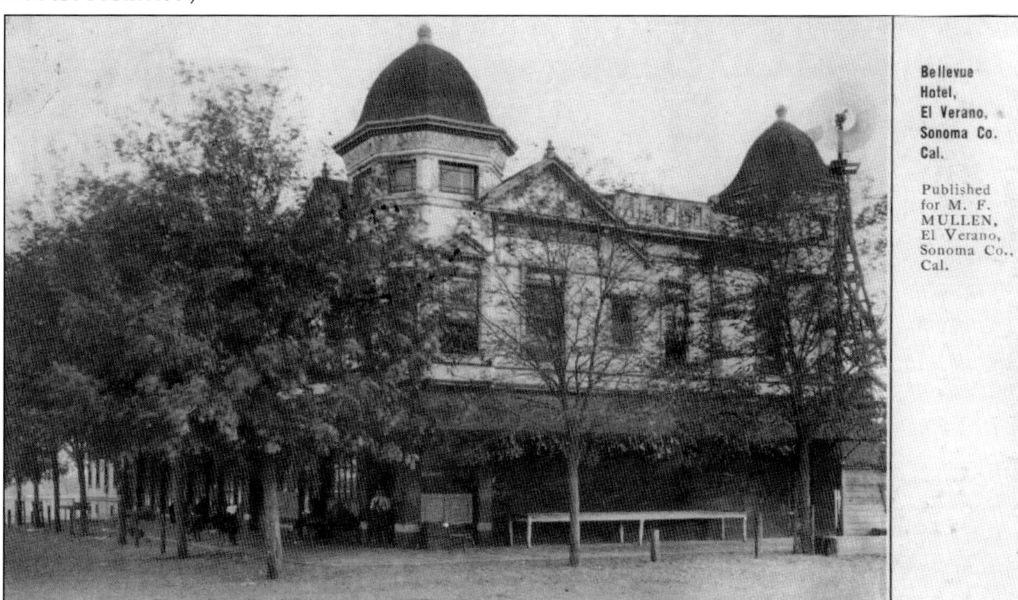

This large brick building was erected as a business block by the Southern Pacific Railroad in 1894 at Linden and Grove Streets and converted into the Bellevue Hotel by John Lounibos by 1900. Subsequent owners included John Serres and Emma Fetters. According to the July 1, 1905, edition of the *Sonoma Index-Tribune*, "The Pinkey Club visited the Bellevue Hotel last Sunday. . . . The club arrived on the 12 o'clock train accompanied by a brass band."

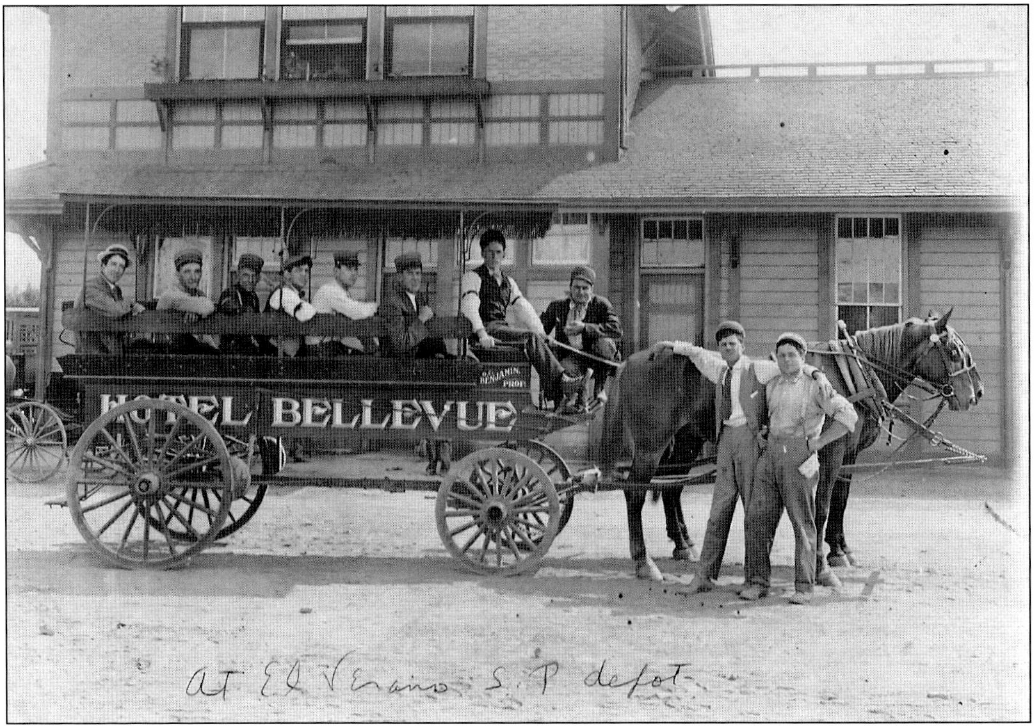

The fine wagon of the Bellevue Hotel waits outside of the Santa Rosa & Carquinez Railroad Station in El Verano sometime between 1888 and 1894. (Courtesy of the Sonoma Valley Historical Society.)

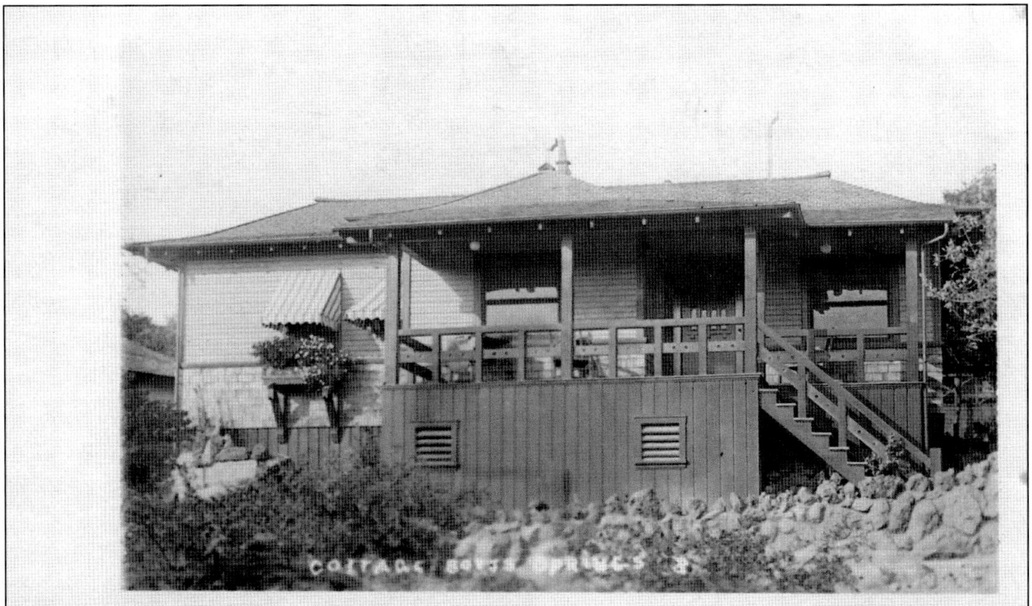

At the top of Central Avenue in Boyes Hot Springs sits this cottage, shown in 1913. Named Rocky Haven, it still exists today (see page 125) and has a large boulder in front with the words "Rocky Haven" carved into it. If only the boulder was visible in this image.

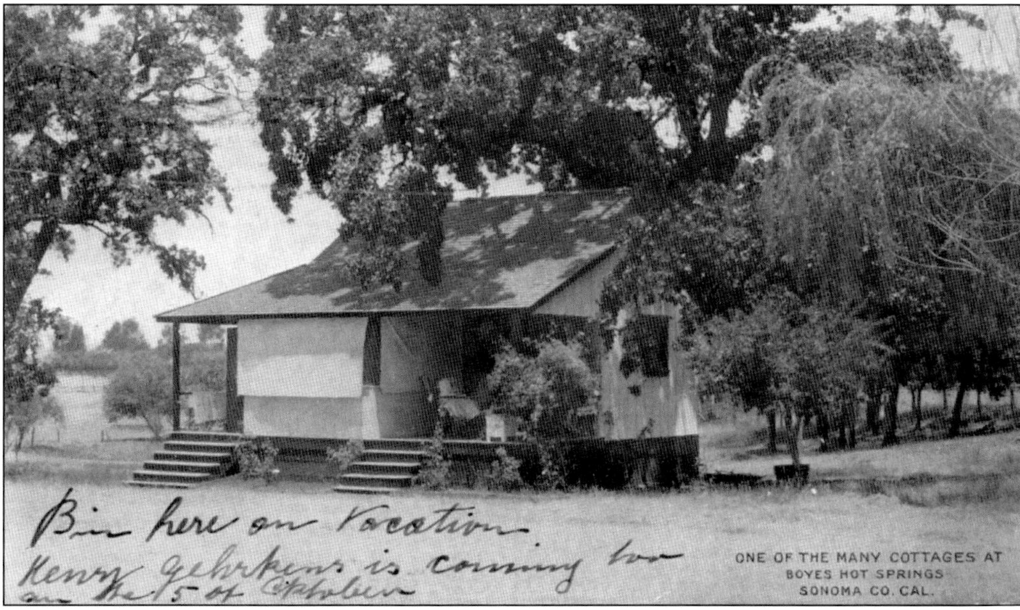

Many of the cottages in Boyes Hot Springs that were available for rent in 1908 are still standing and are now occupied as year-round residences.

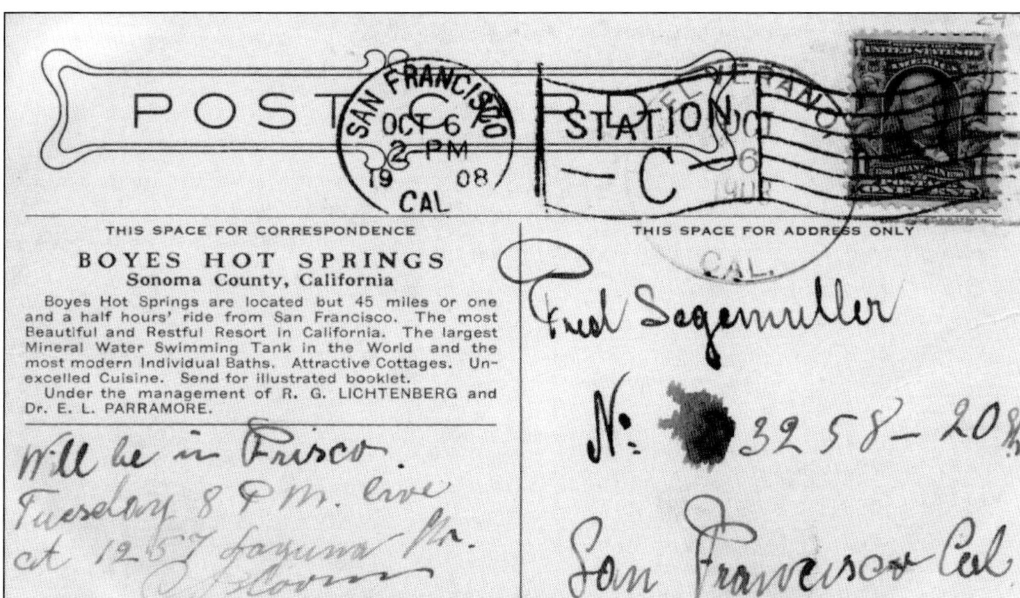

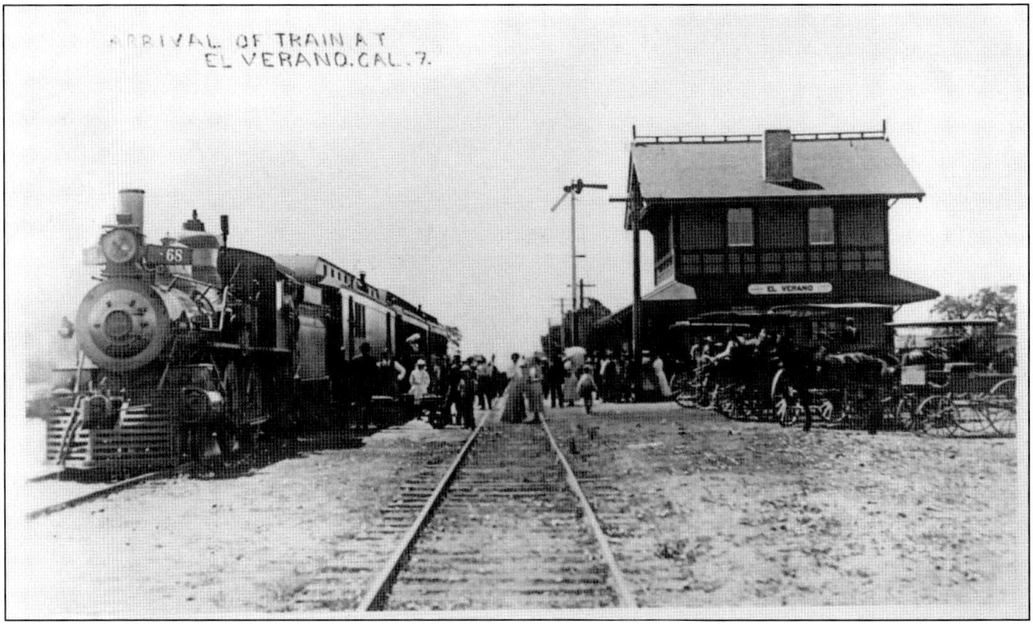

On June 2, 1888, the *Sonoma Index-Tribune* reported that the San Francisco & North Pacific Railroad's El Verano depot was nearing completion. The El Verano land boom lasted only a few years, and the rail line was abandoned in 1934. The depot was converted into apartments in 1949 and torn down in 1984 to make way for the Valley of the Moon Water District office building. (Courtesy of the Sonoma Valley Historical Society.)

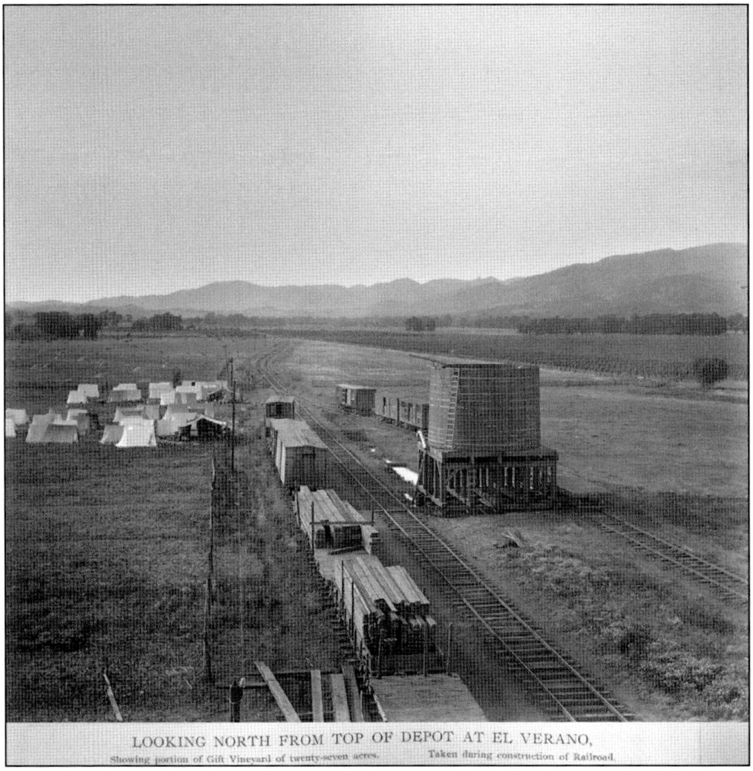

Carleton Watkins was born in New York State in 1829. He came to California during the Gold Rush and became a professional photographer in 1852. His acclaimed photographs of Yosemite Valley were influential in the establishment of the Yosemite National Park. He was hired by real estate developers in 1888 to photograph Sonoma Valley to promote land sales in El Verano. (Courtesy of the Sonoma Valley Historical Society.)

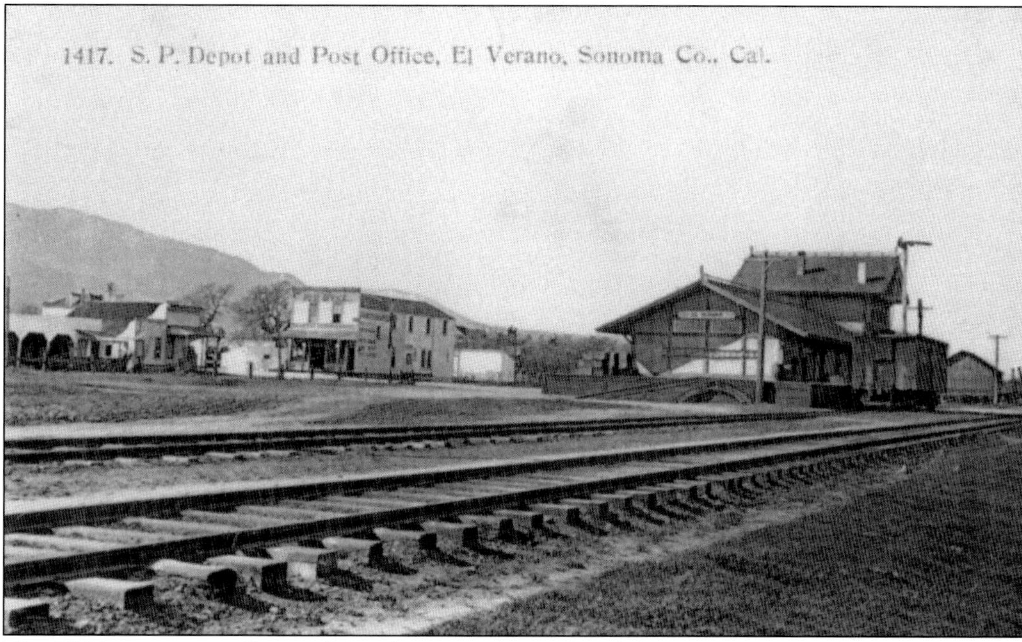

The El Verano post office and Southern Pacific Railroad depot are pictured here around 1900. (Courtesy of the Sonoma Valley Historical Society.)

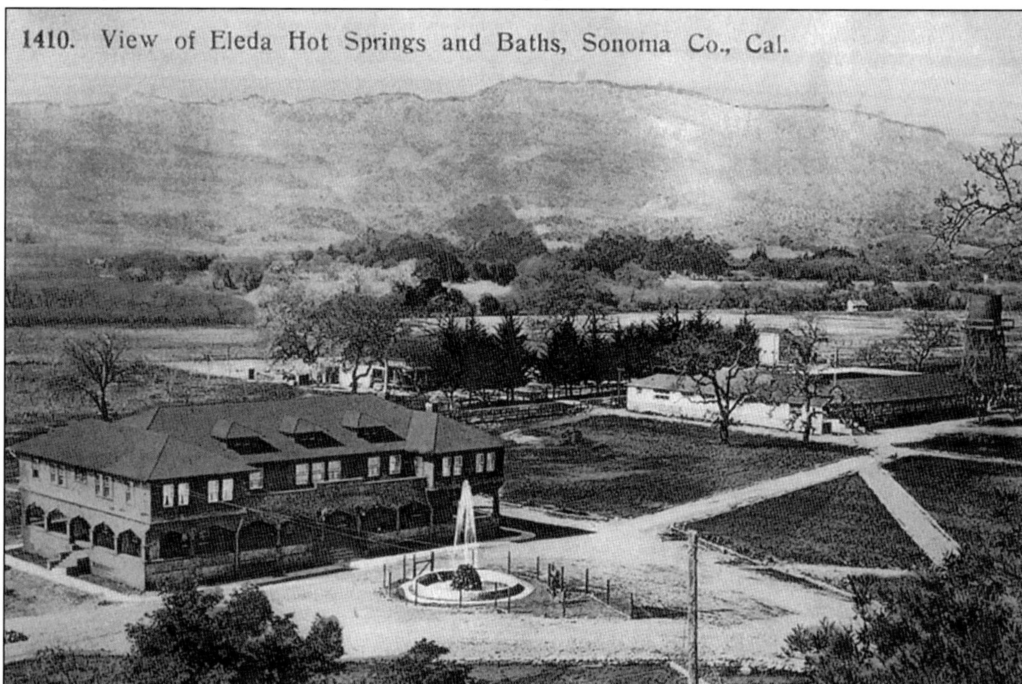

George Fetters was originally from Pittsburgh, Pennsylvania. His wife, Emma, was born in Austria. They came to Sonoma Valley in 1907 and bought property known as the Halstead Ranch, upon which they founded their resort. Shortly after, they leased the resort to Morris Levy, who ran the resort as Eleda Hot Springs until 1911, when the Fetterses took back the lease. (Courtesy of Gordon Lindberg.)

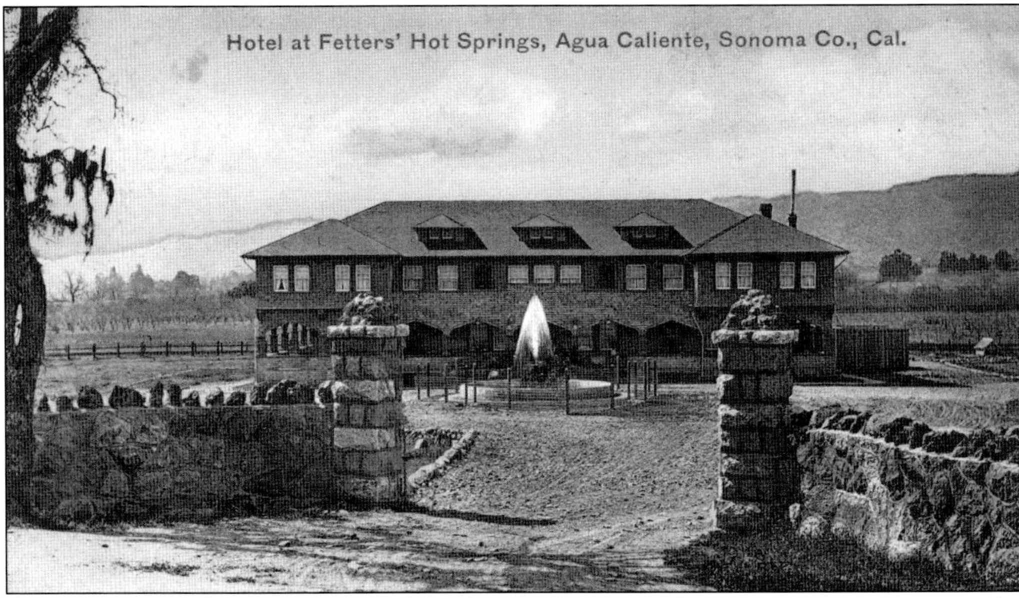

In 1913, apparently bearing a grudge over losing the lease to the resort, Morris Levy testified in opposition to a liquor license being granted to Fetters. They received the license, but this was not the only time the Fetters got into legal trouble over liquor; in 1918, they were tried for the offense of providing liquor to enlisted men (a crime under the War Emergency Act). The *Sonoma Index-Tribune* reported that testifying in the Fetterses' defense were "Fred Boynton, the well known lumber yard man, E.G. Koenig of Boyes Hot Springs, and Lillian the entertainer," among others. Both were convicted, but George's conviction was overturned on appeal. Both George and Emma were in and out of court many times; they were sued for damages by resort guests and, once, for libel.

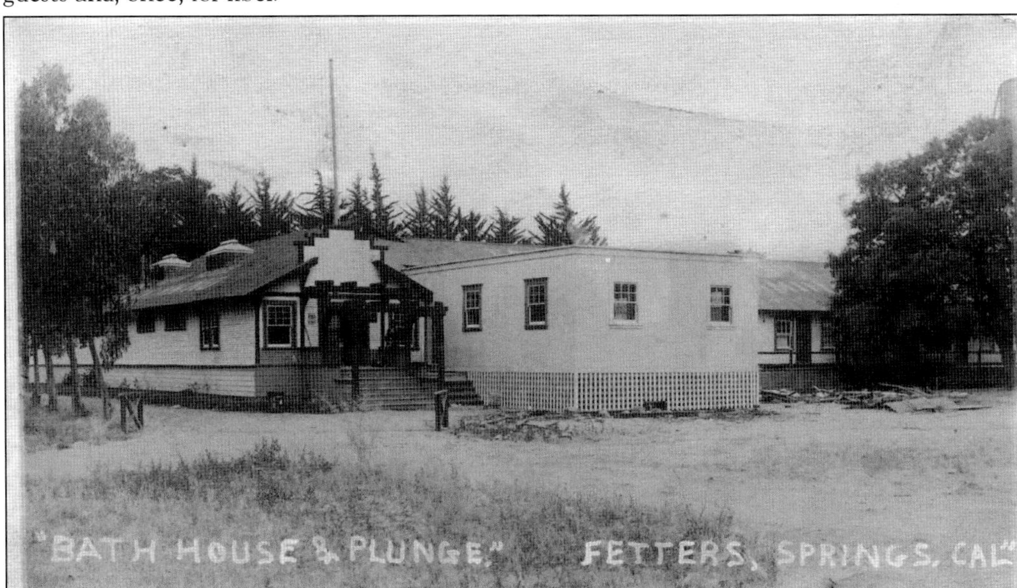

George and Emma Fetters were constantly improving the resort, bringing in moving pictures in 1923, sidewalks in 1924, and a new dance hall in 1925. George donated the land for the new Boyes Hot Springs ballpark, and he threw out the first ball at its dedication in 1940.

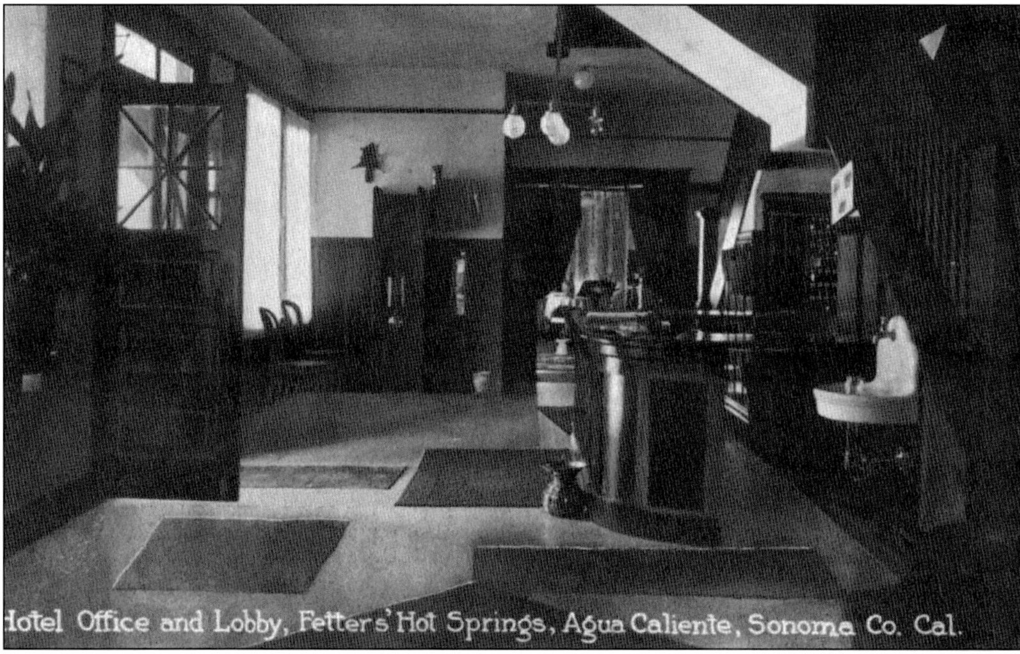

According to the *Sonoma Index-Tribune*, Emma Fetters was "an energetic woman of wealth and enterprise." The Fetterses not only built the resort—with its hotel, swimming pavilion, and theater—but also the Fetters depot of the Northwestern Pacific Railroad. Emma also owned much real estate in the area and once owned the Chauvet Hotel in Glen Ellen.

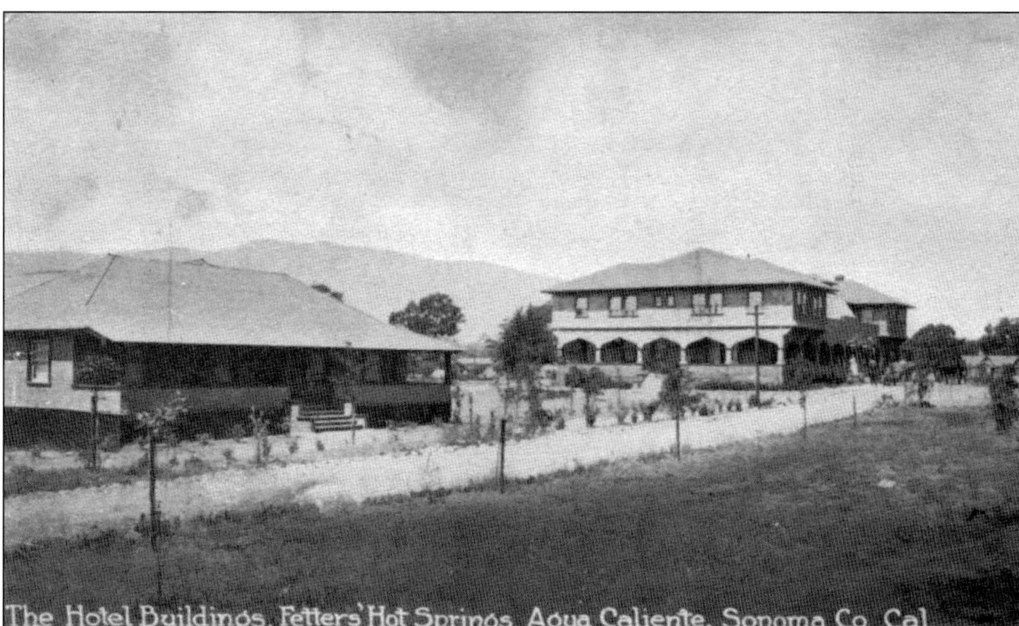

Emma Fetters died of pneumonia in 1922. George Fetters was a prominent member of the community and continued to run the resort until he sold it in 1944. He died in 1964. (Courtesy of Gordon Lindberg.)

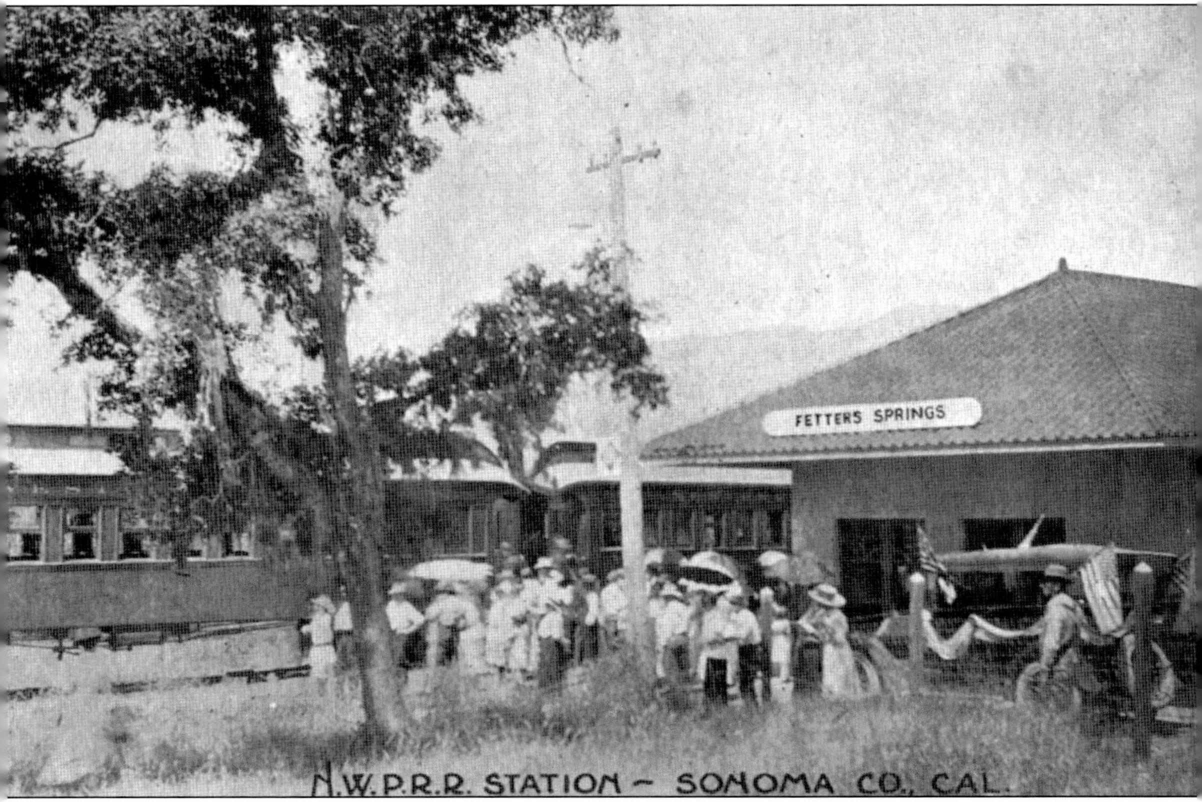

On February 1, 1913, the *Sonoma Index-Tribune* reported: "The new depot opposite Fetters Hot Springs on Northwestern Pacific Railroad has been commenced. It will cost, it is said $4,000. . . . It will be Monolithic in style, the first depot of its style to be built in California." Its construction was unique in that the exterior was sheathed in terrazzo, an ancient Roman material usually used for floors. This building still stands today, but few of the other railroad depots in the valley have survived. The stone walls and tile roof of the Fetters depot may have preserved it from the many fires that ravaged the area, including the inferno of 1923. See page 123 to view a photograph of this building in 2016. (Courtesy of Gordon Lindberg.)

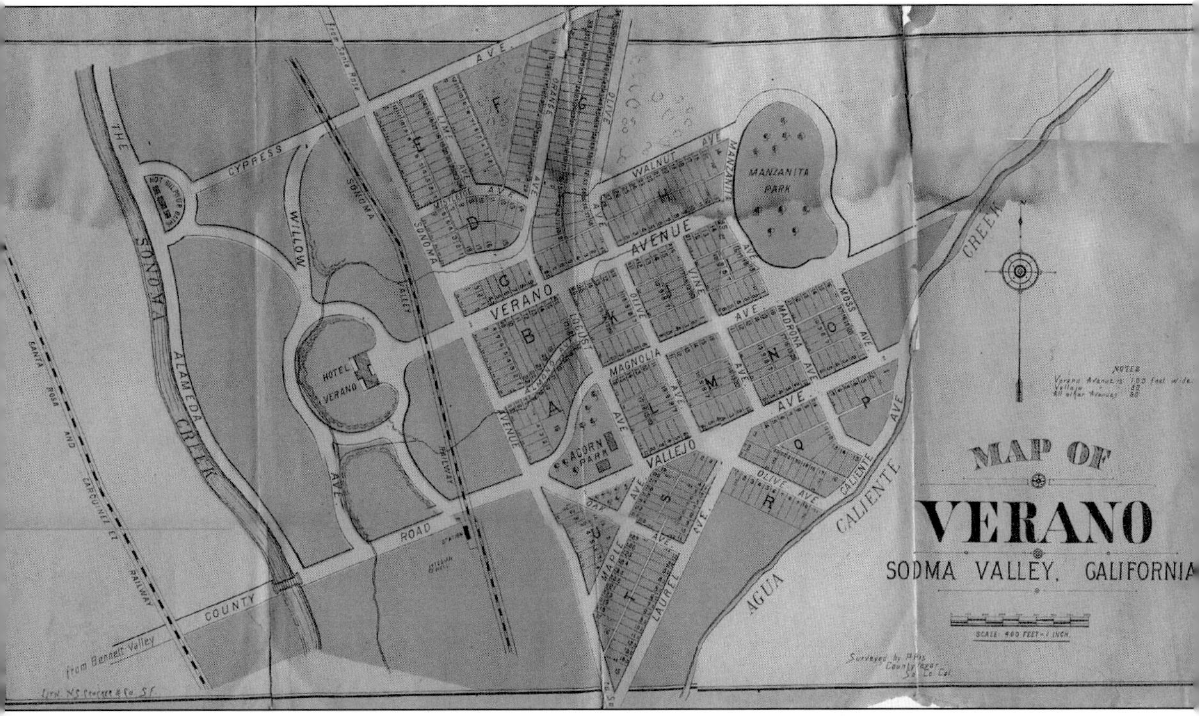

In 1888, the *Sonoma Index-Tribune* opined that "Sonoma Valley, after years of uninterrupted quietude, has at last attracted the attention of men of capital. . . . The new Town of Verano, backed as it is by men of wealth will also help things along." Verano was across Sonoma Creek from El Verano. It was served by one of the two rail lines in the valley, the San Francisco & North Pacific, which was later purchased by Northwestern Pacific Railroad. Verano was part of the real estate boom that created El Verano. Colorful maps such as this were created—complete with fantasy streets, parks, and resorts—to attract buyers. In the opinion of the newspaper, "Farms, villa sites and town lots that can now be bought for a mere song in and adjacent to this city will double and quadruple in value in the course of a few years." (Courtesy of the Sonoma Valley Historical Society.)

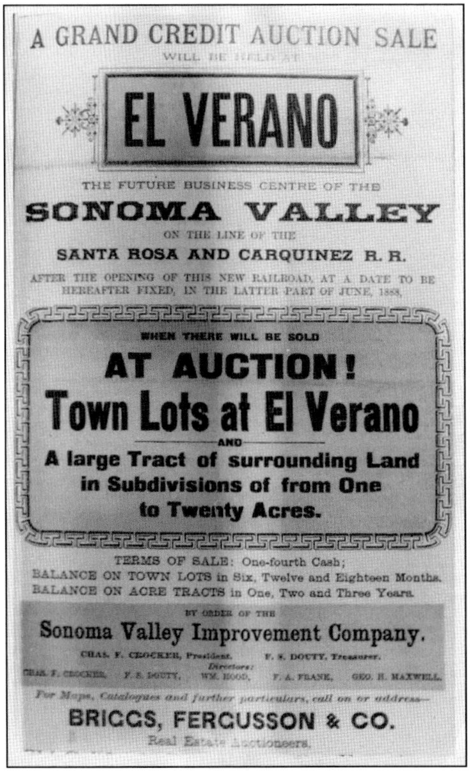

In 1887, the Sonoma Valley Improvement Company was founded by George Maxwell with participation from Charles Crocker, one of the "Big Four" of transcontinental railroad fame. The company's purpose was to sell home and business lots in the area just south of Boyes Hot Springs, which Maxwell named El Verano ("summer" in Spanish). In July 1888, an auction of lots in El Verano netted $30,000, an amount "more than the most sanguine expectations," reported the *Sonoma Index-Tribune*. However, by 1890, "The boulevards and avenues and lovely residence sites and orange groves, which had an existence on paper only, will now have to give way to the horrid potato, the festive bean and the conceited pumpkin." Maxwell's real estate scheme fell victim to a legal dispute over the title to the land, but El Verano would bounce back to become a prosperous resort town. (Courtesy of the Sonoma Valley Historical Society.)

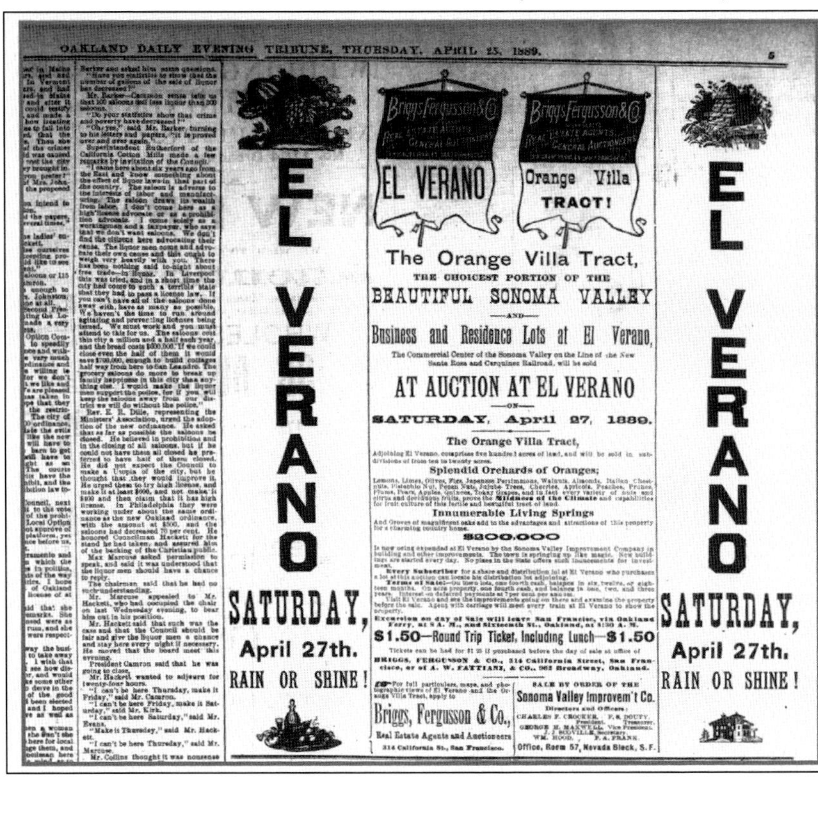
OAKLAND DAILY EVENING TRIBUNE, THURSDAY, APRIL 25, 1889.

EL VERANO

SATURDAY, April 27th. RAIN OR SHINE!

Briggs Fergusson & Co. — EL VERANO — Orange Villa TRACT!

The Orange Villa Tract, THE CHOICEST PORTION OF THE BEAUTIFUL SONOMA VALLEY —AND— Business and Residence Lots at El Verano, The Commercial Center of the Sonoma Valley on the Line of the New Santa Rosa and Carquinez Railroad, will be sold

AT AUCTION AT EL VERANO —ON— SATURDAY, April 27, 1889.

The Orange Villa Tract, Adjoining El Verano, comprises five hundred acres of land, and will be sold in subdivisions of from ten to twenty acres.

Splendid Orchards of Oranges; Lemons, Limes, Olives, Figs, Japanese Persimmons, Walnuts, Almonds, Italian Chestnuts, Pistachio Nut, Pecan Nuts, Jujube Trees, Cherries, Apricots, Peaches, Prunes, Plums, Pears, Apples, Quinces, Tokay Grapes, and in fact every variety of nuts and citrus and deciduous fruits, prove the **Mildness of the Climate** and capabilities for fruit culture of this fertile and beautiful tract of land.

Innumerable Living Springs And Groves of magnificent oaks add to the advantages and attractions of this property for a charming country home.

$200,000 Is now being expended at El Verano by the Sonoma Valley Improvement Company in building and other improvements. The town is springing up like magic. New buildings are started every day. No place in the State offers such inducements for investment.

Every Subscriber for a share and distribution lot at El Verano who purchases a lot at this auction can locate his distribution lot adjoining.

Terms of Sale:—On town lots, one fourth cash, balance in six, twelve, or eighteen months. On acre property, one fourth cash, and balance in one, two, and three years. Interest on deferred payments at 7 per cent per annum.

Visit El Verano and see the improvements going on there and examine the property before the sale. Agent with carriage will meet every train at El Verano to show the property.

Excursion on day of Sale will leave San Francisco, via Oakland Ferry, at 8 A. M., and Sixteenth St., Oakland, at 8:30 A. M.

$1.50—Round Trip Ticket, Including Lunch—$1.50

Tickets can be had for $1 25 if purchased before the day of sale at office of BRIGGS, FERGUSSON & CO., 314 California Street, San Francisco, or of A. W. FATTIANI, & CO., 962 Broadway, Oakland.

For full particulars, maps, and photographic views of El Verano and the Orange Villa Tract, apply to Briggs, Fergusson & Co., Real Estate Agents and Auctioneers, 314 California St., San Francisco.

SALE BY ORDER OF THE Sonoma Valley Improvem't Co. Directors and Officers: CHARLES F. CROCKER, President. F. S. DOUTY, Treasurer. GEORGE H. MAXWELL, Vice President. J. J. SCOVILLE, Secretary. WM. HOOD, F. A. FRANK. Office, Room 57, Nevada Block, S. F.

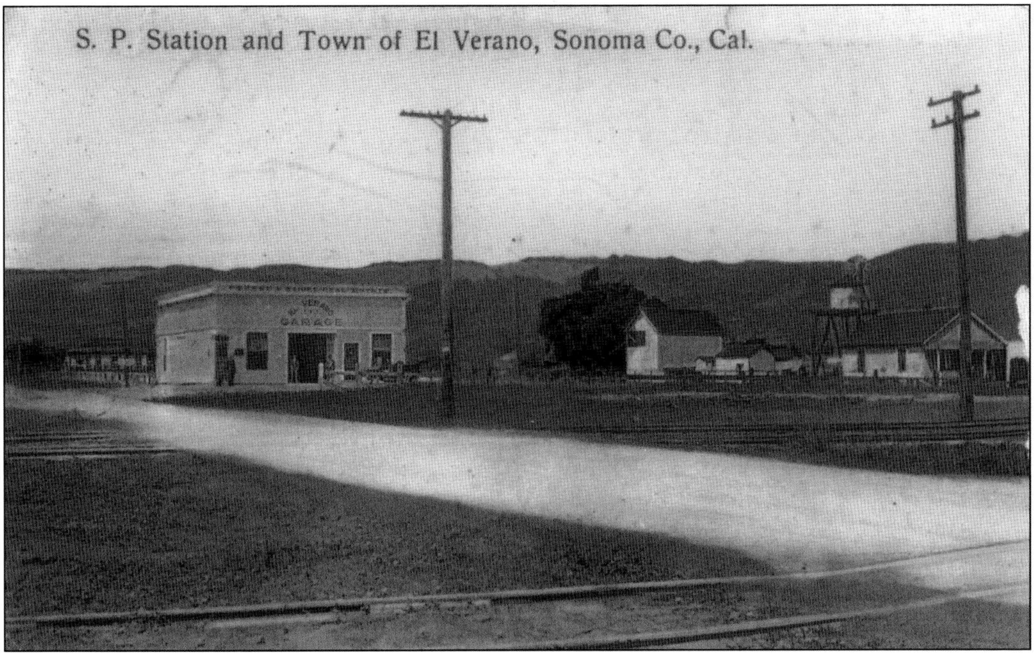

Early in the 20th century, El Verano was still largely open space with few trees. The prominent building at left, located at Bay and Grove Streets, was the El Verano Garage. This building still exists today. (Courtesy of the Sonoma Valley Historical Society.)

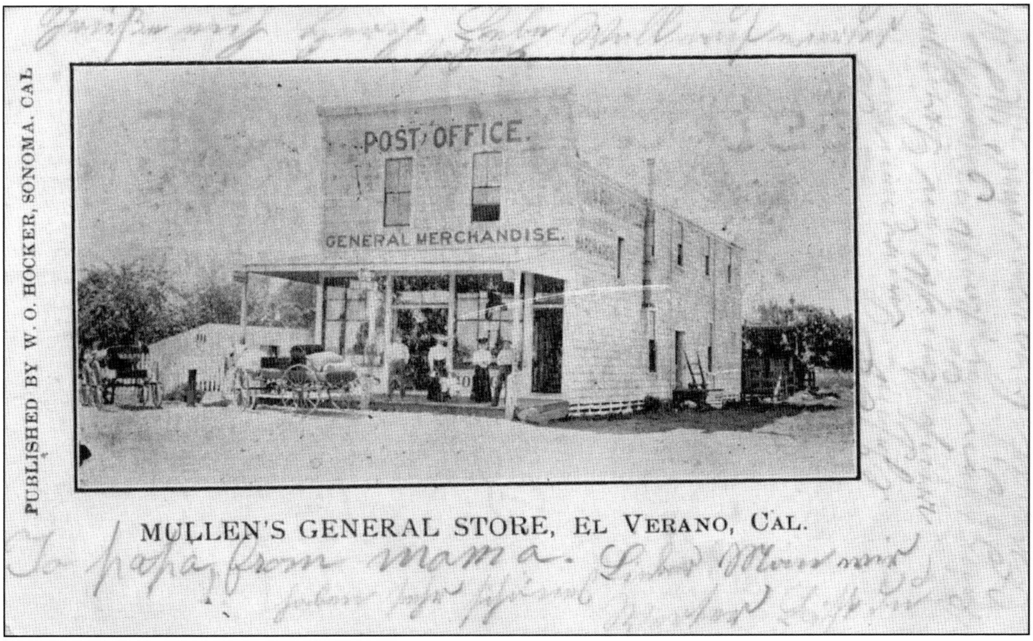

The building at Laurel and Bay Streets that became Mullen's General Store was built in 1887 during the first El Verano land boom. Emmett Mullen took over around 1900 and ran it until the 1950s. It housed the post office until 1949, with Mullen serving as postmaster. In 1933, Henry Paso walked into the store and shot Emmett's brother Tom Mullen four times. At his sentencing to life in San Quentin, Paso was asked why he did it; he replied, "I dunno, I dunno."

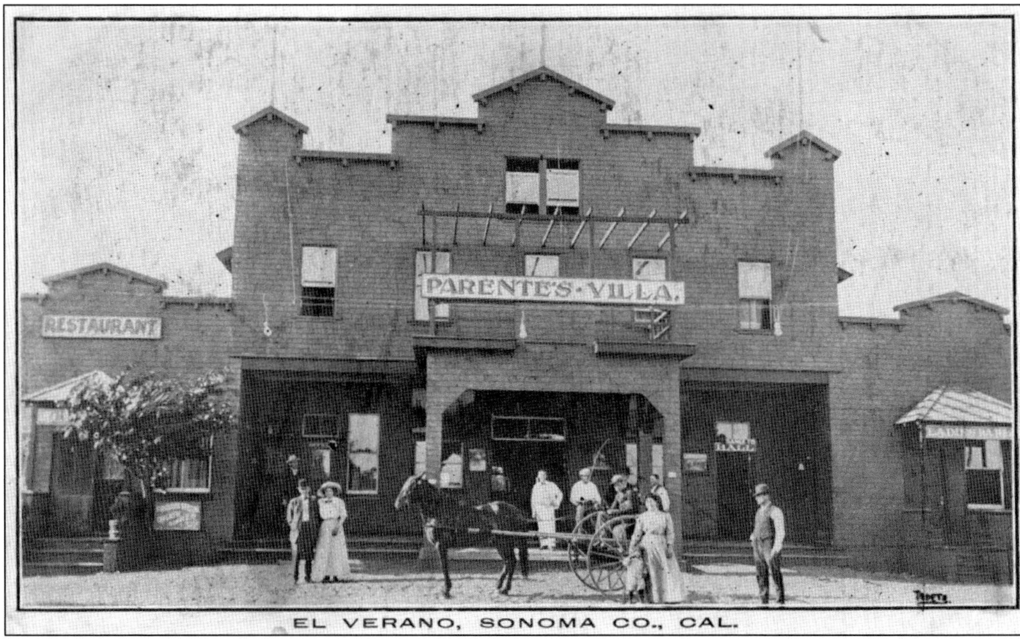

Louis Parente ran a popular resort on Verano Avenue from 1909 until well into the 1930s. Parente was a boxing promoter and backed many prizefighters. In 1919, the *Sonoma Index-Tribune* reported, "Sonoma Valley raises prize fighters as well as prize tomatoes and [Joe] White, who is a protégé of Louis Parente, is the real guy on both. In fact there is such phenom [*sic*] wonder connection between the prize fighter and the prize tomatoes he raises, that it is whispered that Luther Burbank is going to come down and get the dope from scientific investigation." (Courtesy of the Sonoma Valley Historical Society.)

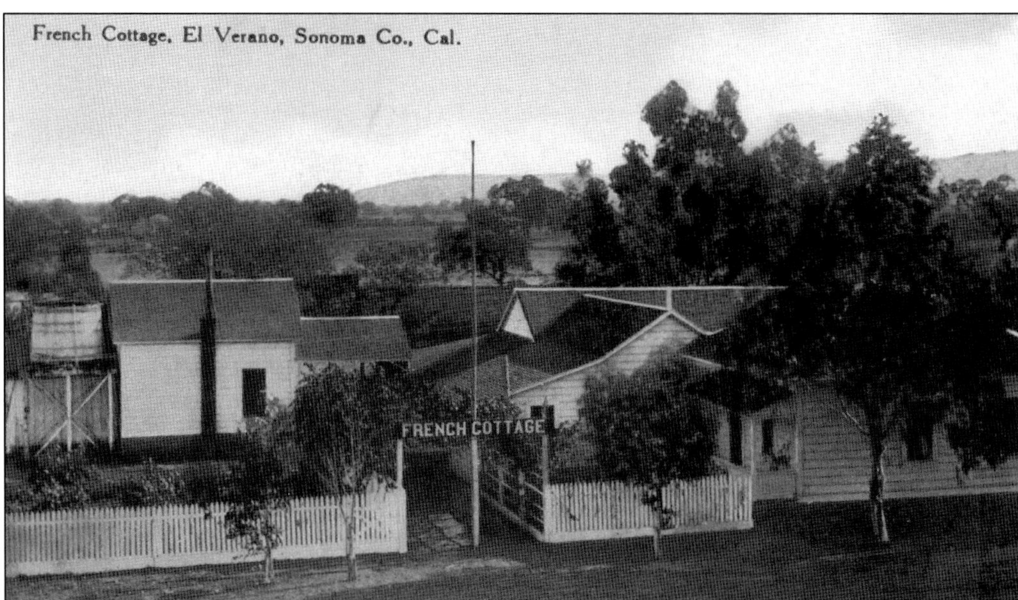

J. Dutil established French Cottage around 1902 in the heart of El Verano at Oak and Linden Streets. In the 1950s, it was still going strong as Verdier's Resort.

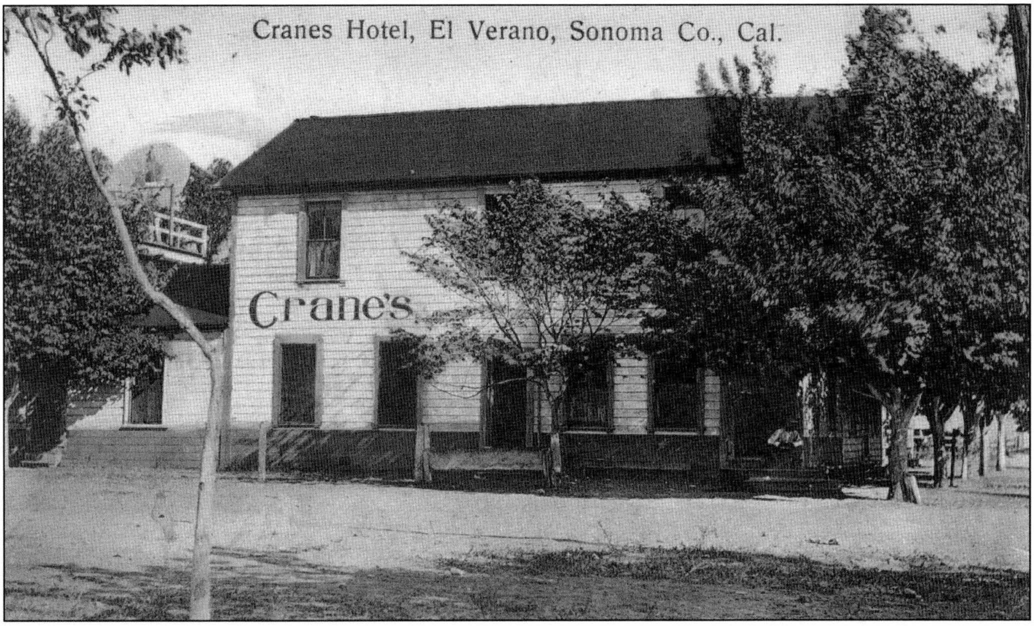

Crane's Hotel is first mentioned in the *Sonoma Index-Tribune* in 1912. Located at the corner of Verano Avenue and Maple Street, it went on to become Our Resort in the 1930s and, finally, McNeilly's Tavern in 1981 (McNeilly's closed in the early 2000s).

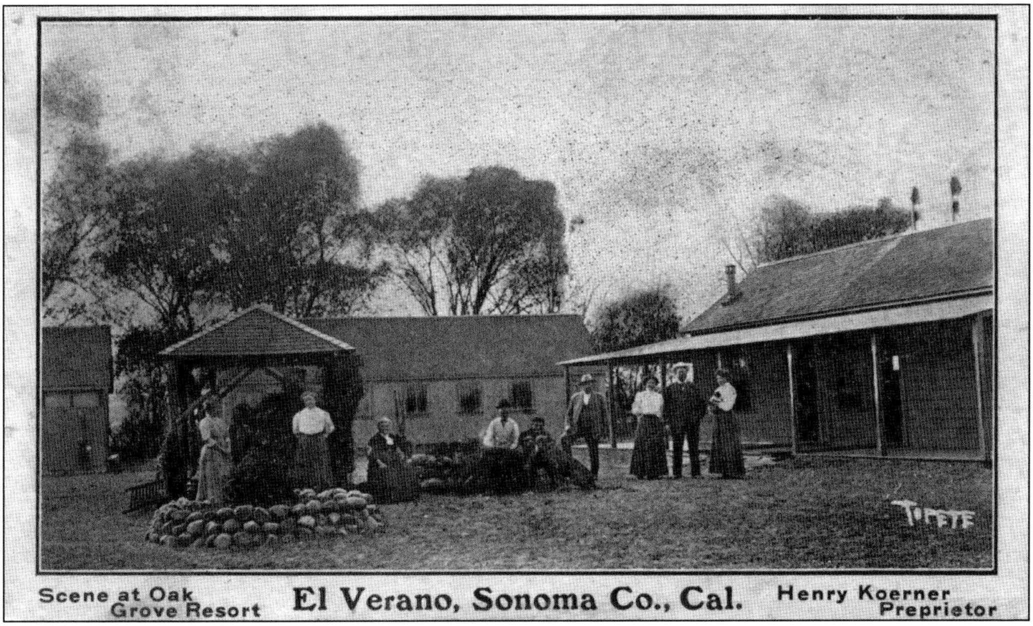

In late June 1939, the Petaluma Eagles held their 11th Annual Picnic and Barbecue—featuring a frog-jumping contest, turtle races, a greased pig, and free dancing—at the Oak Grove Resort on Petaluma Road. In July of that year, the Cork Athletic and Social Club held its Fourth of July Picnic at Oak Grove. Admission was 25¢, and all were welcome.

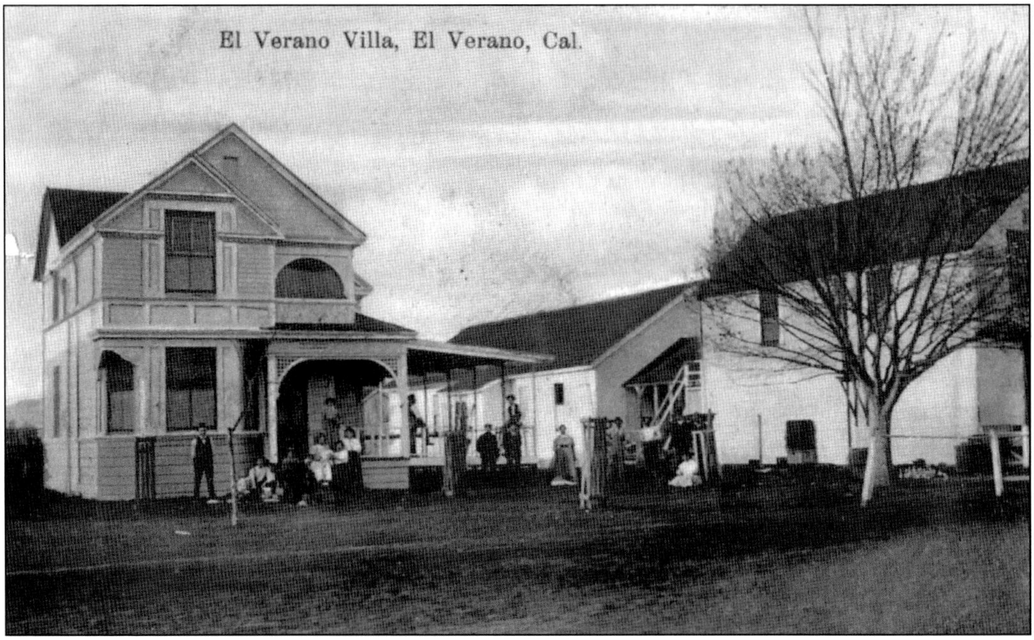

According to the *San Francisco Call*, El Verano Villa was incorporated in 1891, making it one of the first resorts in the valley. In 1902, Mrs. A. Nevaurmont, the owner, planted a large number of trees on the grounds, and the *Sonoma Index-Tribune* stated: "This will add much to the appearance of this popular resort and will no doubt please the large number of guests that make it their rendezvous every summer." (Above, courtesy of Gordon Lindberg.)

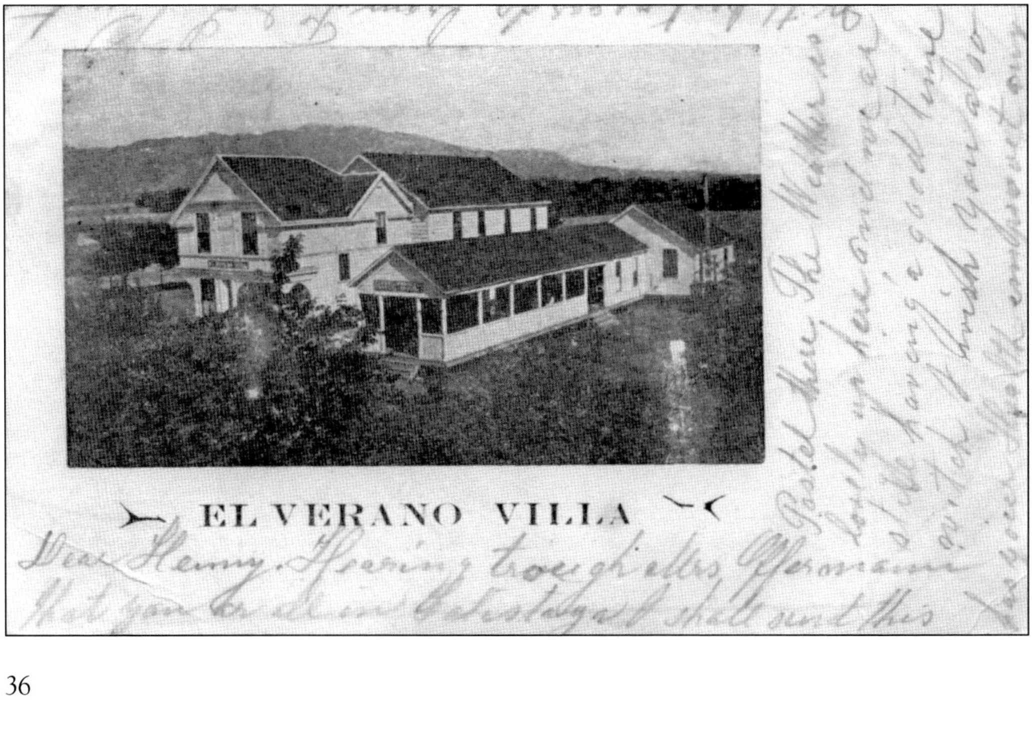

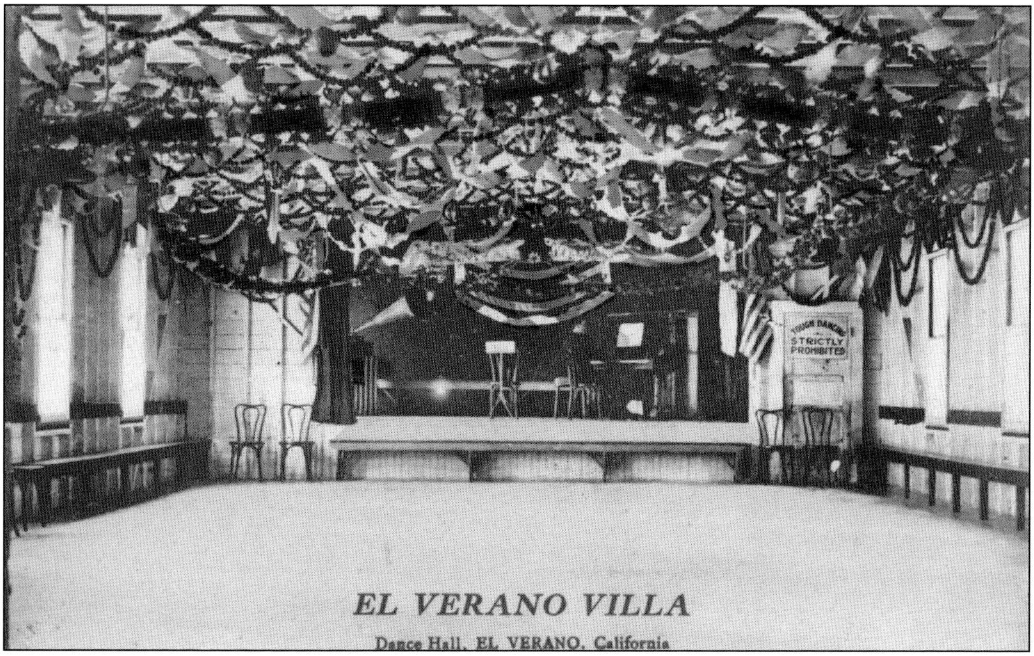

On July 1, 1904, Happy Hooligan wrote in the El Verano column in the *Sonoma Index-Tribune*, "There will be a dance at El Verano Villa on Saturday evening, also on the 3rd of July. Ghirardelli's Orchestra will furnish the music. All are invited." By 1924, Captain Tullet was owner of the resort. He announced the opening dance, featuring the Jack Delaney Palace Hotel Orchestra, on May 30 of that year.

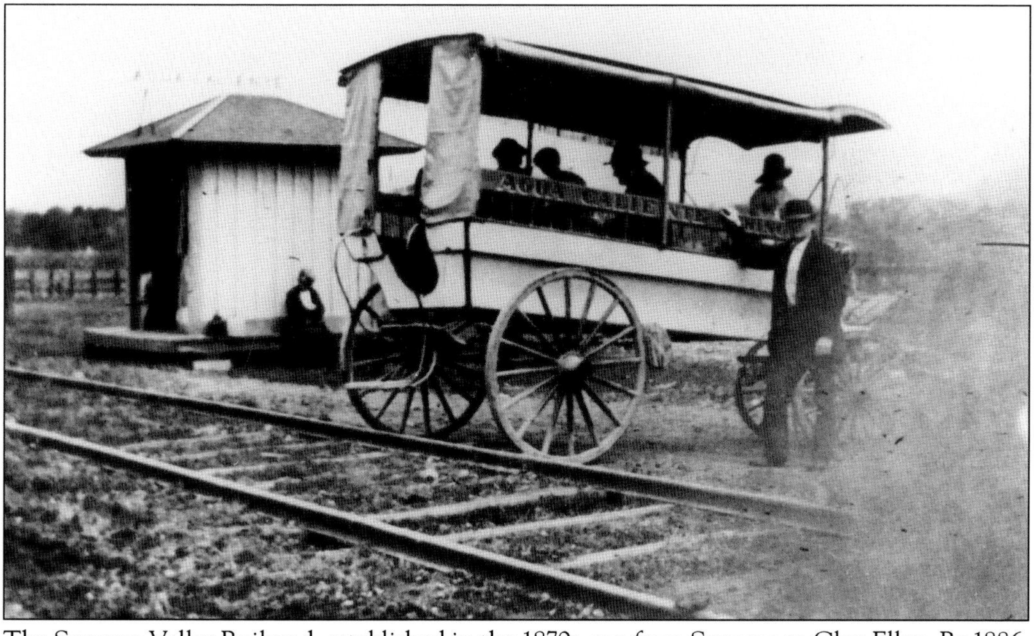

The Sonoma Valley Railroad, established in the 1870s, ran from Sonoma to Glen Ellen. By 1886, the Sonoma Valley Railroad's passenger train stopped in Agua Caliente twice daily, serving M.K. Cady's Agua Caliente Springs Hotel and the burgeoning town. (Courtesy of the Sonoma Valley Historical Society.)

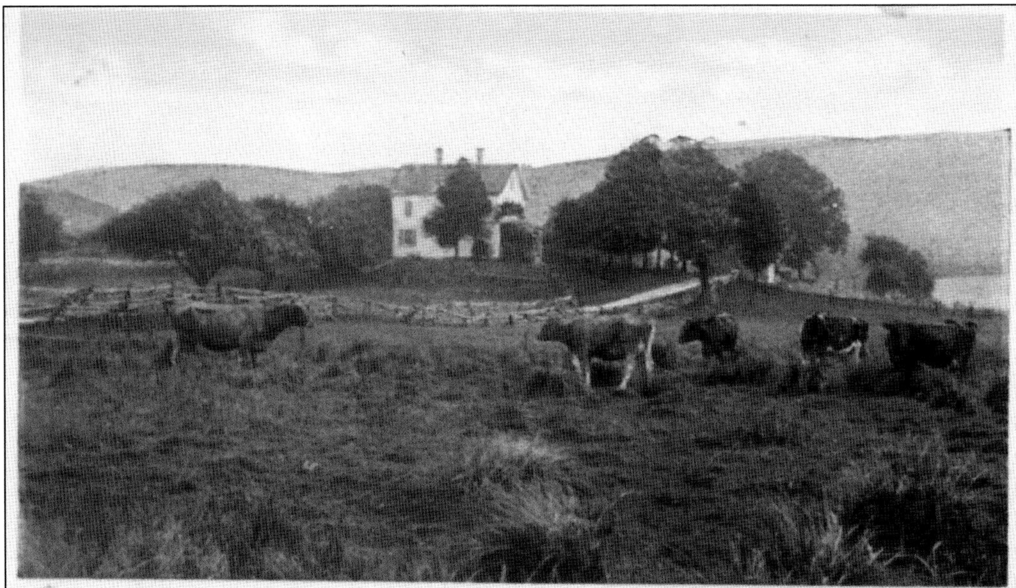

Scene near El Verano, California

In 1888, the Sonoma Valley Improvement Company bought the 700-acre Clark ranch to establish the town of El Verano. Despite the grand plans of Charles Crocker and George Maxwell, El Verano did not lose its rural quality. In 1888, when pioneer resort owner M.K. Cady was selling his Agua Caliente Springs Hotel, he put an advertisement in the *Sonoma Index-Tribune* announcing the sale of "thoroughbred and graded Jersey cows." The same year, the newspaper reported that "The copious rains of December and the fine growing weather the past month has been of vast advantage to the dairying interests of Sonoma Valley. . . . The milch cows on our dairies are sleek and fat and are giving large quantities of rich milk." (Both, courtesy of Gordon Lindberg.)

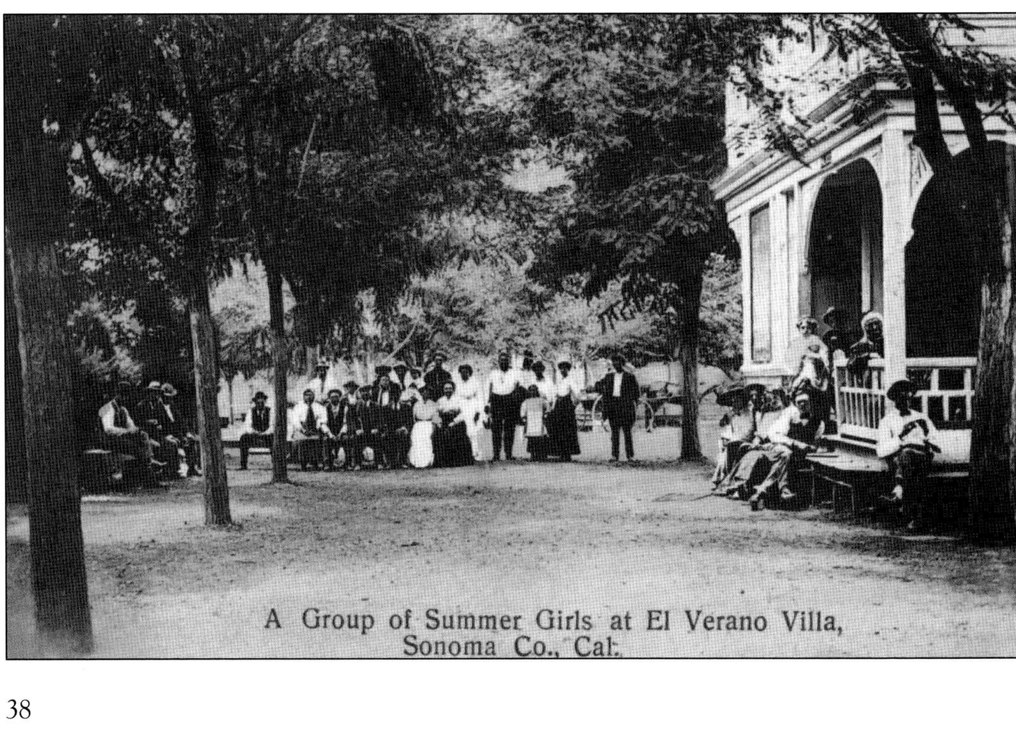

A Group of Summer Girls at El Verano Villa, Sonoma Co., Cal.

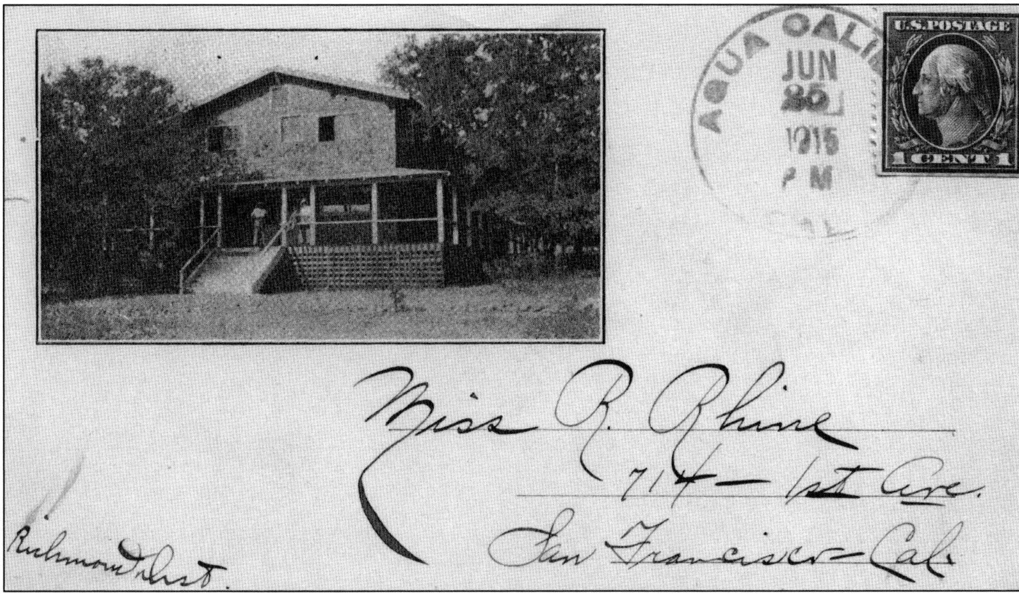

Judging from a contemporaneous map of Agua Caliente that shows an "iron spring," as advertised on the back of this card sent in 1915, it can be deduced that the Caliente Park Hotel was on the east side of the road to Santa Rosa. The "two minutes walk to swimming tank and dancing pavilion" would have led one to Agua Caliente Villa, most likely.

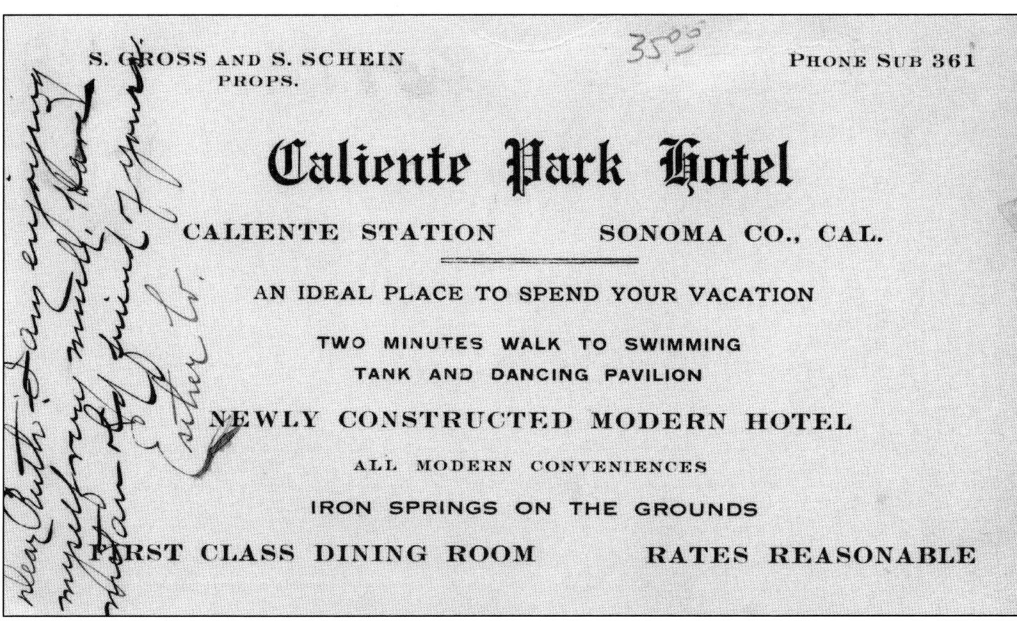

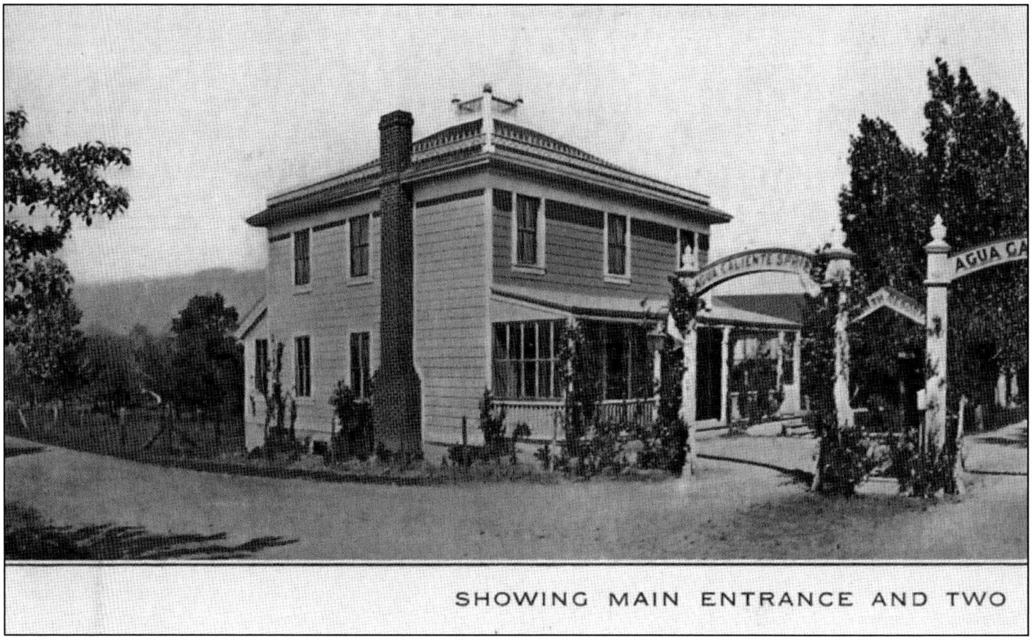

The Agua Caliente Springs Hotel, founded by M.K. Cady, opened in the summer of 1885. In 1887, the *Sonoma Index-Tribune* noted that "The new swimming baths at the Agua Caliente Warm Springs are completed and now open to the public. They are the largest and best appointed mineral baths in the state. The water of these springs are of delightful temperature for bathing and their curative properties are highly endorsed by our leading physicians."

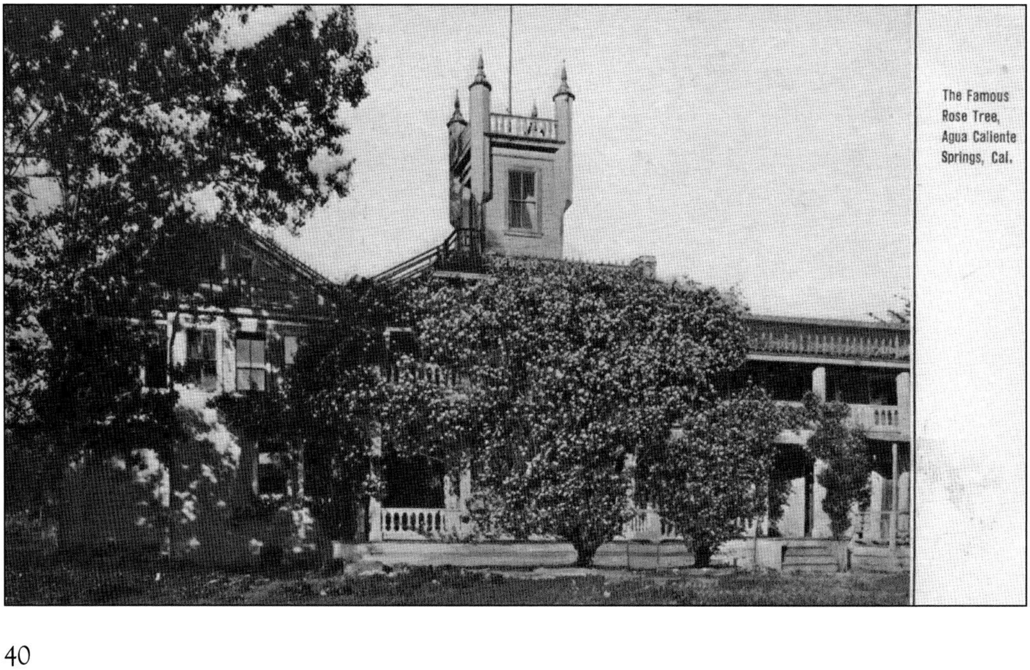

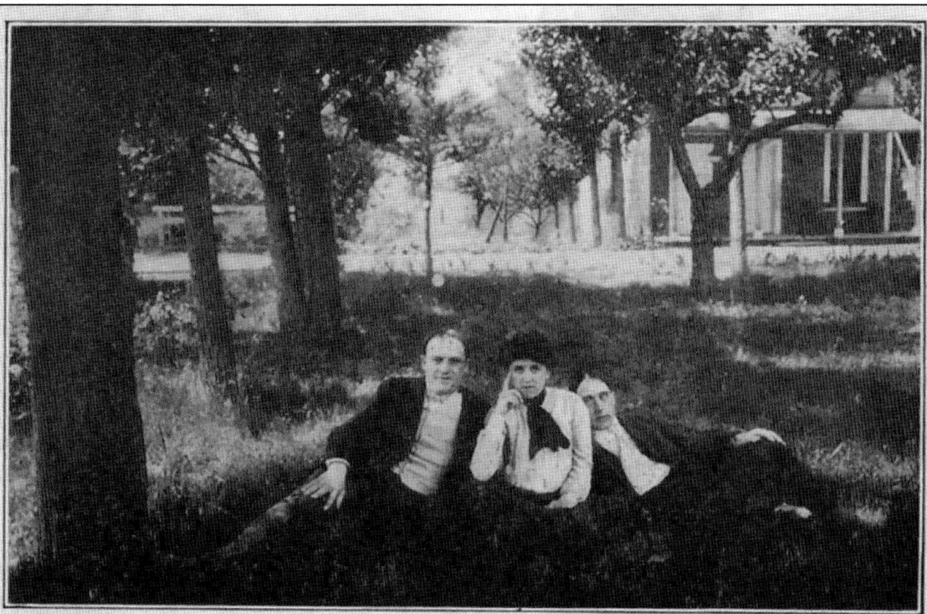

Taking Life Easy at Agua Caliente Springs.

"No more pleasant holiday can be taken than a drive to Agua Caliente Springs where the best of lunches and dinners are served at reasonable rates, and a glorious swim may be enjoyed in one the finest mineral baths in America," reported the *Sonoma Index-Tribune* in October 1887. (Courtesy of Gordon Lindberg.)

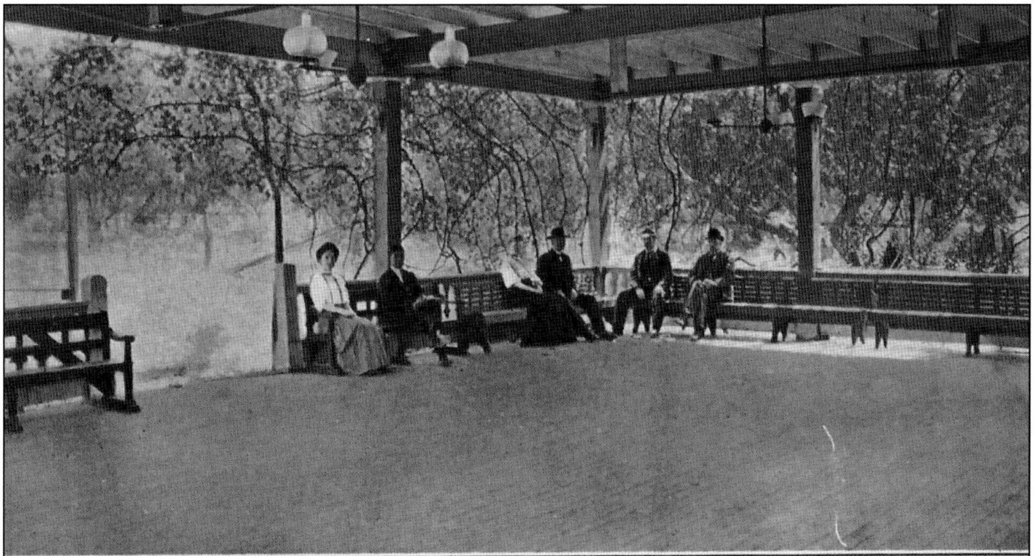

DANCING PAVILION, AGUA CALIENTE SPRINGS, CAL.

The pavilion at Agua Caliente Springs was open to the air and surrounded by trees, imbuing it with an air of gentility. The April 29, 1905, *Sonoma Index-Tribune* stated: "There will be a grand time next Saturday evening when the grand [season] opening of this popular resort will take place. Fine music has been engaged and there will be a program followed by dancing and a supper."

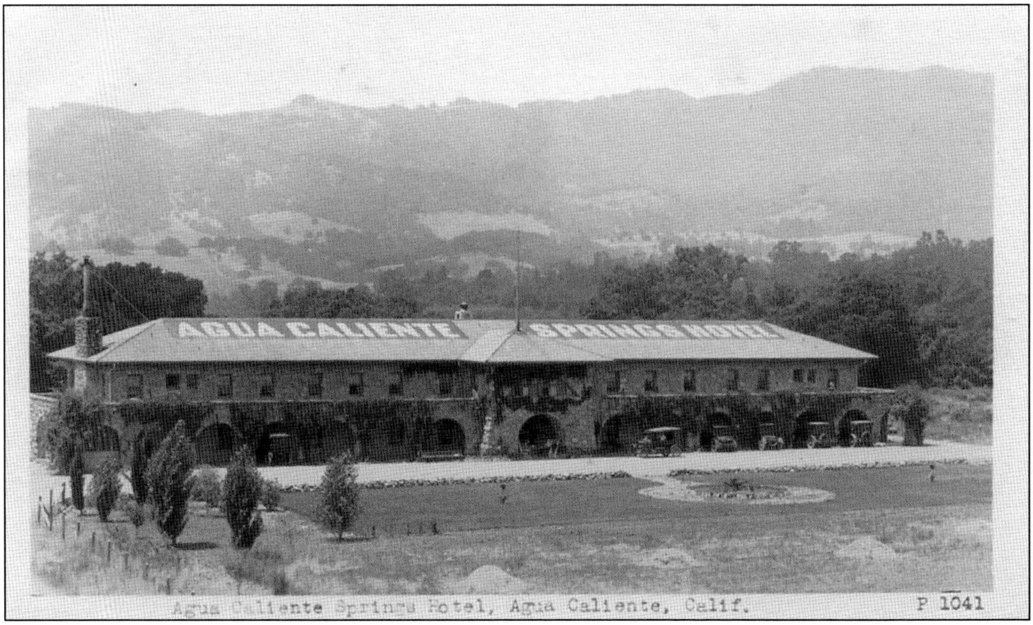

"Fireproof and steam heated, sulphur baths in rooms," read an advertisement for the "new" Agua Caliente Springs Hotel, which opened in 1917. Since it was made entirely of native stone, it was indeed fireproof. The building, located on Vailetti Road, is currently in use as an assisted-living facility. (Courtesy California State Library.)

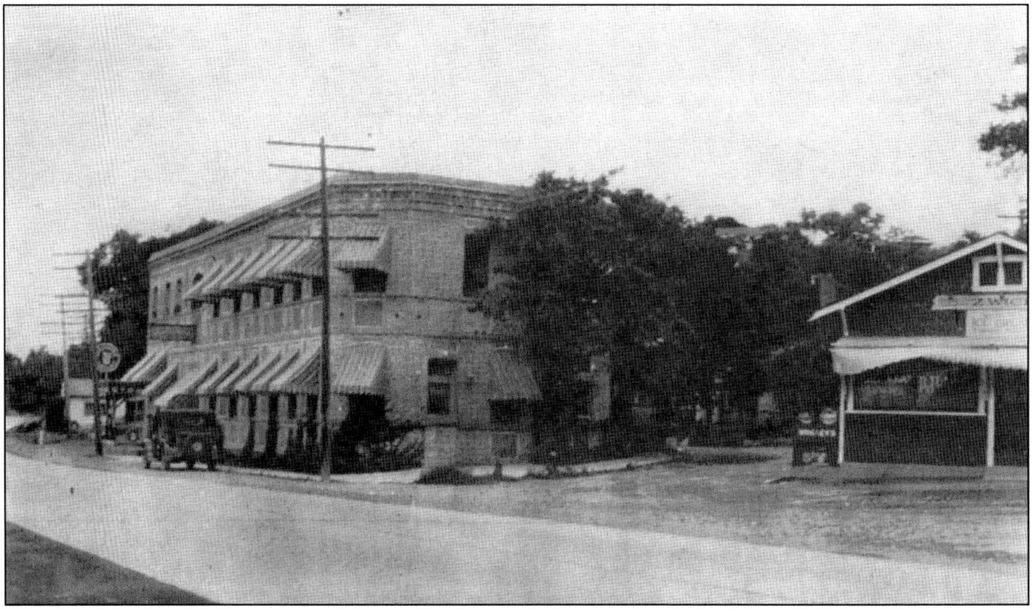

The Clementi Inn, built around 1910, continued under many names, including the Robin Hood Inn, Lafayette Hotel, and Paul's Castle. It was converted to apartments in 1940. The building was eventually abandoned and fell into disrepair, and it was demolished in 2009. (Courtesy of Gary Heon and the Sonoma Valley Historical Society.)

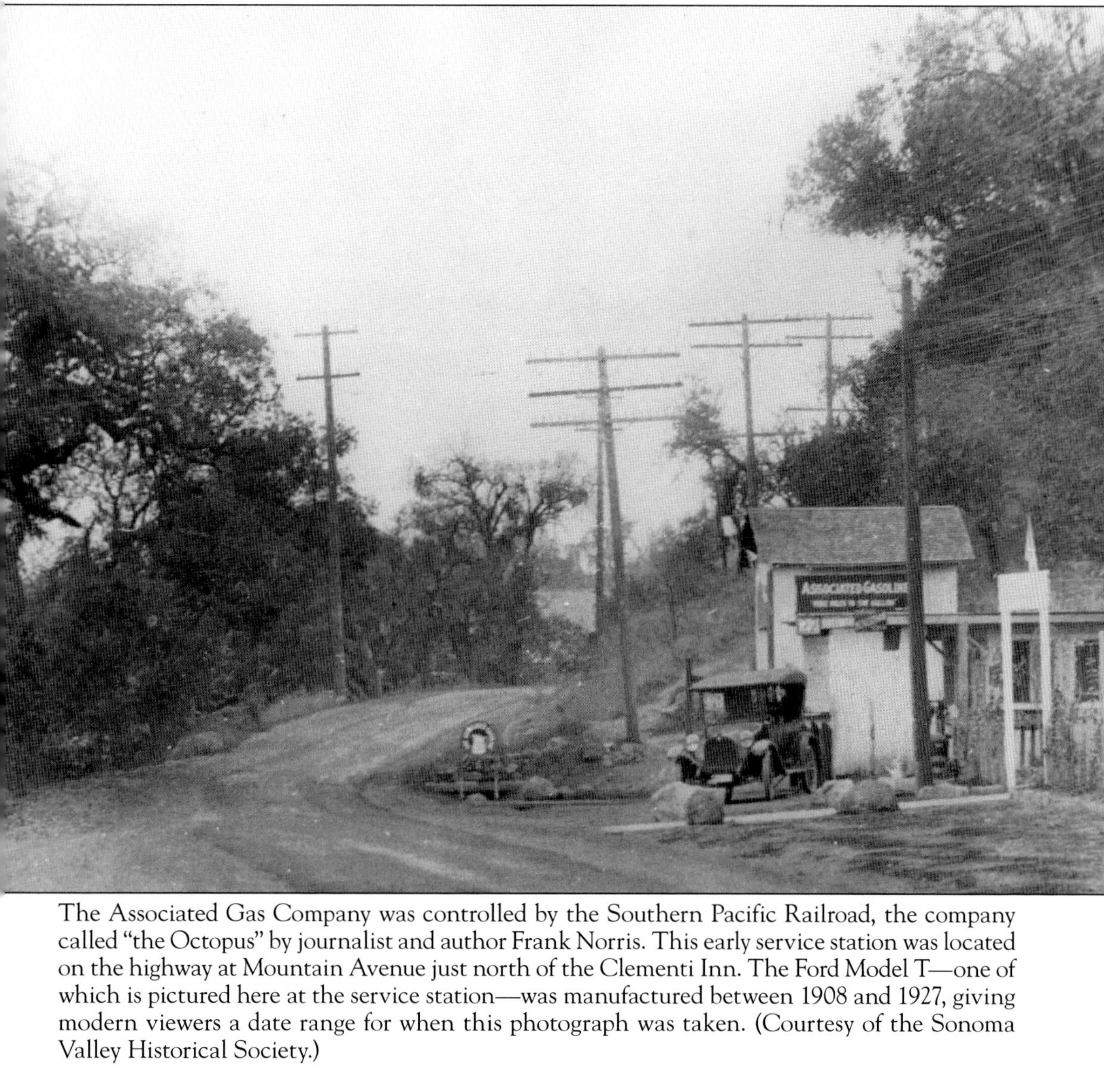

The Associated Gas Company was controlled by the Southern Pacific Railroad, the company called "the Octopus" by journalist and author Frank Norris. This early service station was located on the highway at Mountain Avenue just north of the Clementi Inn. The Ford Model T—one of which is pictured here at the service station—was manufactured between 1908 and 1927, giving modern viewers a date range for when this photograph was taken. (Courtesy of the Sonoma Valley Historical Society.)

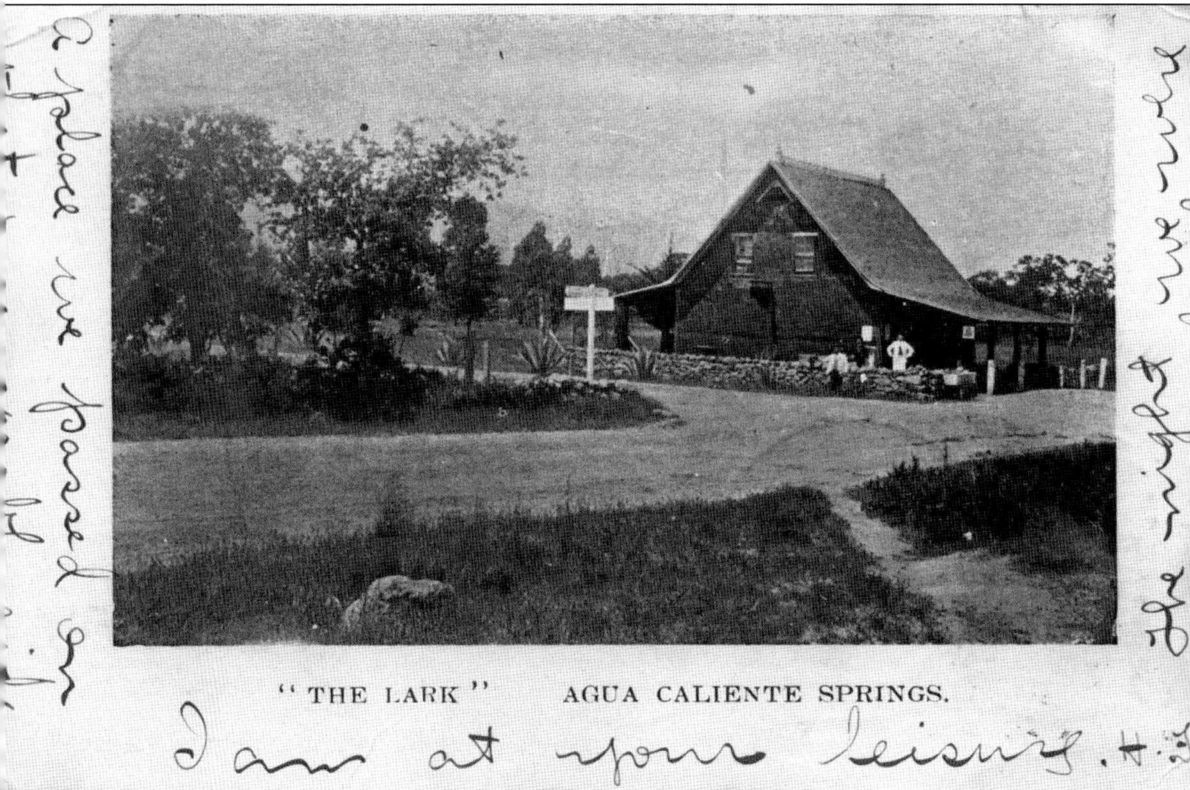

On October 9, 1906, "H.J.G." wrote to Anna Silva of Larkspur, Marin County, "A place we passed on that memorable ride, the night we went out on a lark." In the 1920s, the Lark was owned by Sal Carlo, a well-known prizefighter. In 1922, the *Sonoma Index-Tribune* reported that Carlo "made a big investment on the site of the ole Caliente Hotel where he conducts his extensive resort and attractive café, the Lark." In 1924, he added a garage to the back of the Lark. In 1925, like many other valley resort hosts, he was briefly arrested for violation of the Volstead Act (Prohibition).

Two

THE GREAT DEVELOPMENT

In 1911, the Boyes Hot Springs post office was established in Graham's Cash Store. The already thriving town was thus informally founded, though it would celebrate its centennial in 1949. By 1911, there were dozens of resorts in the Springs ranging from humble cottages to large hotels with swimming plunges, picnic grounds, and dance halls.

Entertainment was abundant and varied. According to the *Sonoma Index-Tribune*, in March 1913, a half-day of school was declared so that the children, along with most of the rest of the populace, could attend a baseball game between the Chicago White Sox and the San Francisco Seals at the ballpark in Boyes Hot Springs.

Dancing and dance music were very popular during the early 20th century. According to an article in the *San Francisco Call-Bulletin*, band leader Art Hickman was said to have picked up the term "jazz" from baseball players when he was performing during the evenings for them at training camp in Boyes Hot Springs in the 1910s.

A catastrophic fire in 1923 destroyed much of the Springs, but shortly afterward, thanks to the remarkable resilience of its people, optimism was in the air and rebuilding was vigorous. A headline in the *Index-Tribune* on September 23, 1923, the day after the fire, read: "A Bigger and Better Boyes Hot Springs."

The Boyes Bath House survived the fire and was remodeled and expanded many times. The Boyes Hot Springs Hotel was rebuilt, and its name was changed to the Sonoma Mission Inn in 1928.

The big resorts at Fetters Hot Springs and Agua Caliente Springs were in their prime. El Verano boasted resorts such as El Verano Villa, French Cottage, and Rossi's, which later became Little Switzerland.

Boyes Hot Springs even had its own movie studio for a short time when Harold "Josh" Binney came to the valley to make silent comedies in 1923 and set up his Sonoma Photoplay Studio right on Sonoma Highway (now known as Highway 12).

As early as 1934, the railroads started to diminish in importance, and that year, the El Verano station of the Southern Pacific was eliminated. In 1942, the Boyes Hot Springs line was pulled up, and the era of the railroad came to an end.

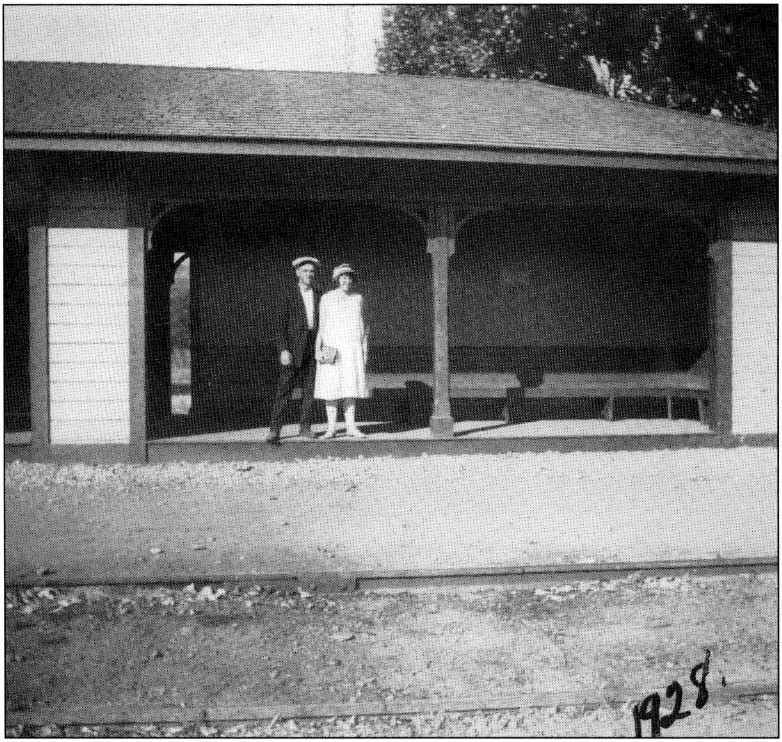

This photograph is from a series taken by tourists in 1928. The unidentified couple is standing on the depot platform at Boyes Hot Springs. As wonderful as old postcards can be, even more precious are the candid pictures that offer slice-of-life snapshots a commercial photographer would never make.

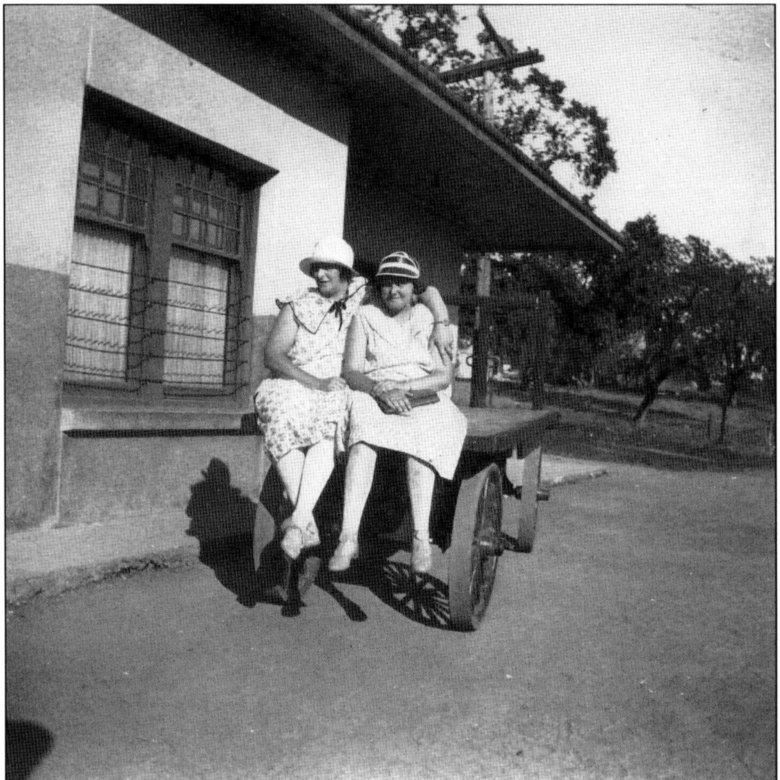

In this 1928 picture, two unidentified vacationers pose on a railway wagon outside the monolithic Fetters depot, which was built in 1913.

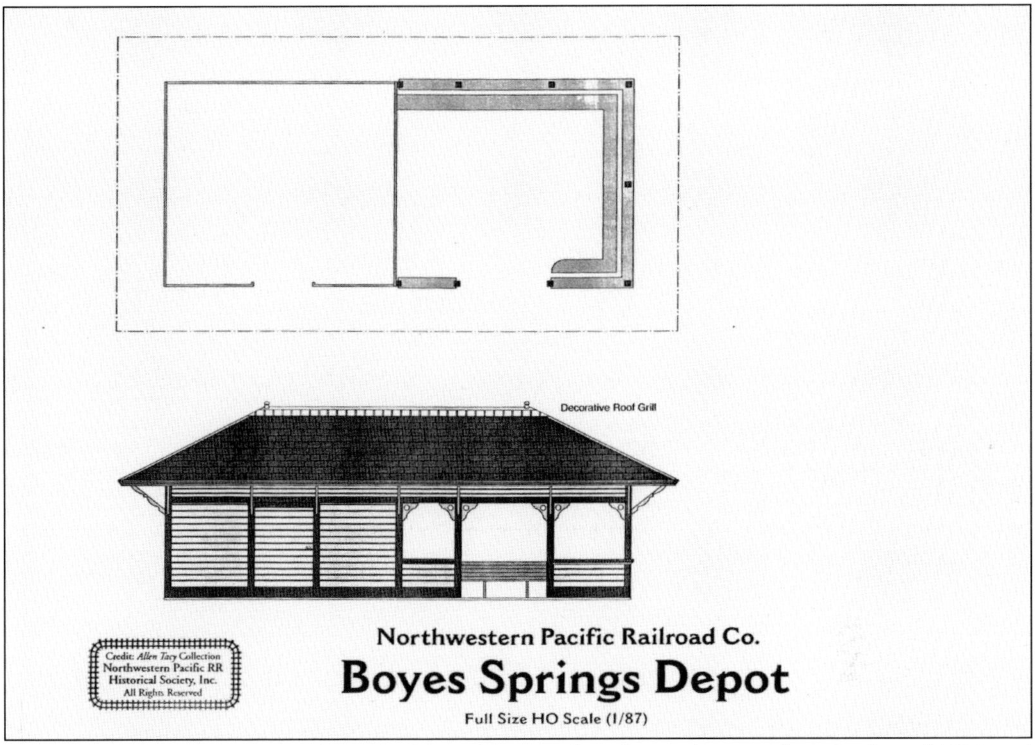

The first Boyes Hot Springs depot building (shown above) was destroyed in the fire of 1923 and rebuilt in 1925. The new building was "of the standard suburban type, rustic finish and cement floors. The waiting room will be 12x40 feet, the platform 16x48 feet, and the freight shed 12x20 feet. There will also be an agent's office," according to a June 1925 article in the *Sonoma Index-Tribune*. (Courtesy of the Northwestern Pacific Railroad Historical Society, Allen Tacy Collection.)

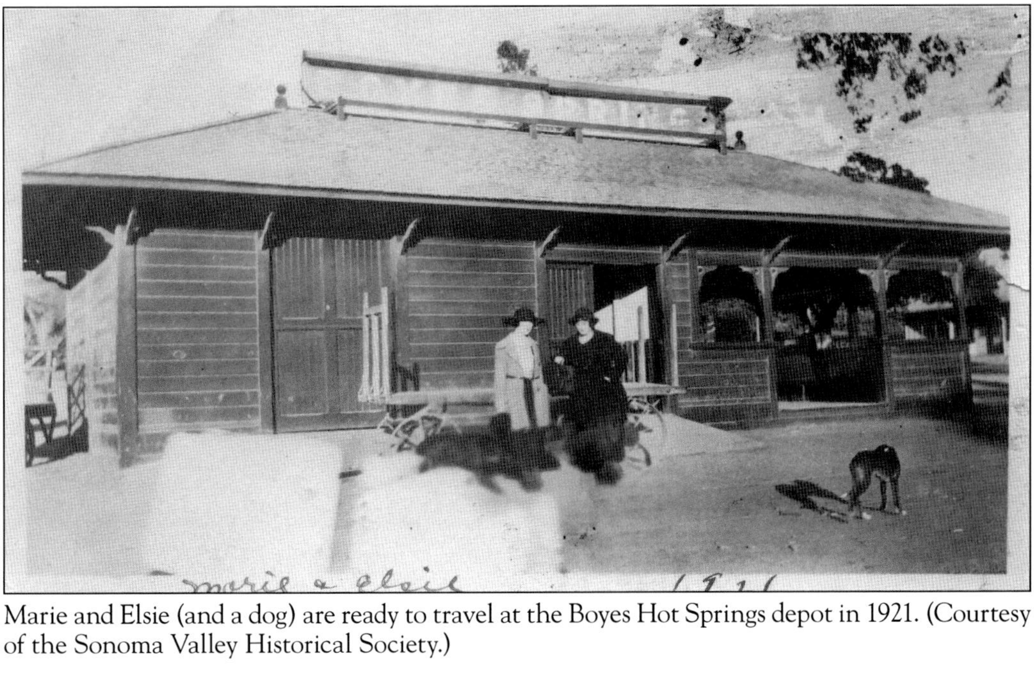

Marie and Elsie (and a dog) are ready to travel at the Boyes Hot Springs depot in 1921. (Courtesy of the Sonoma Valley Historical Society.)

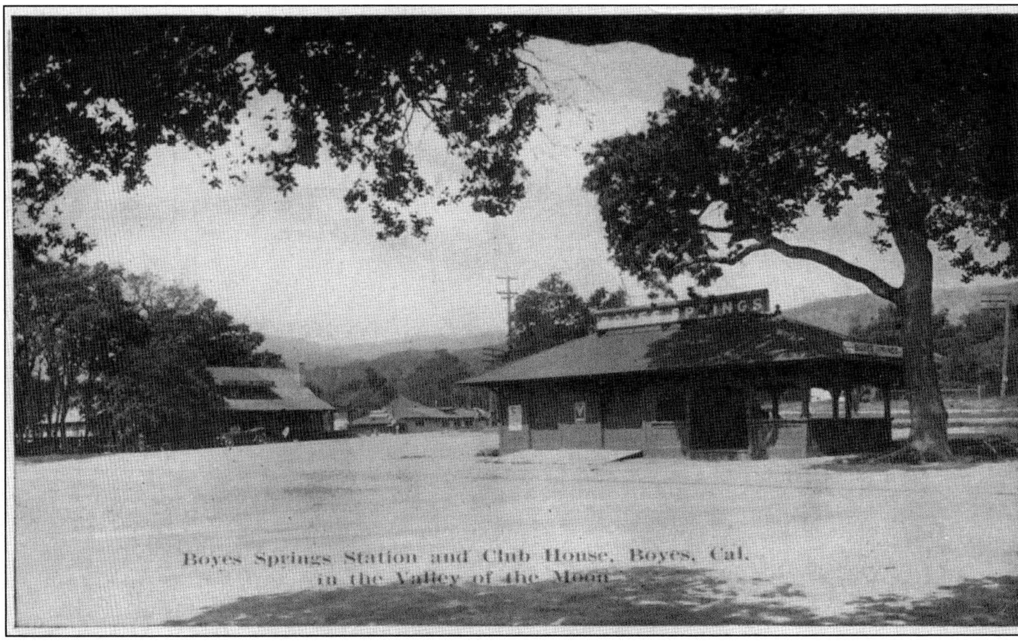

This photograph shows the Boyes Hot Springs depot and clubhouse as arriving passengers saw them before the 1923 fire. Fetters Springs also had a clubhouse. The qualification for membership was the price of a drink.

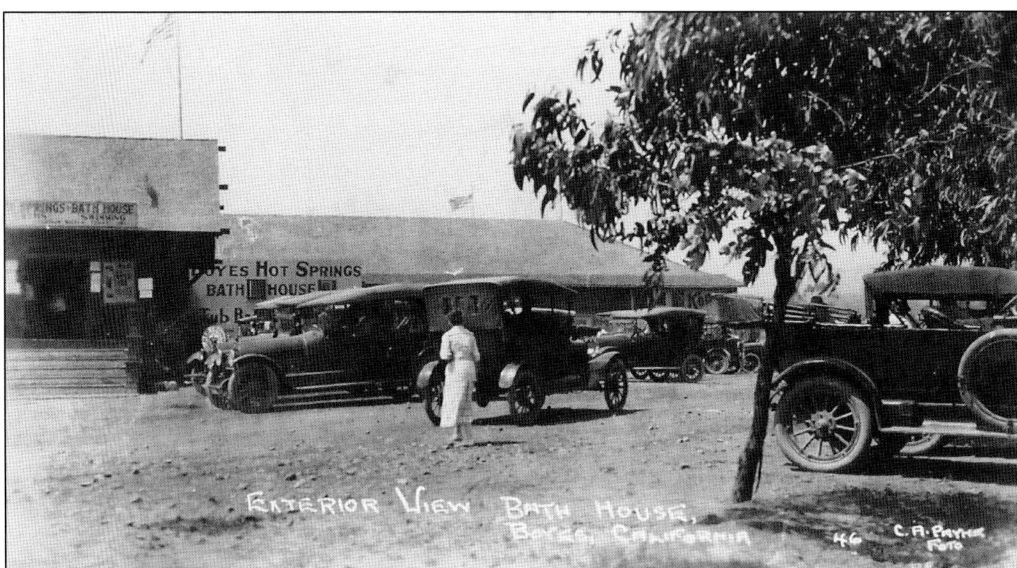

In the spring of 1925, the Boyes Bath House was completely remodeled. The new owners, Partridge and Lichtenberg, demolished the old buildings and brought in an "army of carpenters" to raise a new establishment. That May, the *Sonoma Index-Tribune* reported that the new owners celebrated the grand opening with a three-day carnival.

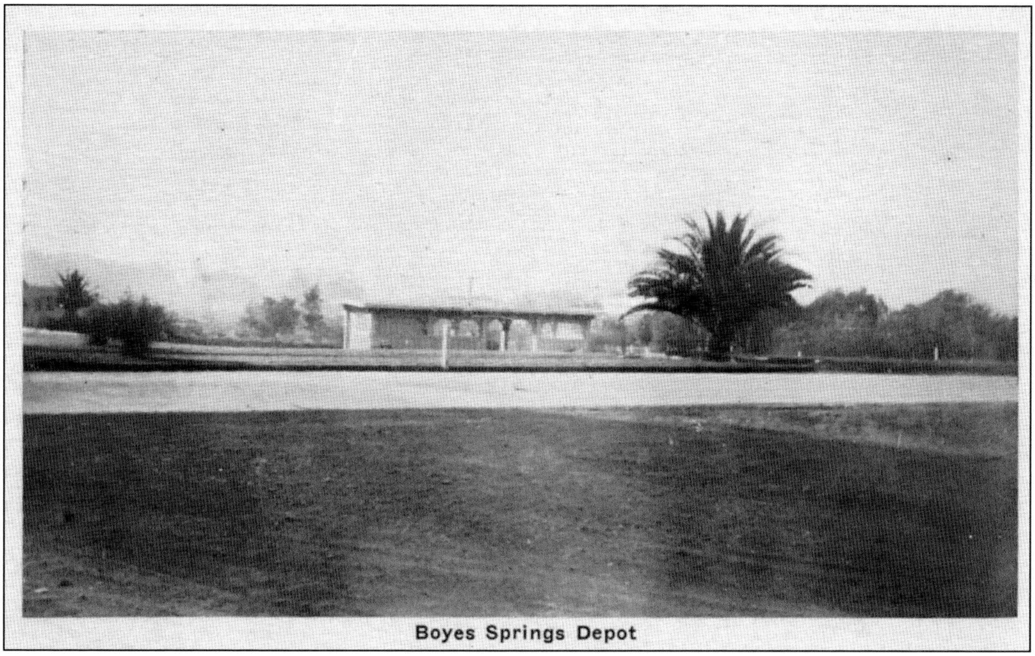

In this photograph, the depot at Boyes Hot Springs has the companionship of a vigorous palm tree. This tree remained a fixture of the center of the Boyes Plaza, as it came to be known, until it was cut down in 1956 to make way for the Plaza Center Building. (Courtesy of the Sonoma Valley Historical Society.)

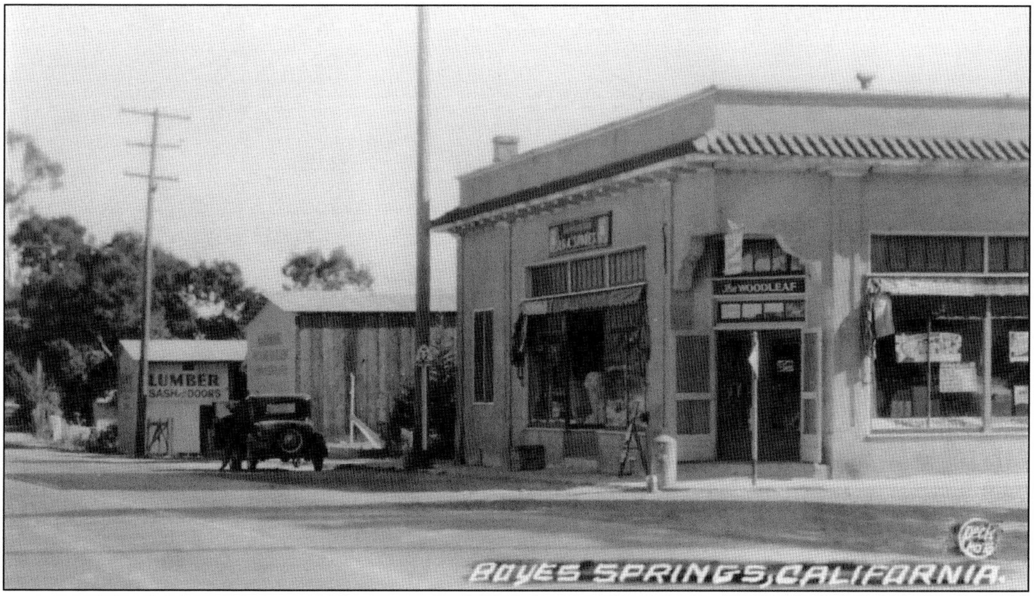

Marion Greene took over management of the Woodleaf Store in 1921, the year the original building was constructed. After the fire of 1923, a new store was built for H. Cabanot in 1924. Greene ran the business for 29 years, during which time she was twice elected president of the Sonoma County Retail Grocers Association—the only woman to hold that position. Along with Rudy Lichtenberg, she founded the Boyes Hot Springs Improvement Club. (Courtesy of the Sonoma Valley Historical Society.)

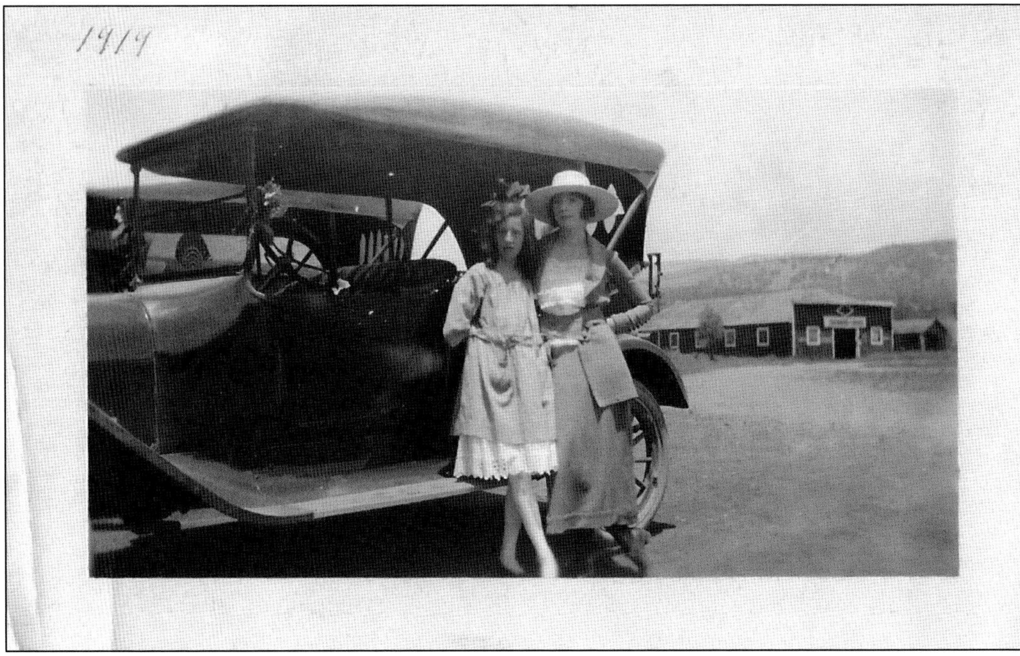

Two unidentified, stylish women pose in front of their automobile, with one sporting her summer hat. The photograph is helpfully inscribed with "Boyes Hot Springs, 1919." The buildings in the background do not help to establish the exact location. (Courtesy of the Sonoma Valley Historical Society.)

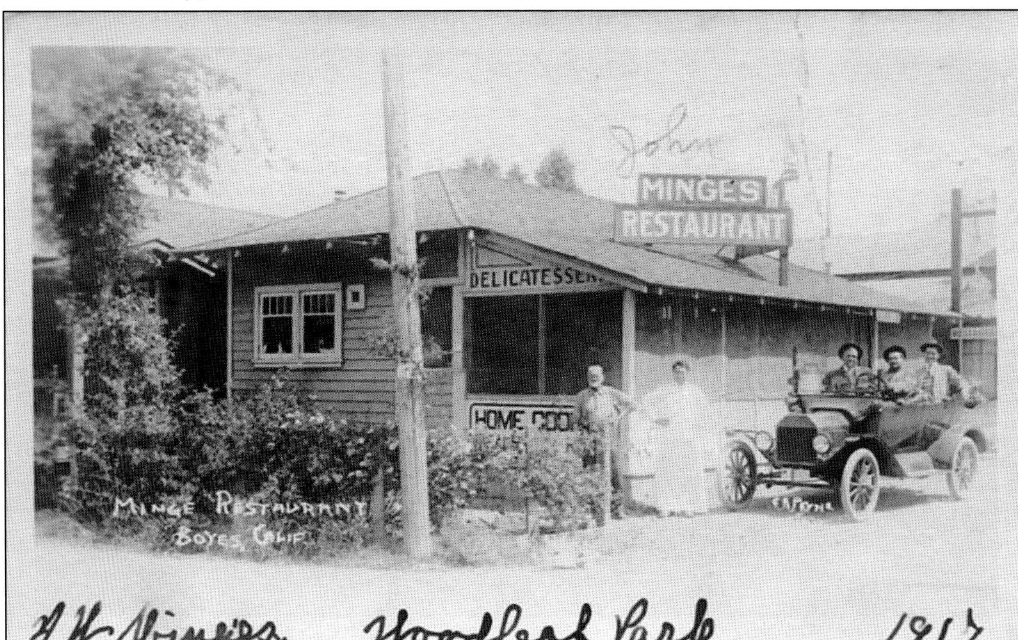

William Minges was a prominent businessman and landowner in Boyes Hot Springs during the first three decades of the 20th century. He owned cottages, a restaurant (pictured), a water company, and a store. He was an officer in the Boyes Hot Springs Improvement Club and greatly boosted rebuilding after the 1923 fire that destroyed so much, including most of his buildings.

In 1925, the *Sonoma Index-Tribune* reported that "Boyes Hot Springs Mineral Water, as bottled at the Springs by H. Peterson, gives California one of its finest natural products and has brought fame to Sonoma Valley. The water comes direct from the springs to your table in attractive bottles, quarts or pints or nips. It is soft, pure and sparkling, and superior to any imported water on the market. Physicians recommend the use of this water as a corrective for stomach and related troubles." (Right, courtesy of Robert Parmelee; below, author's collection.)

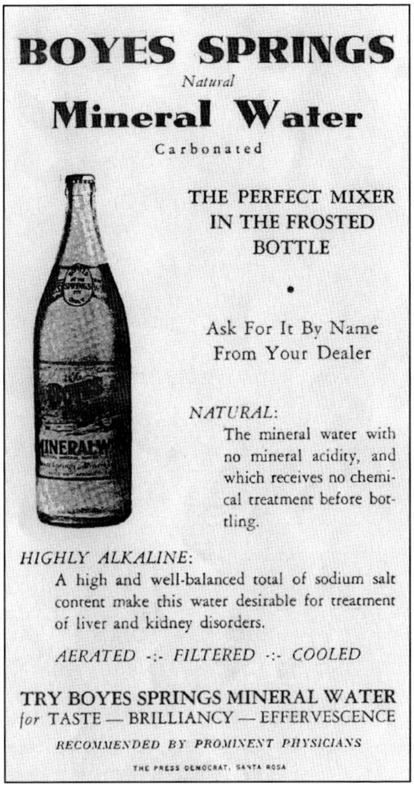

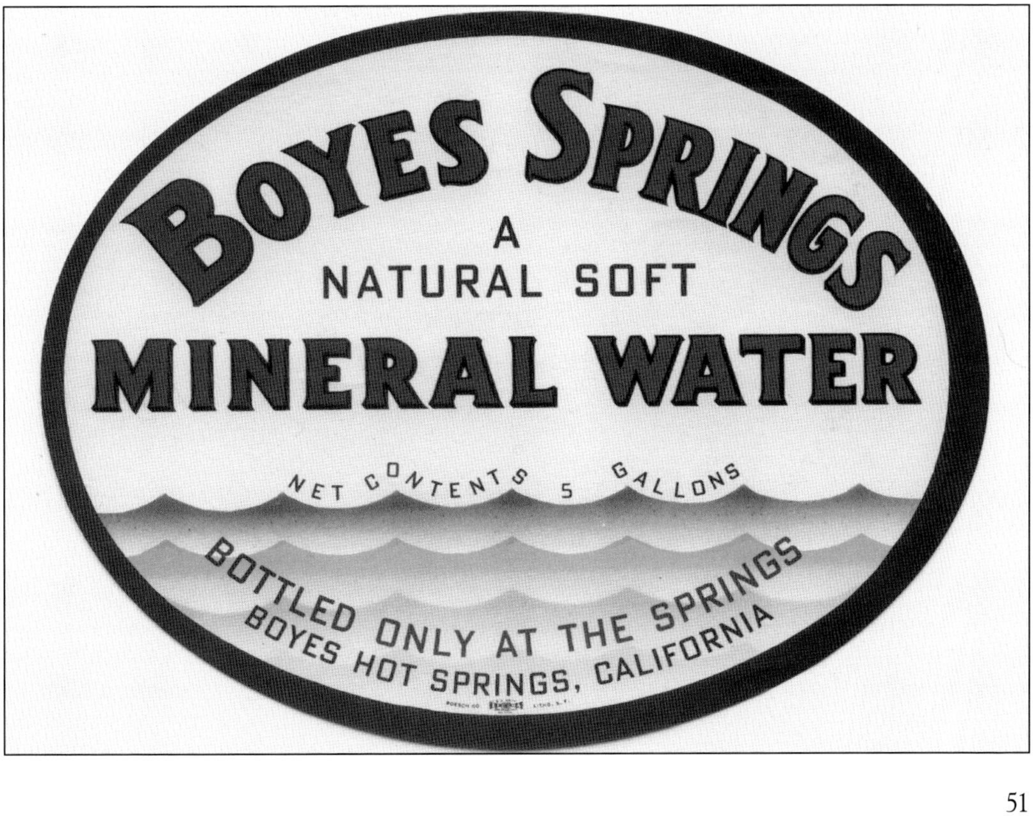

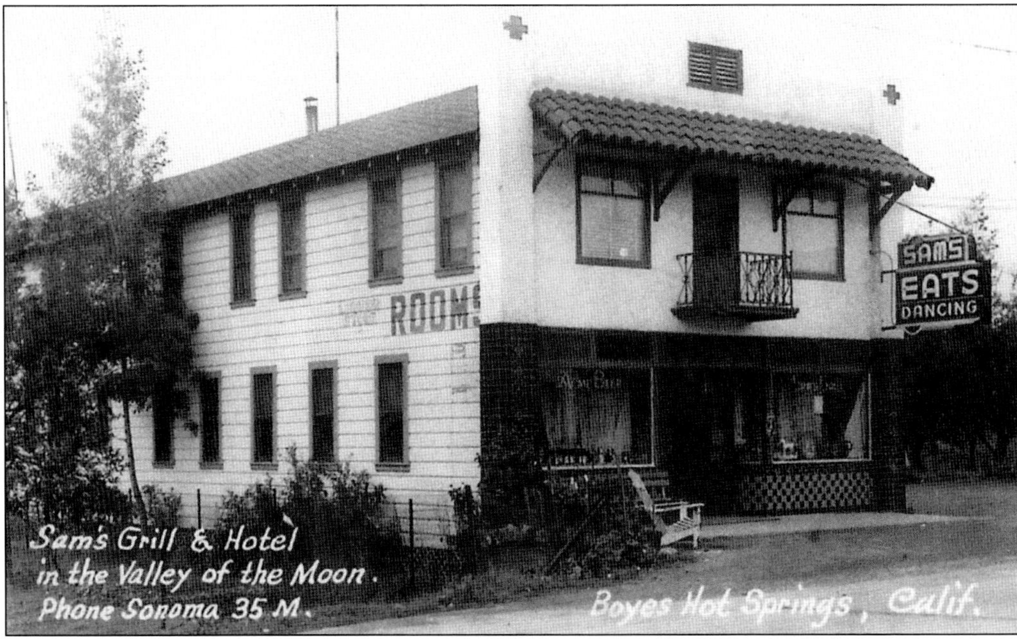

Sam Ganos purchased his restaurant building on the highway across Central Avenue from the Boyes Hot Springs Hotel Subdivision in 1918. The *Sonoma Index-Tribune* reported that during the 1923 fire he "fought like a Trojan and succeeded in putting out the fire as it repeatedly attacked the two-story frame structure, which was saved." Ganos and his family ran restaurants in Boyes Hot Springs through the 1960s. (Courtesy of the Sonoma Valley Historical Society.)

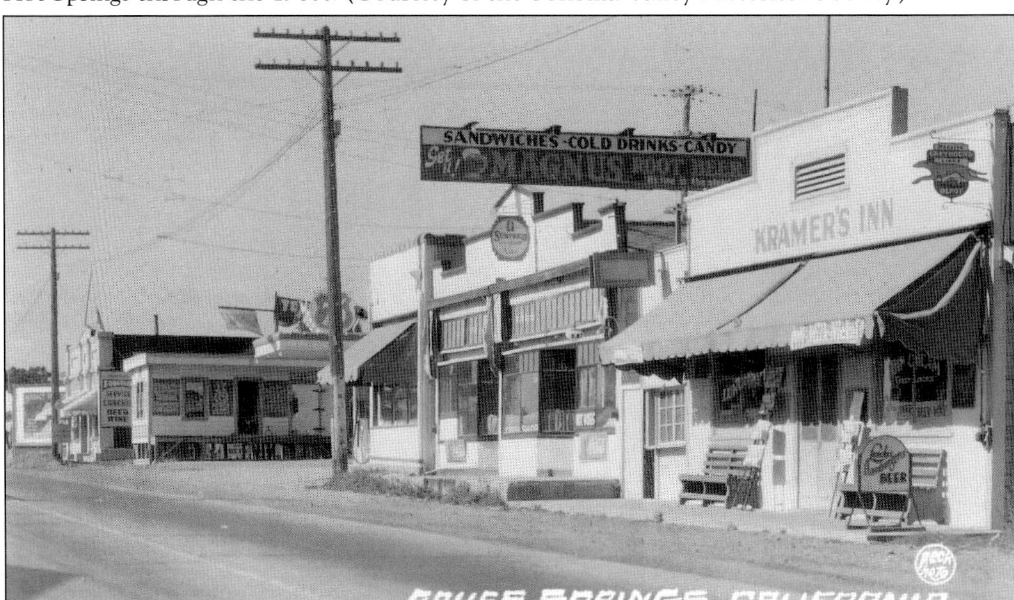

In 1924, the *Sonoma Index-Tribune* reported that "Among the recently rebuilt stores of Boyes Hot Springs is that of N. Kramer, who continues to make improvements. The store is soon to have a stucco front and the interior is being nicely improved, also." In 1930, the *Index-Tribune* featured an advertisement for the Pacific Greyhound Lines, with Kramer as the Boyes Hot Springs agent. The Greyhound sign is visible at far right. (Courtesy of the Sonoma Valley Historical Society.)

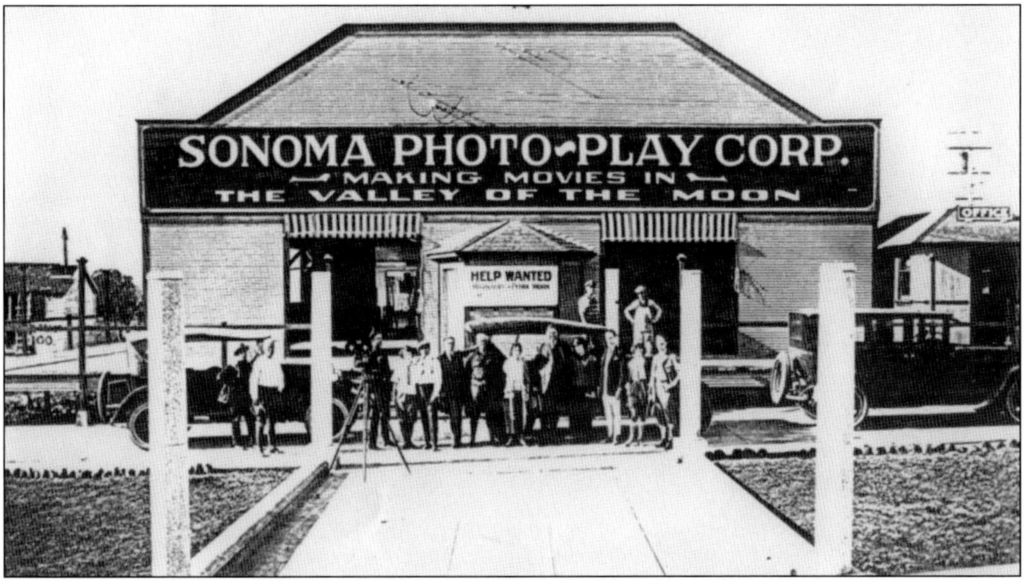

Director and actor Harold "Josh" Binney came to Sonoma in 1923, setting up a movie studio on the main highway in Boyes Hot Springs and arousing great excitement in the populace. He produced three short comedies before skipping town, pursued by angry creditors. After serving a short prison sentence for fraud, Binney went on to direct movies in Hollywood. His studio was located on Sonoma Highway across from the current location of the Grange Hall. (Courtesy of the Sonoma Valley Historical Society.)

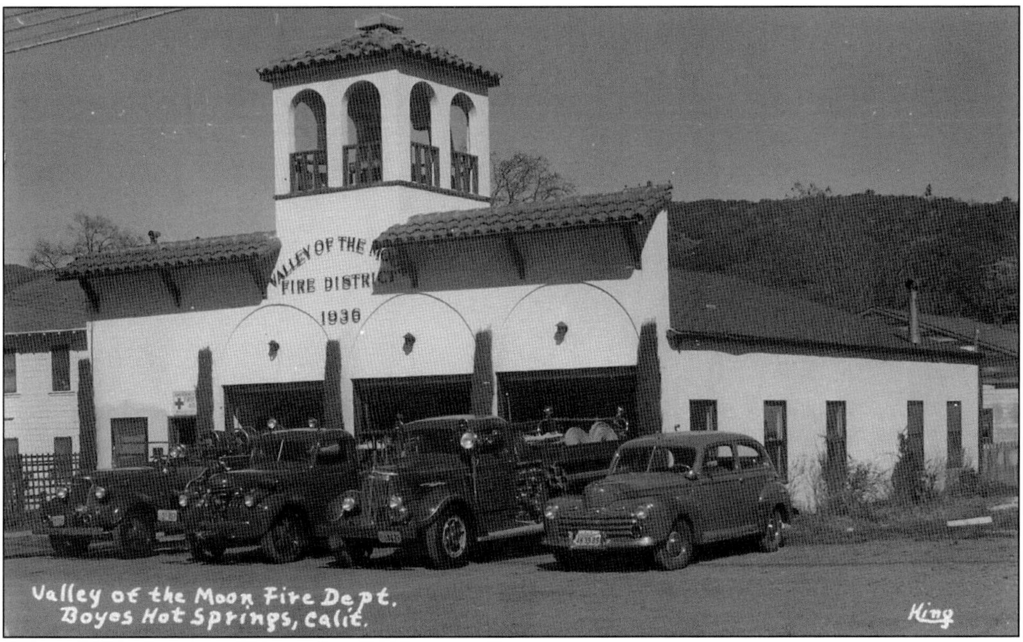

The Valley of the Moon Fire District was founded in 1916. In 1936, the new, Mission-style fire station was constructed on the Sonoma Highway at Central Street. It was built at a cost of $6,000 using workers from the New Deal's Public Works Administration. According the *Sonoma Index-Tribune*, "The tower which looms from the building and houses the siren, has changed the skyline of the Springs district and gives it a metropolitan air." (Courtesy of Robert Parmelee.)

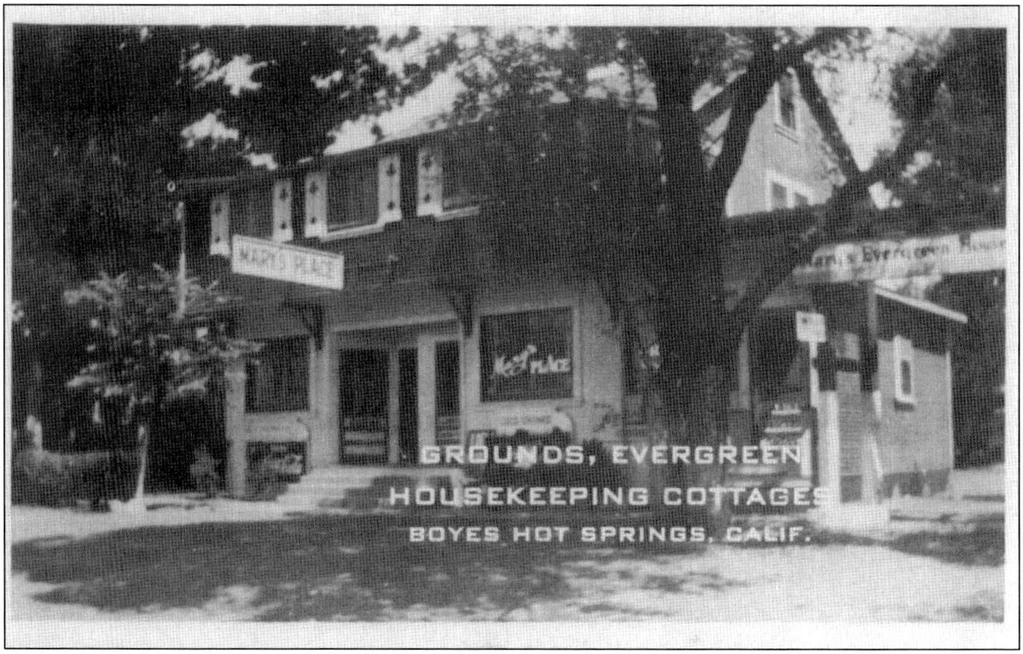

The Evergreen Cottages resort existed from at least the 1920s through the 1950s. The handsome main building still stood on Pine Street in Boyes Hot Springs in 2016. (Courtesy of Gordon Lindberg.)

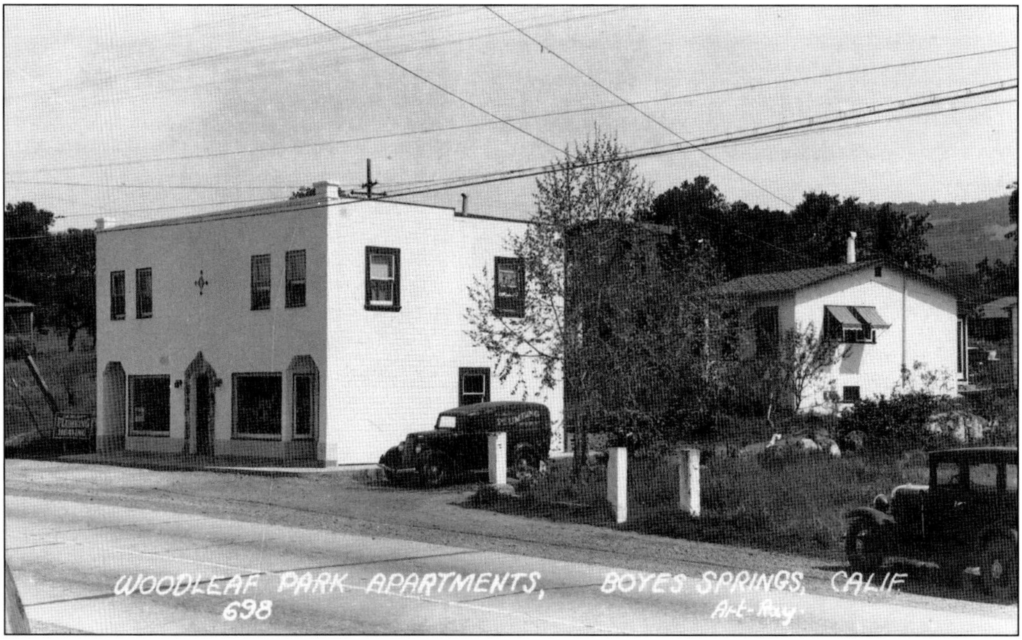

In the 1930s, the Woodleaf Park Apartments building housed the E.A. Delaney plumbing company. From the mid-1950s to 2016, barber John Mazza cut the hair of generations of men in the shop at right. Keeping that tradition alive is the new barber, Antonio Juan. (Courtesy of Gordon Lindberg.)

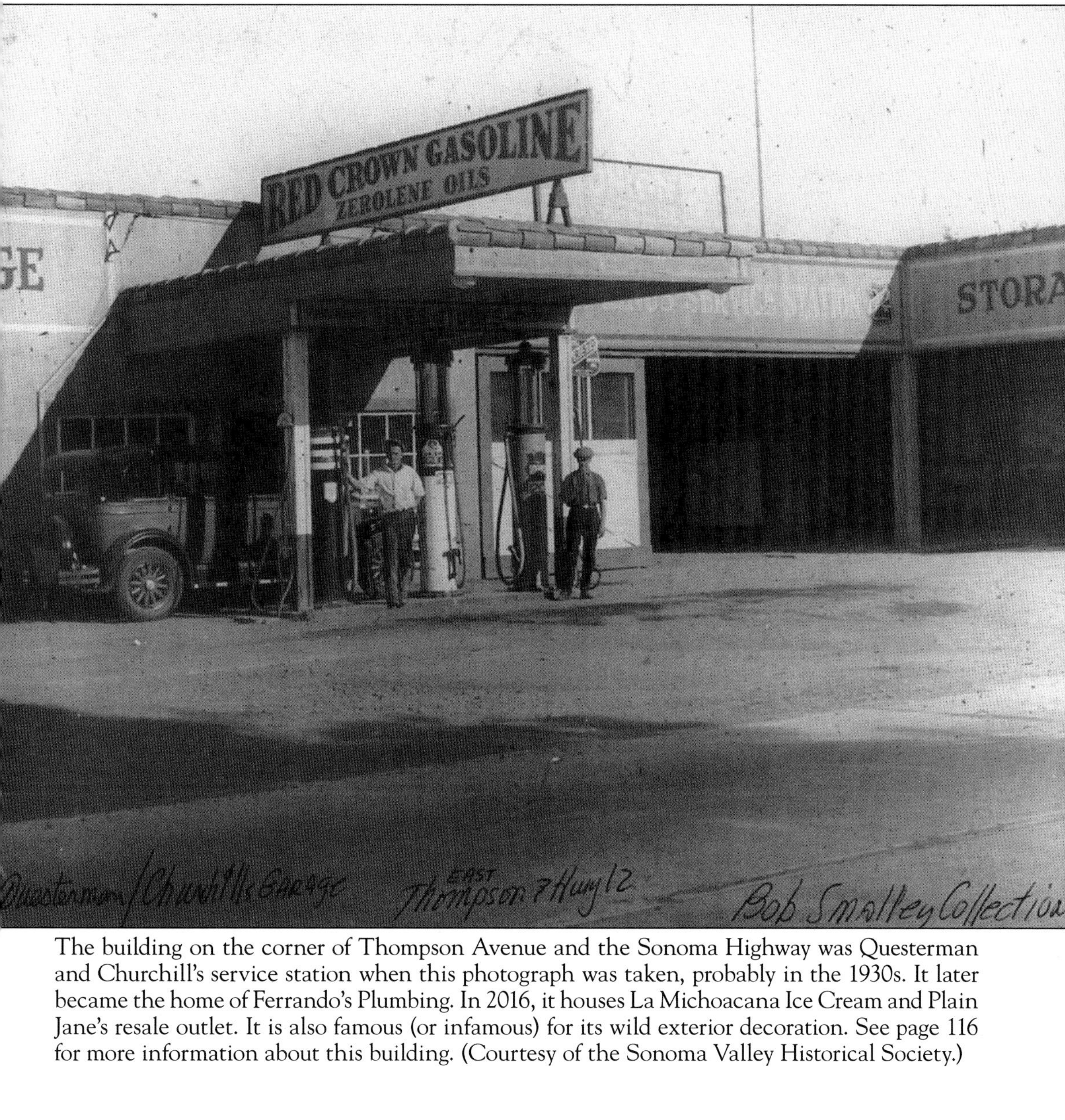

The building on the corner of Thompson Avenue and the Sonoma Highway was Questerman and Churchill's service station when this photograph was taken, probably in the 1930s. It later became the home of Ferrando's Plumbing. In 2016, it houses La Michoacana Ice Cream and Plain Jane's resale outlet. It is also famous (or infamous) for its wild exterior decoration. See page 116 for more information about this building. (Courtesy of the Sonoma Valley Historical Society.)

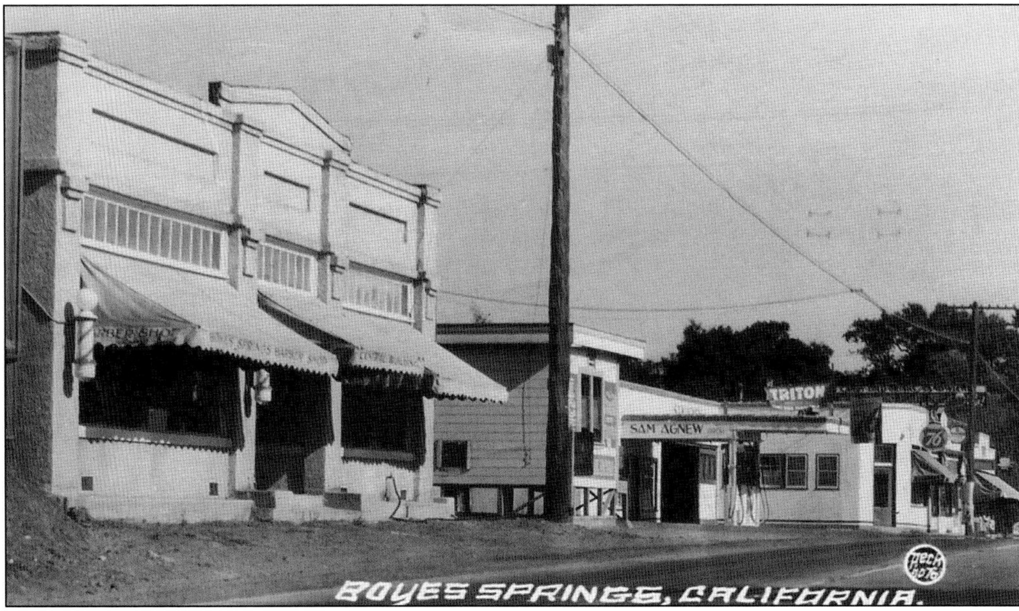

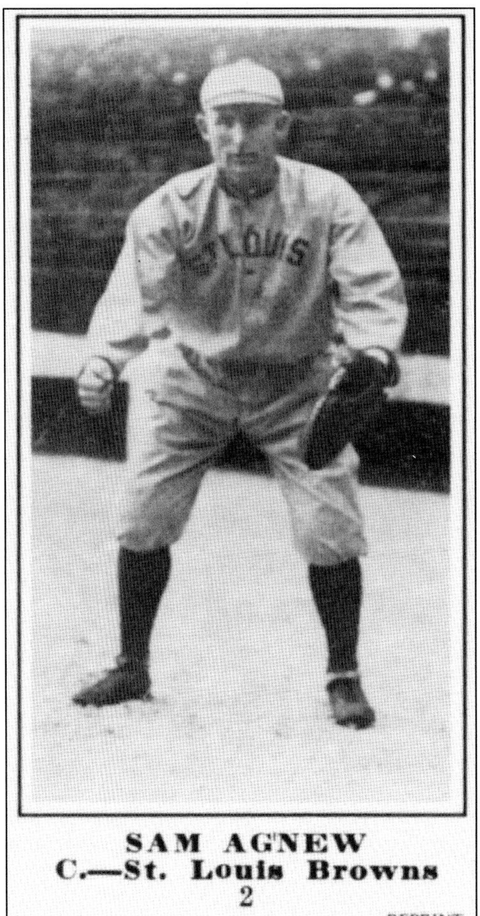

In a view looking south on the highway near Vallejo Street, the Central building, constructed by barber Bob Liaros in the 1920s, is in the foreground, and just past the center is the service station of Sam Agnew. Between the two is the Ice House. Kramer's Inn is in the distance. Agnew was a former Major League Baseball catcher and manager who moved to Sonoma Valley and opened his business in 1935. He played for the St. Louis Browns, the Boston Red Sox, and the Washington Senators in the years between 1913 and 1919.

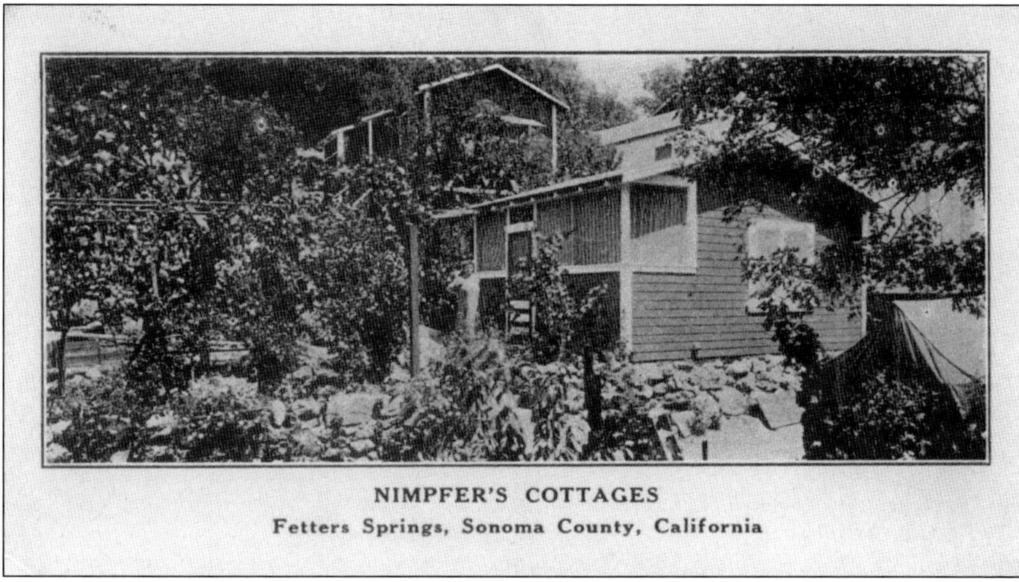

George Nimpfer ran a resort in Agua Caliente, across the highway from Fetters Springs, in the 1930s and 1940s. Earlier, the resort was called Leixner's, and its owner, Martin Leixner, was business partners with Nimpfer in various ways over many years. At one point, they bought the orchards of Fetters resort. Nimpfer's Cottages are up the steep rocky hill from the main building on the highway, which still stands in 2016, although it is in very poor condition. (Courtesy Sonoma Valley Historical Society.)

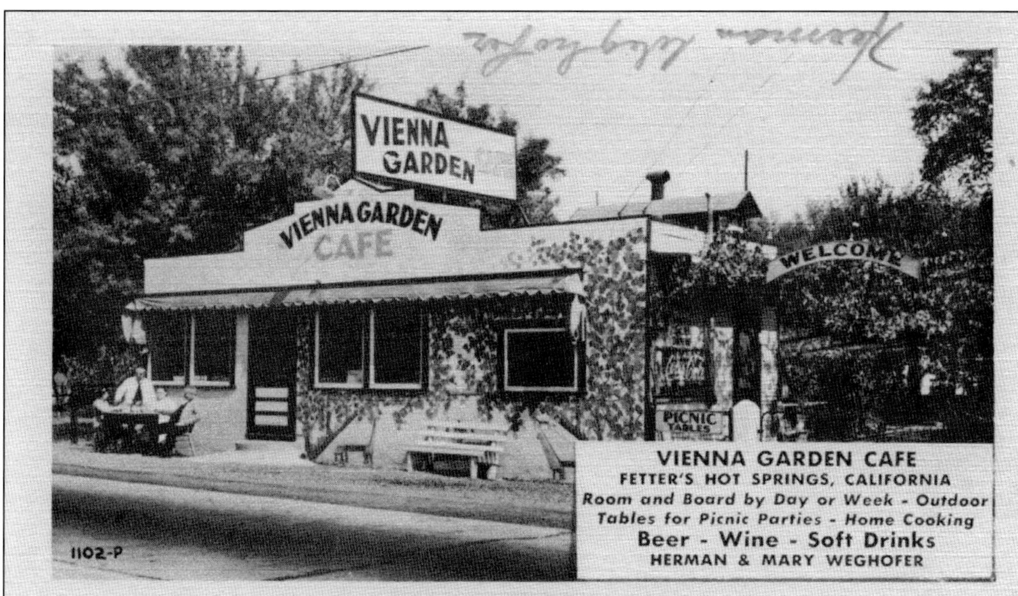

On Friday, September 10, 1937, the *Sonoma Index-Tribune* reported that a large group of tailors "visited their friend, Herman Weghofer, at Vienna Gardens, in Fetters Springs. . . . This was a veritable tailor's convention and Mr. Weghofer, who formerly tailored for the City of Paris, was very happy."

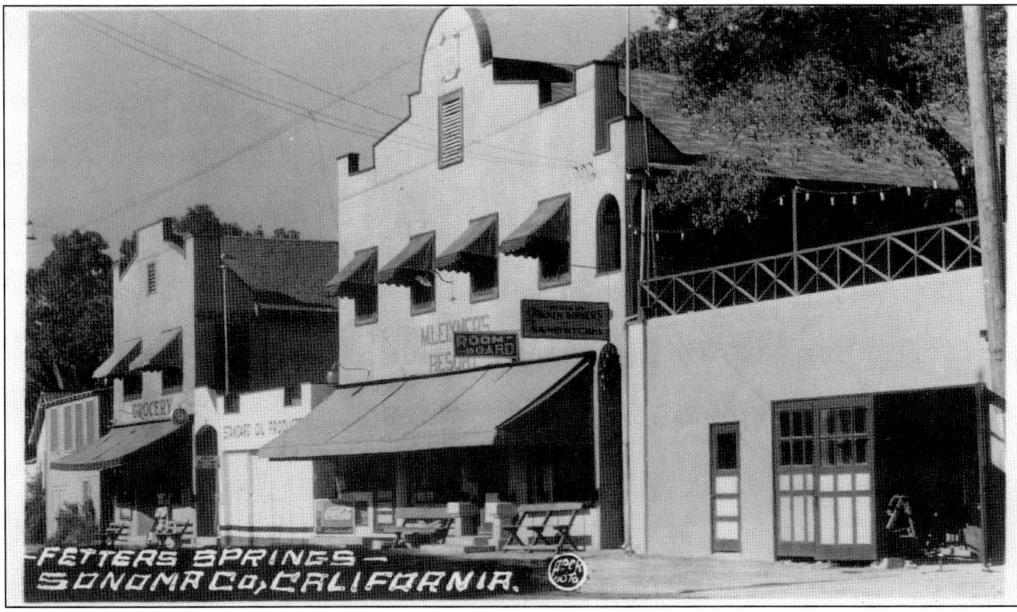

Martin Leixner started a tailoring business in Sonoma in 1919. He was among a group of Viennese immigrants that settled in the area. In 1923, he joined with another Viennese tailor, Herman Weghofer, to enlarge the business, which was advertised in the *Sonoma Index-Tribune* as being located "in Fetters Springs, on the Highway, opposite the Hotel (Fetters)." Herman Weghofer opened his Vienna Garden Café just a few hundred feet south of there, near Mountain Avenue, a few years later.

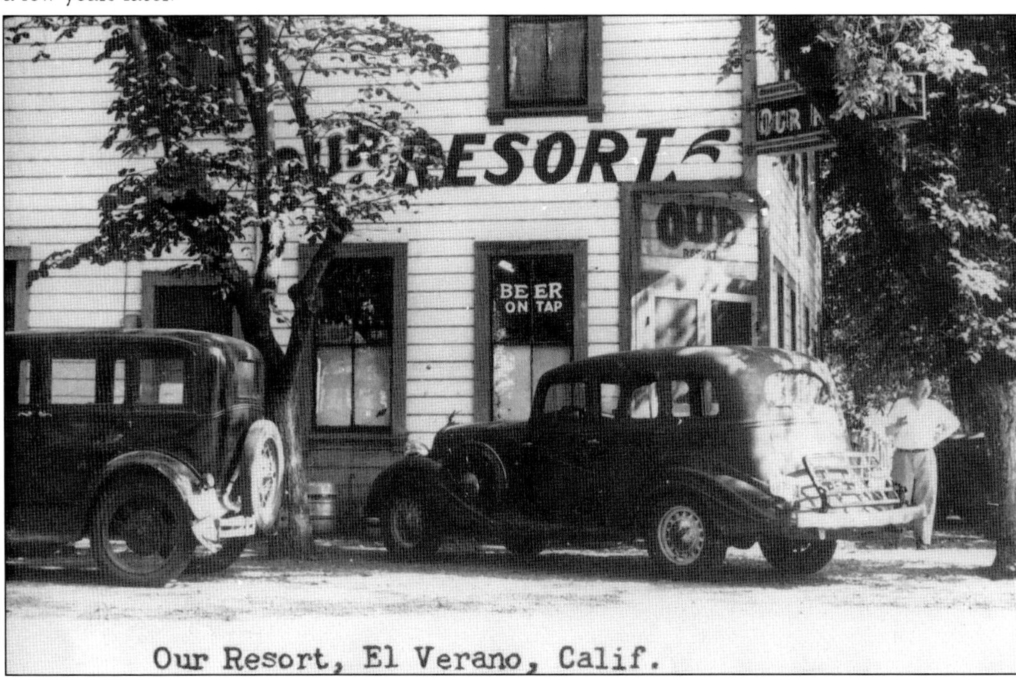

Our Resort was originally Crane's Hotel. The buildings at the corner of Maple and Verano Avenues still stand in 2016 but have been empty for many years. (Courtesy of the Sonoma Valley Historical Society.)

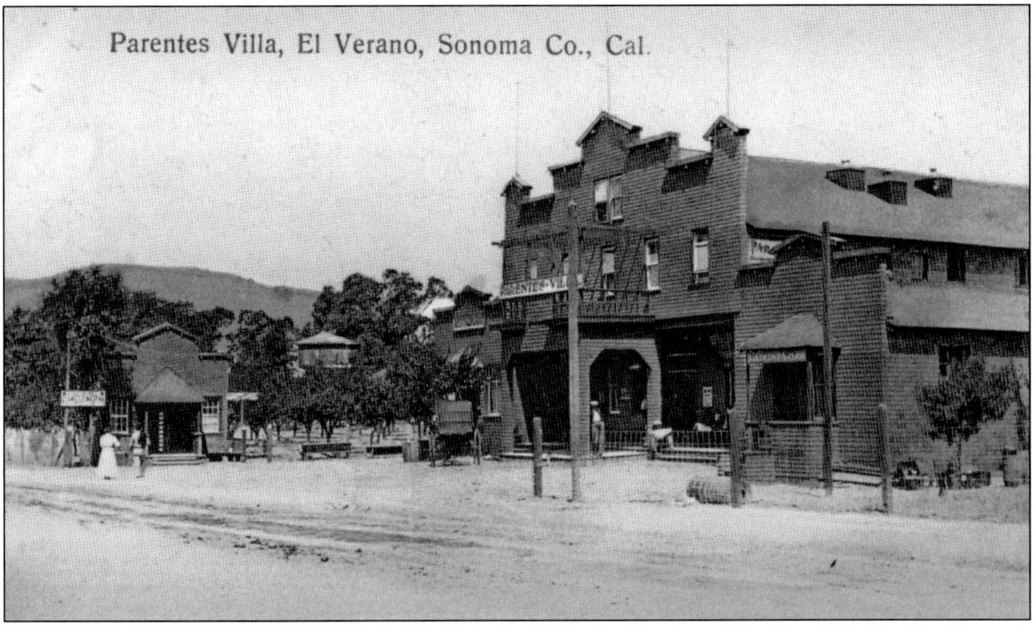

Sometime before 1910, Louis Parente started his long run as one of the top resort owners in the valley. His complex on Verano Avenue, located next to Paul's Resort, would eventually become Rozario's, then the El Verano Inn (not the one in the Mullen's General Store building), and was later replaced by an addition to the Finnish American Home Association housing complex in 1985. (Courtesy of the Sonoma Valley Historical Society.)

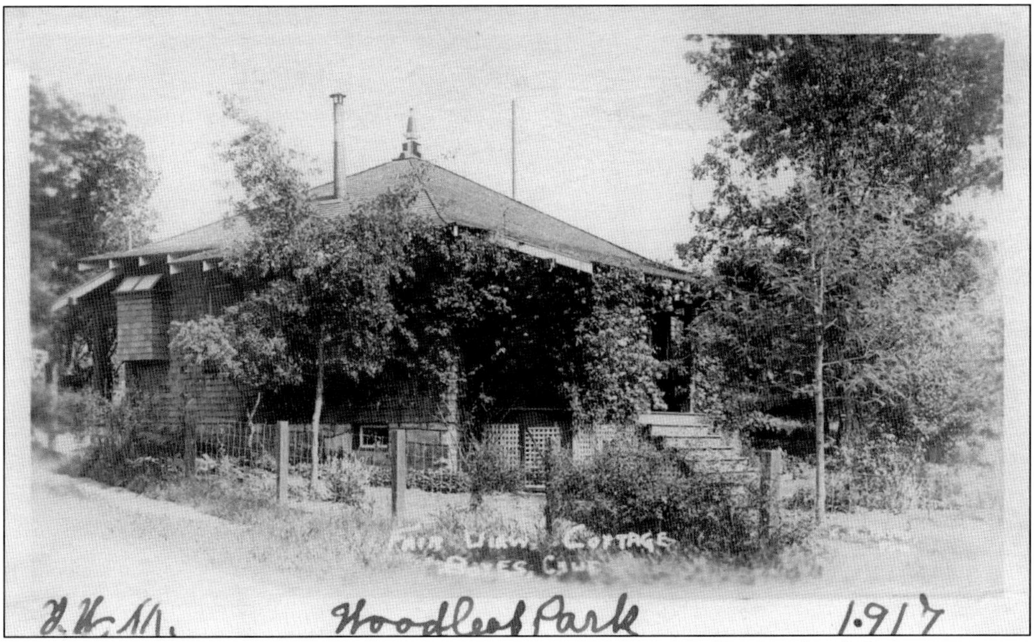

Fairview Cottage was one of G.W. Minges's properties in the Woodleaf Park subdivision. Minges was the "mayor" of Boyes Hot Springs.

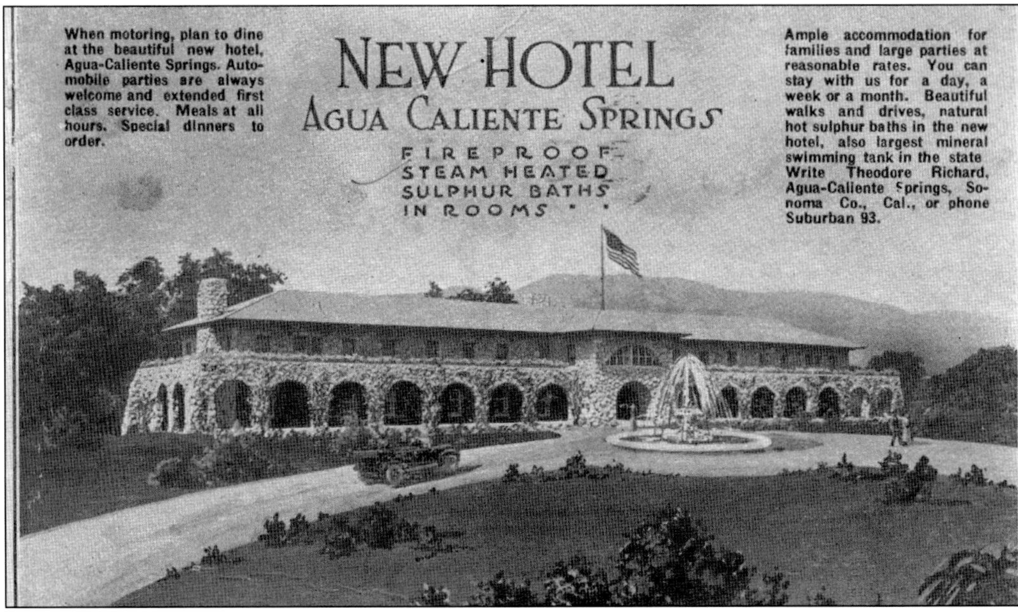

At the Agua Caliente Springs Bath House in 1925, Dr. W. Riedle practiced his "combined scientific application of the best there is in Massage, Chiropractic and Hydro-therapy, Electro-therapy, etc. If combined with bathing and drinking of Agua Caliente Radio-Active mineral water, this treatment will cure most the so-called hopeless ailments." This claim was printed in an advertisement in the *Sonoma Index-Tribune*.

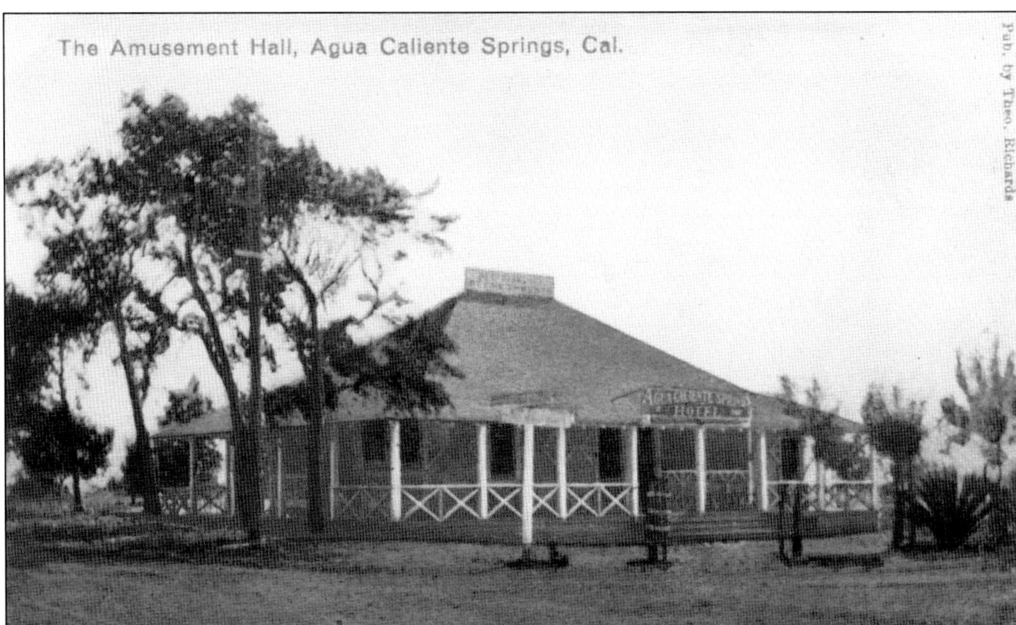

In 1912, when this postcard was mailed, there was a movement in Sonoma County called the Anti-Road House League, which had the goal of shutting down establishments in unincorporated areas where alcohol was served. An initiative was passed, and on January 1, 1913, the county went dry. The amusement hall at Agua Caliente Springs would undoubtedly have been considered a roadhouse.

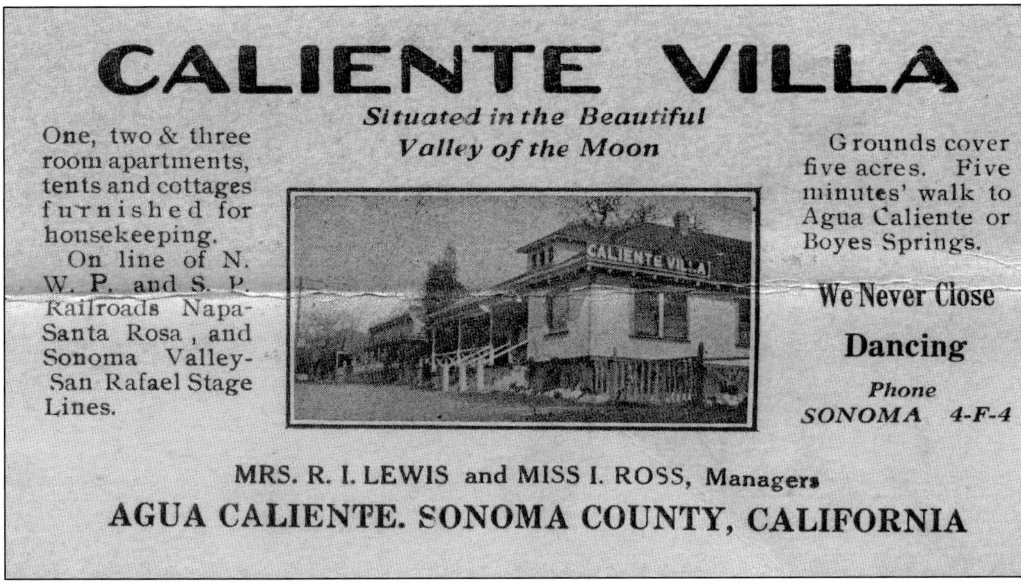

Caliente Villa billed itself as an "auto camp," which meant it catered to the new vacationists who arrived by car. A 1920 advertisement in the *Sonoma Index-Tribune* lists the daily specials in the restaurant, which included Spanish beans on Wednesdays and tamales on Sundays. The establishment was run by Mrs. R.I. Lewis and Miss I. Ross "fifty fifty," according to the 1920 advertisement. (Above, courtesy of Lynn Downey; below, courtesy of the Sonoma Valley Historical Society.)

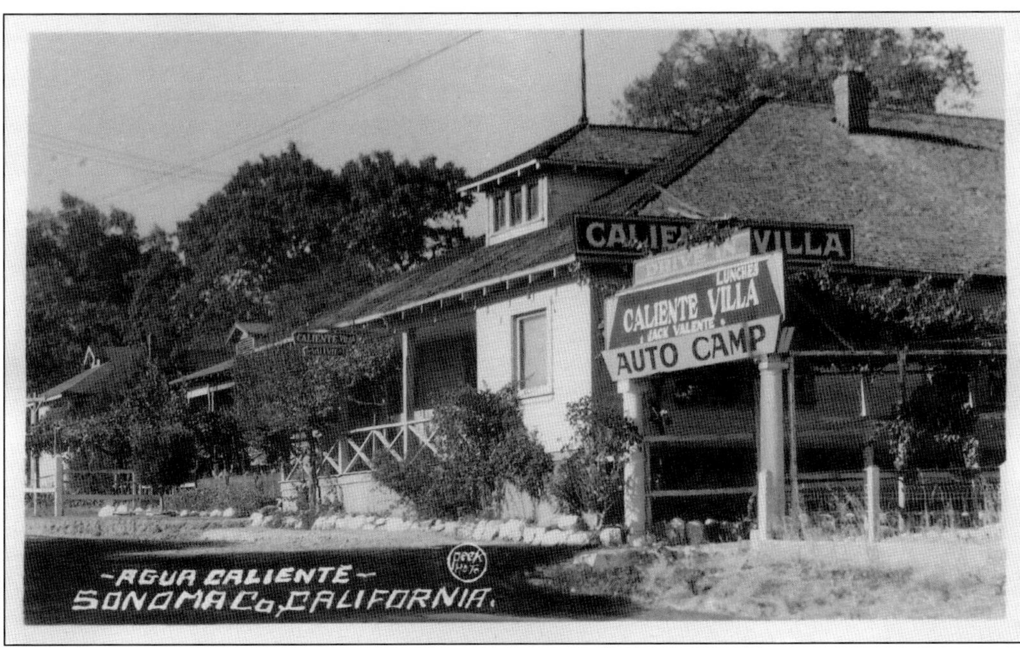

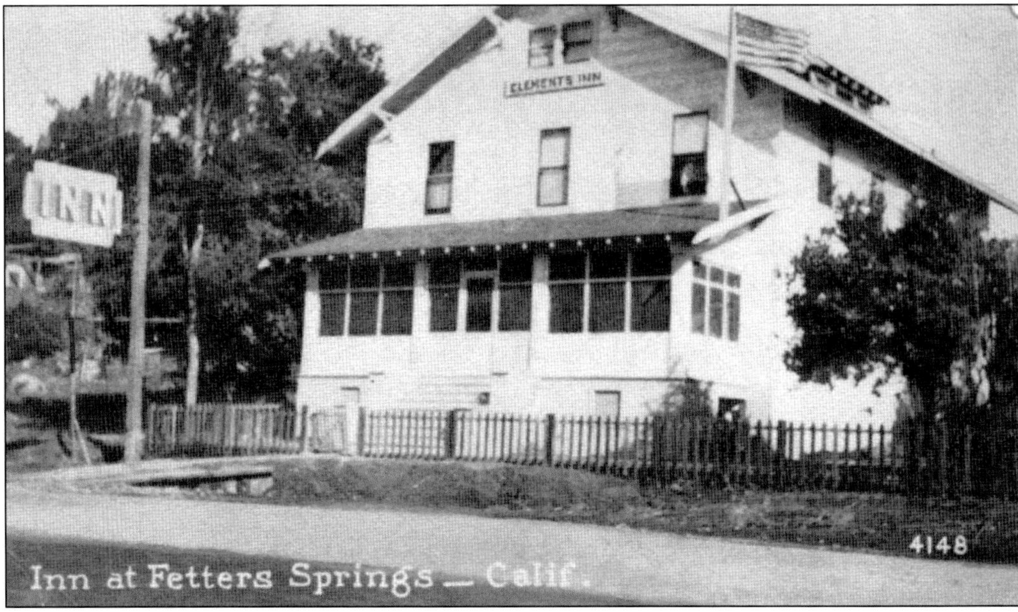

Clements Inn was on the main highway in Fetters Springs. In newspaper stories, the name was sometimes confused with Clementi's, the brick hotel at Mountain Avenue.

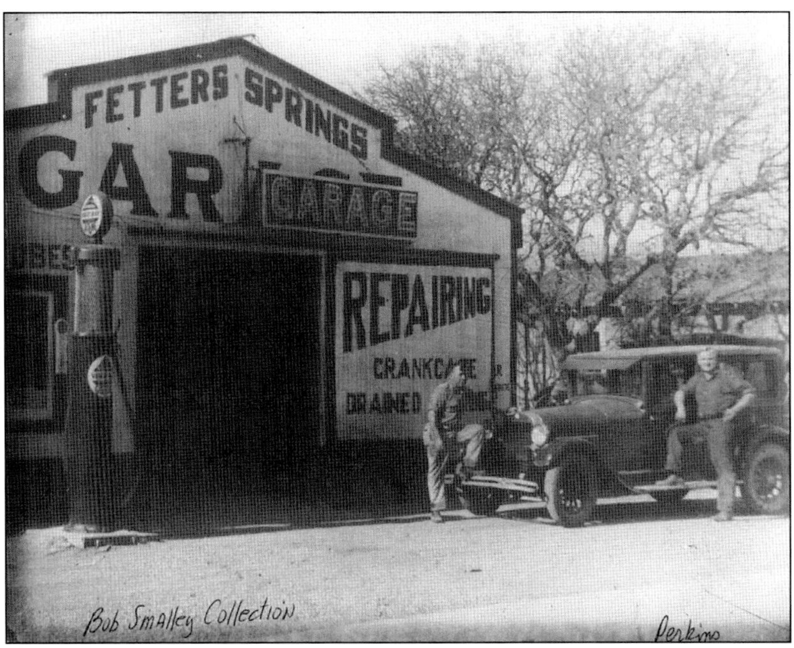

With the ascendancy of the automobile, garages and service stations proliferated in Sonoma Valley. The Fetters Springs Garage prospered in the 1930s and 1940s. It was probably located on the grounds of the resort. (Courtesy of the Sonoma Valley Historical Society.)

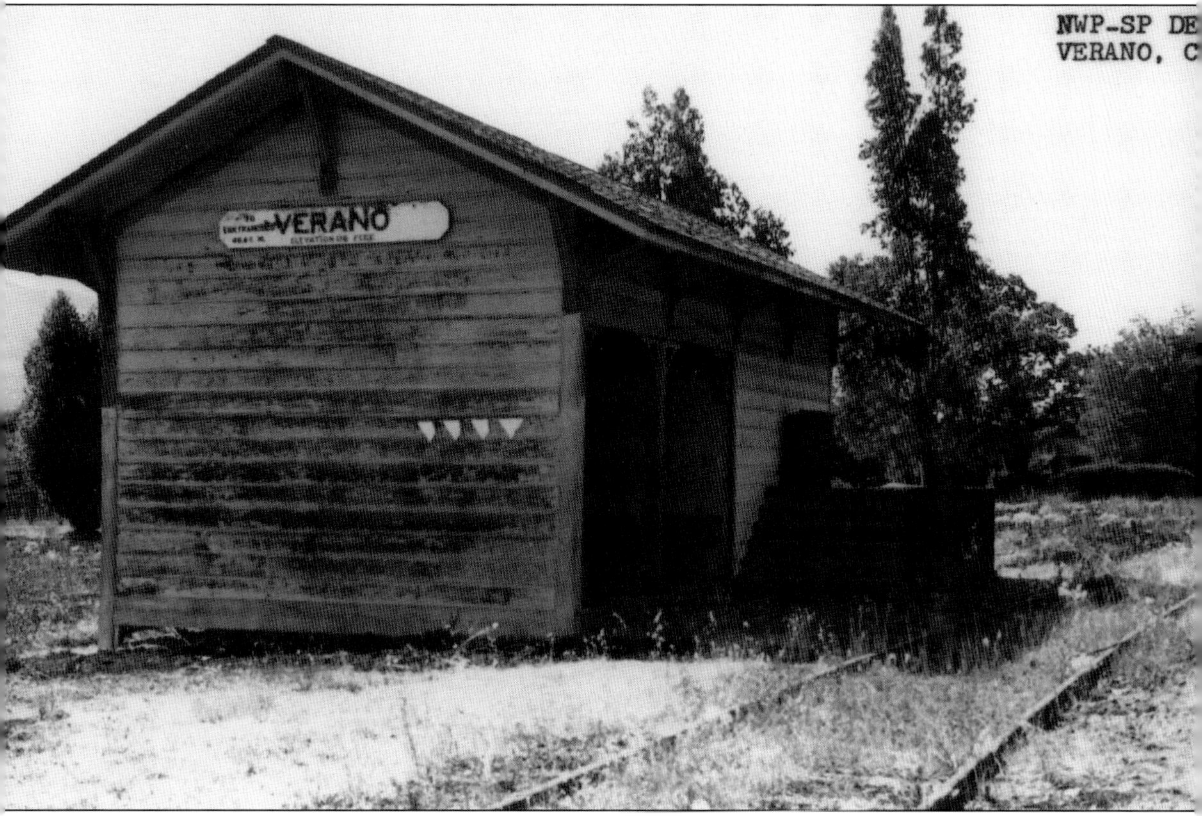

The Verano depot of the Northwestern Pacific Railroad was located on the property that became Paul's Resort near the confluence of Agua Caliente Creek and Sonoma Creek. (Courtesy of the Sonoma Valley Historical Society.)

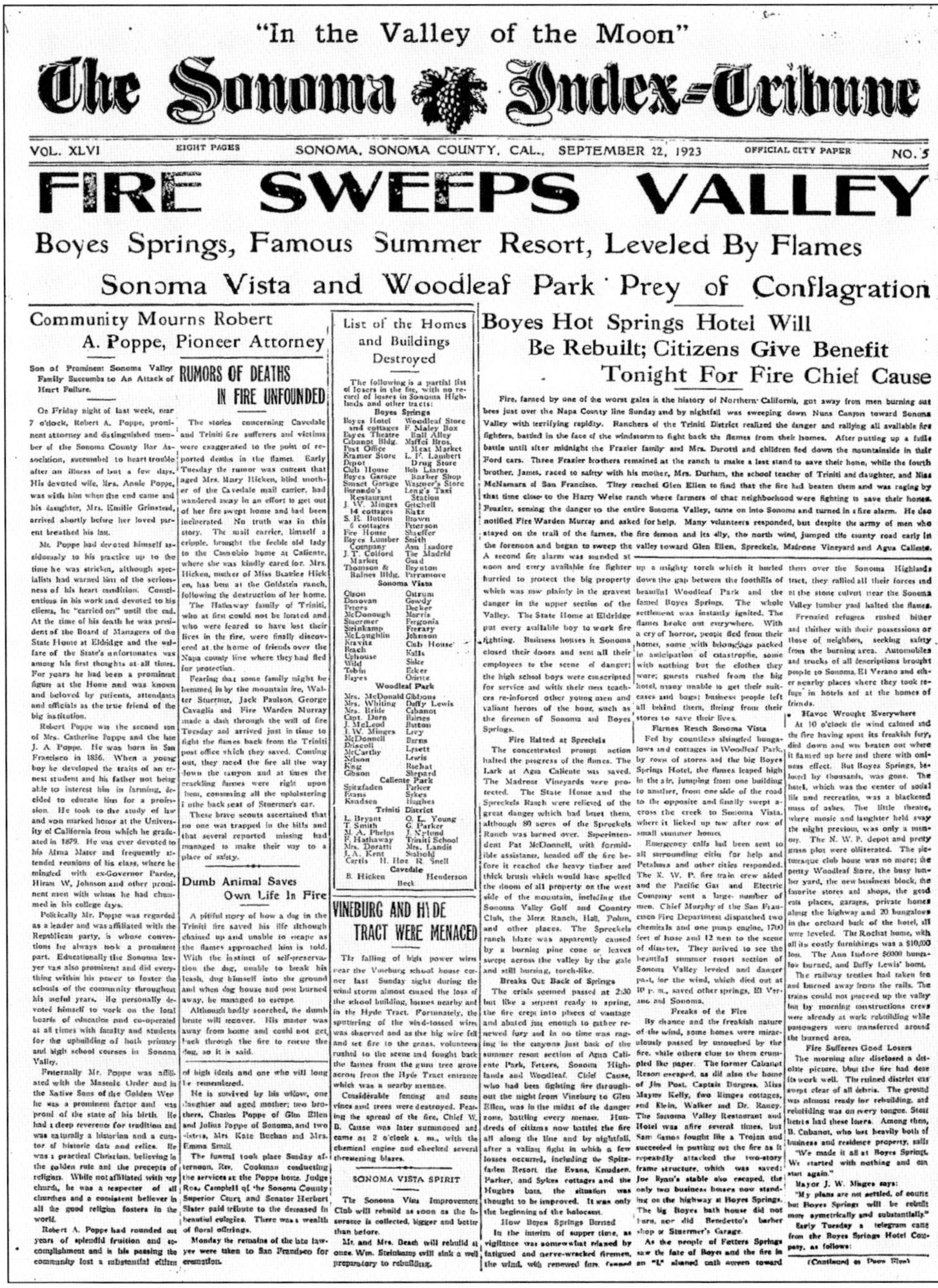

"In the Valley of the Moon"

The Sonoma Index-Tribune

VOL. XLVI | EIGHT PAGES | SONOMA, SONOMA COUNTY, CAL., SEPTEMBER 22, 1923 | OFFICIAL CITY PAPER | NO. 5

FIRE SWEEPS VALLEY

Boyes Springs, Famous Summer Resort, Leveled By Flames

Sonoma Vista and Woodleaf Park Prey of Conflagration

Community Mourns Robert A. Poppe, Pioneer Attorney

RUMORS OF DEATHS IN FIRE UNFOUNDED

List of the Homes and Buildings Destroyed

Dumb Animal Saves Own Life In Fire

VINEBURG AND HYDE TRACT WERE MENACED

Boyes Hot Springs Hotel Will Be Rebuilt; Citizens Give Benefit Tonight For Fire Chief Cause

Fire, fanned by one of the worst gales in the history of Northern California, got away from men burning out bees just over the Napa County line Sunday and by nightfall was sweeping down Nuns Canyon toward Sonoma Valley with terrifying rapidity. Ranchers of the Triniti District realized the danger and rallying all available fire fighters, battled in the face of the windstorm to fight back the flames from their homes.

On September 22, 1923, "Fire, fanned by one of the worst gales in the history of Northern California, got away from men burning out bees just over the Napa County line Sunday and by nightfall was sweeping down Nuns Canyon toward Sonoma Valley with terrifying rapidity." The destruction was massive, though it did not include the Boyes Hot Springs Bath House or Fetters resort. "The morning after disclosed a desolate picture. Soon after the embers died, the ruined district was swept clear of all debris. The ground was almost ready for rebuilding, and rebuilding was on every tongue." Resort owner B. Cabanot said, "We made it all at Boyes Hot Springs. We started with nothing and can start again." (Courtesy of the Sonoma Valley Historical Society.)

Three

The Inn and the Baths

As early as July 1923, a group of investors including Rudy Lichtenberg, manager of the Boyes Hot Springs Bath House, proposed building a luxurious new hotel to be called the Sonoma Mission Inn. This would not be located in the heart of Boyes Hot Springs but nearby, on land that would become the Valley of the Moon Golf and Country Club. The development was to include an enormous natatorium and was designed to rival the big resorts of Southern California. "The Sonoma Mission Inn, when completed, will without a doubt become one of the most famed resorts of all California," said the *Sonoma Index-Tribune*.

As many great plans in the early day of the Springs tended to do, this evaporated like a cloud of steam over a geothermal pool. However, in September 1923, a very real thermal event, the great fire, put many peoples' plans on hold.

The fire destroyed much of Boyes Hot Springs, including the Boyes Hot Springs Hotel. That hotel was rebuilt in 1925–1926 and operated under the same name until 1928, when it was rebranded as the Sonoma Mission Inn. "The new name, calculated to capitalize on Sonoma's romantic and historic background, was thought much better for publicity purposes than Boyes Hot Springs, in that Sonoma has the last of the Missions on El Camino Real and it is an Acknowledged fact that the Mission spots of California were chosen for superior climate, for health giving waters and beauty of surroundings," said an article in the *Index-Tribune* in February 1928.

In 1930, the Sonoma Mission Inn corporation fell on hard times. The American Securities Company tried to force a foreclosure sale of the hotel, which was resisted by Lichtenberg and the other directors. In March 1930, the *Index-Tribune* reported that "Internal disruptions among the stockholders precipitated the present financial trouble which, it is believed, will be finally worked out with no interruption in the business. The last week end was another busy one at the hotel."

During World War II, the inn was used as a rest base for naval personnel. In the decades after the war, owners came and went. The inn has flourished for many years under the management of Fairmont Hotels & Resorts, which now operates it as The Fairmont Sonoma Mission Inn & Spa.

The bathhouse was destroyed by fire in 1969 and was never rebuilt.

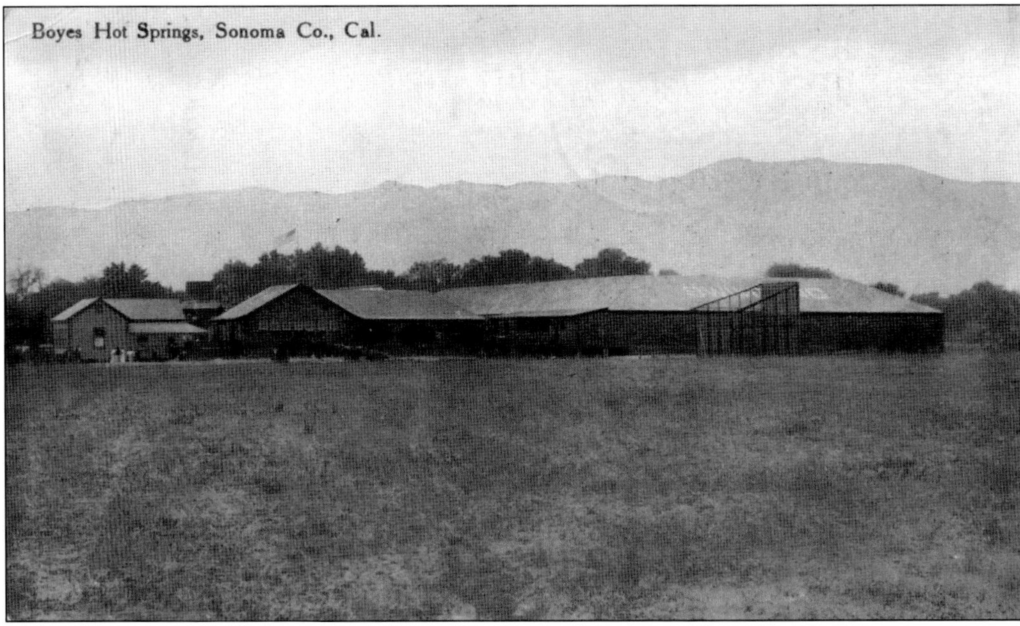

Located along Sonoma Creek at Pine Street and Boyes Boulevard, the bathhouse complex covered some 20,000 square feet at its largest. From its construction in the 1890s and through its expansion over the early decades of the 20th century, the Boyes Bath House remained the vital center of the resort culture of the Springs. Generation after generation of tourists and locals alike swam, relaxed, and created lifelong memories there.

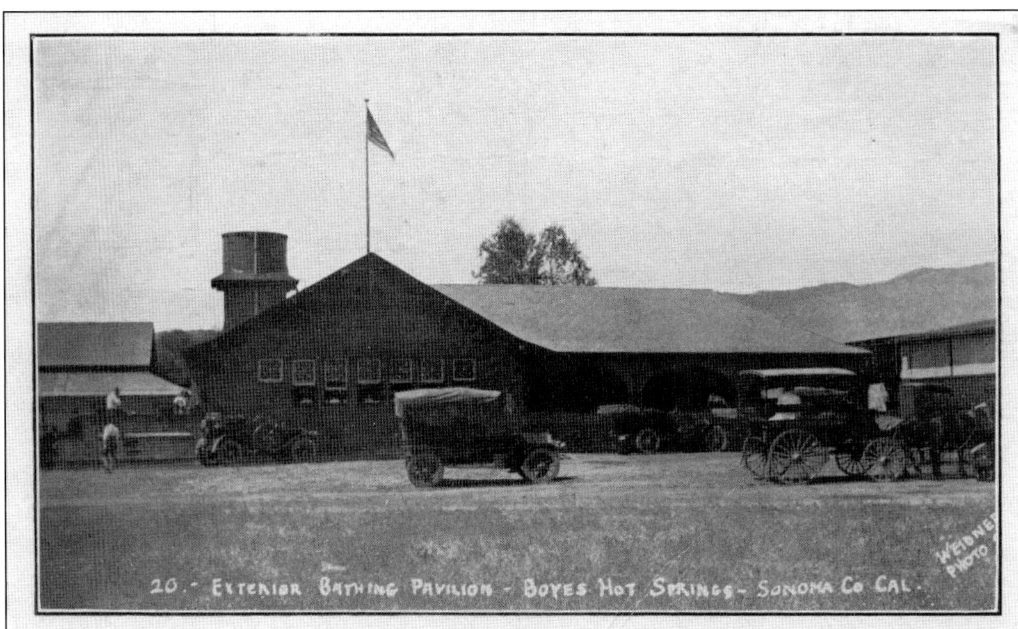

The list of amenities at Boyes Hot Springs was extensive. A *Sonoma Index-Tribune* article mentions them as including "new garage and auto supplies, livery and riding horses, cottages and tents, boating, electric lights, moving pictures, entertainment and dance every night, baseball, perfect climate, local and long distance phones."

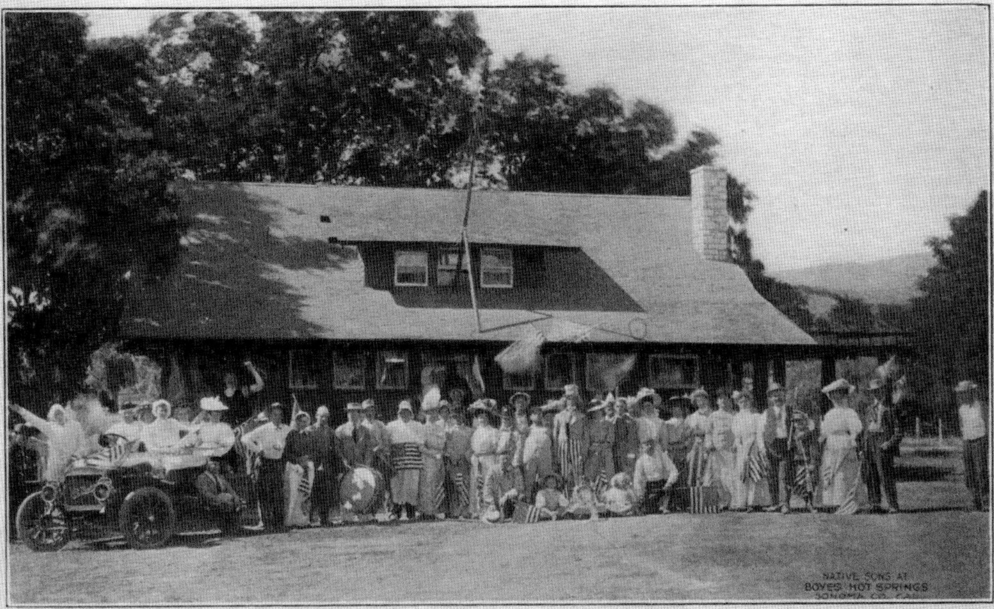

Boyes Hot Springs had a clubhouse, as did Fetters Springs. The clubhouses were often said to employ "mixologists," so they were obviously bars. On New Year's Eve in 1922, people were invited to "a grand time at the Boyes Hot Springs Club House, singing, dancing, refreshments and eats, everything free."

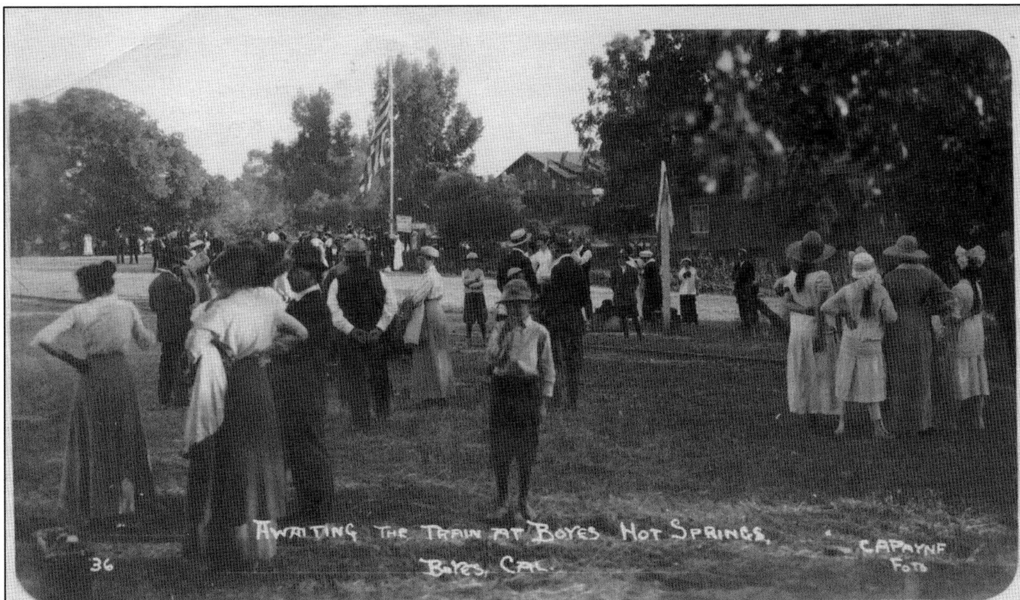

In this 1915 photograph, summer visitors are waiting for the train; the Boyes Hot Springs Hotel is in the background. (Courtesy of the Sonoma Valley Historical Society.)

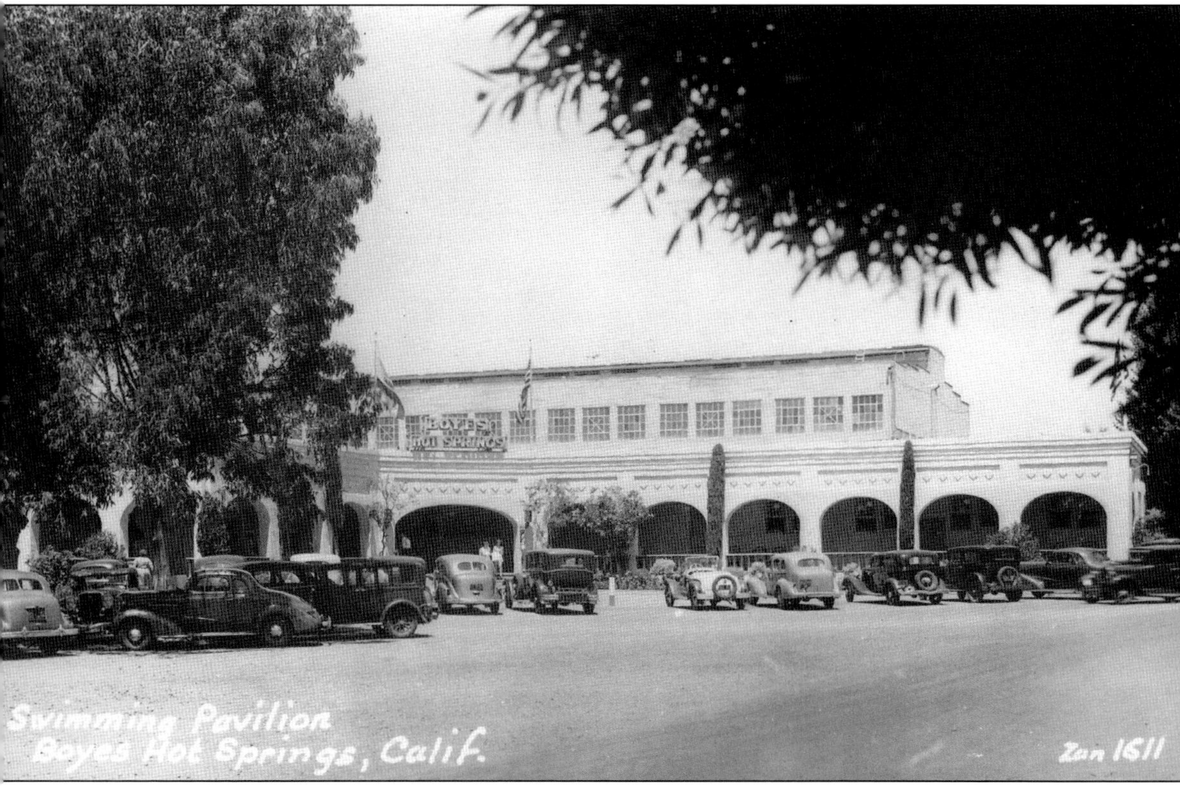

By the 1930s, traveling via automobile had become a popular way to get to the Boyes Bath House.

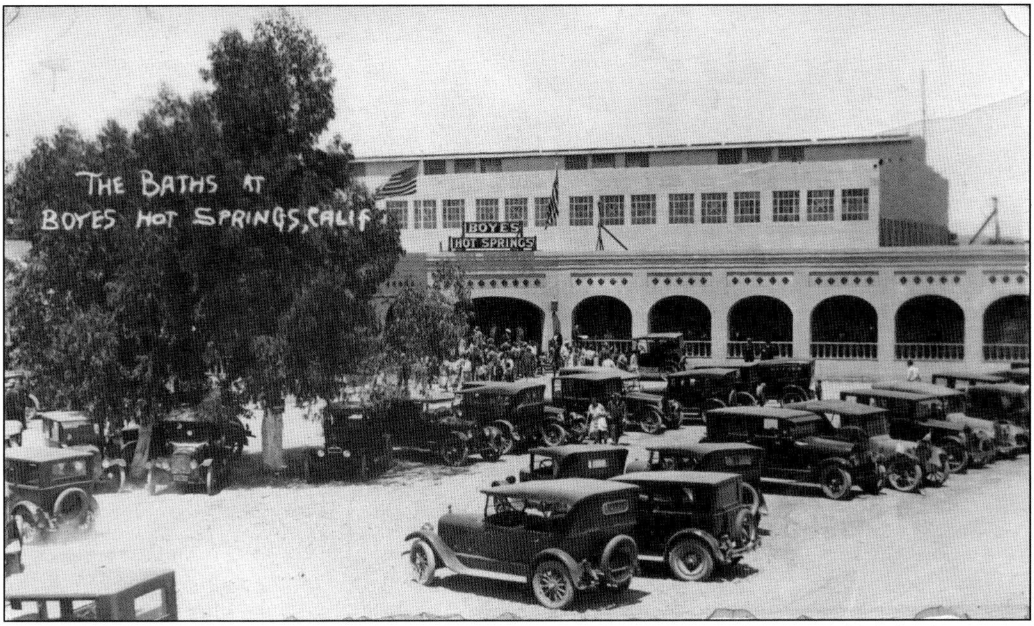

Thank goodness for the real-photo postcard! Most of the photographic record of the history of the Springs is due to the popularity of these cards. The most prolific photographers included Alexander "Zan" Stark, Weidner, Peck, and C.A. Payne. Stark started his photography career in San Francisco and moved to Mill Valley, where he hit on the idea of making postcards of California scenes. He traveled all over the state for 40 years.

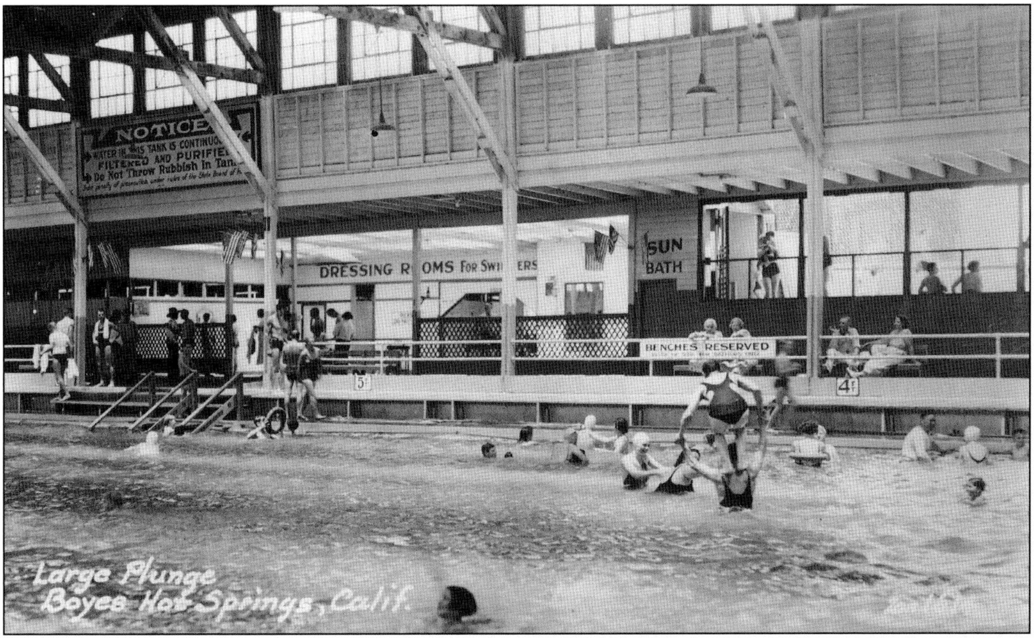

A joyous crowd, including some amateur acrobats, cavort in the large pool at the Boyes Bath House under a sign that reads "Notice: Water in this tank is continuously filtered and purified. Do not throw rubbish in the tank." (Courtesy of the Sonoma Valley Historical Society.)

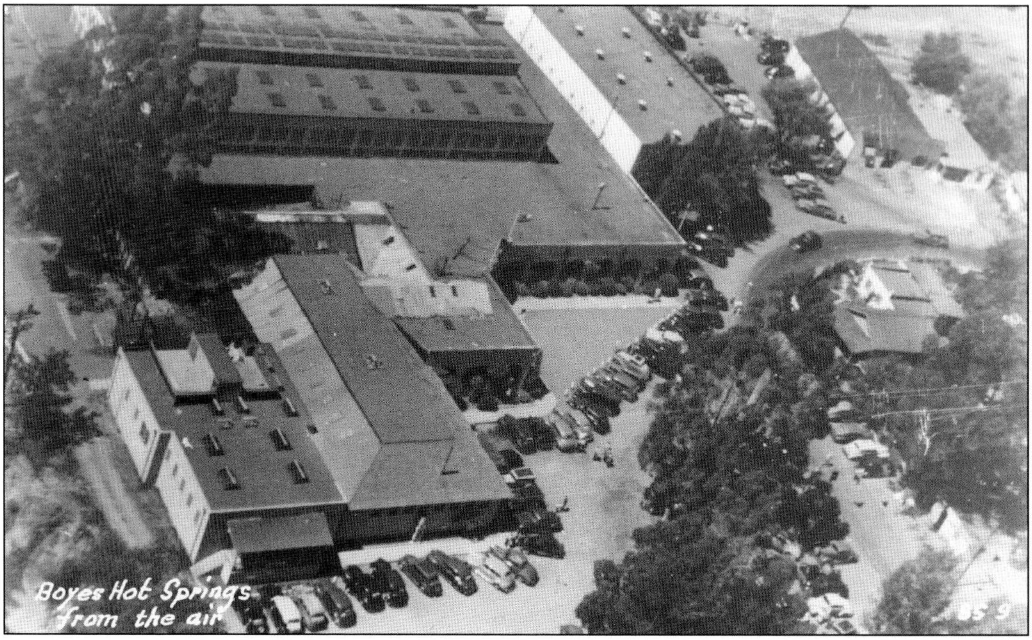

The layout of the Boyes Bath House is visible in this aerial photograph by Zan Stark. The arched grand entrance with the open triangular area in front faces Pine Street, not far from Boyes Boulevard. (Both, courtesy of Stanford University Library, Special Collections.)

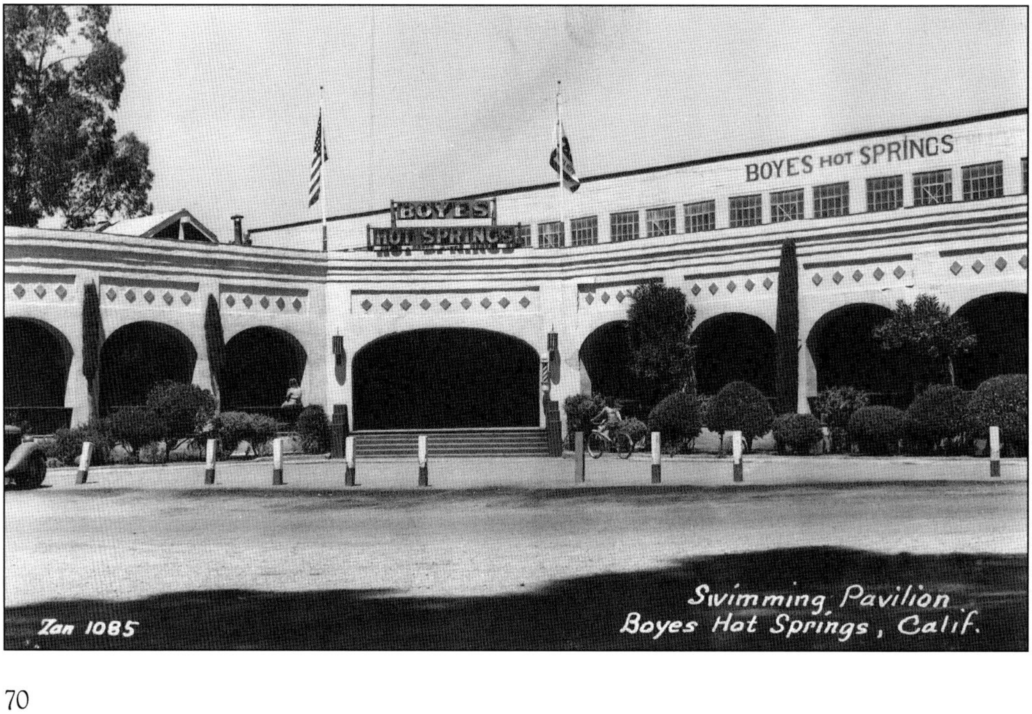

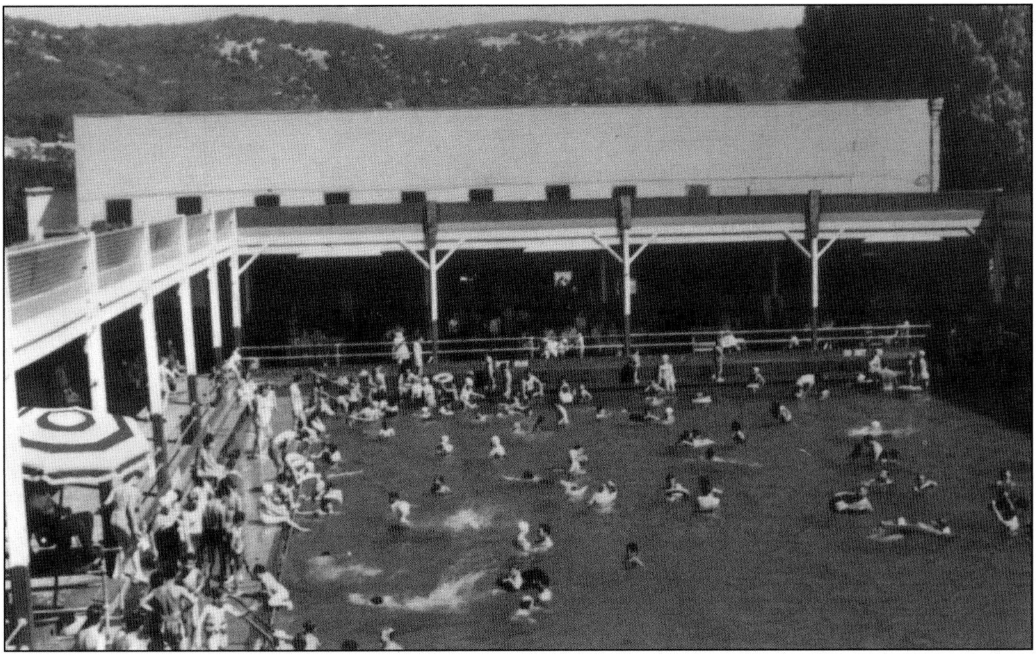

The Boyes Bath House was increasingly popular into the 1950s with both vacationers and locals. Many kids learned to swim in its pool. Its destruction by fire in 1969 signaled the end of the great resort era. (Courtesy of the Sonoma Valley Historical Society.)

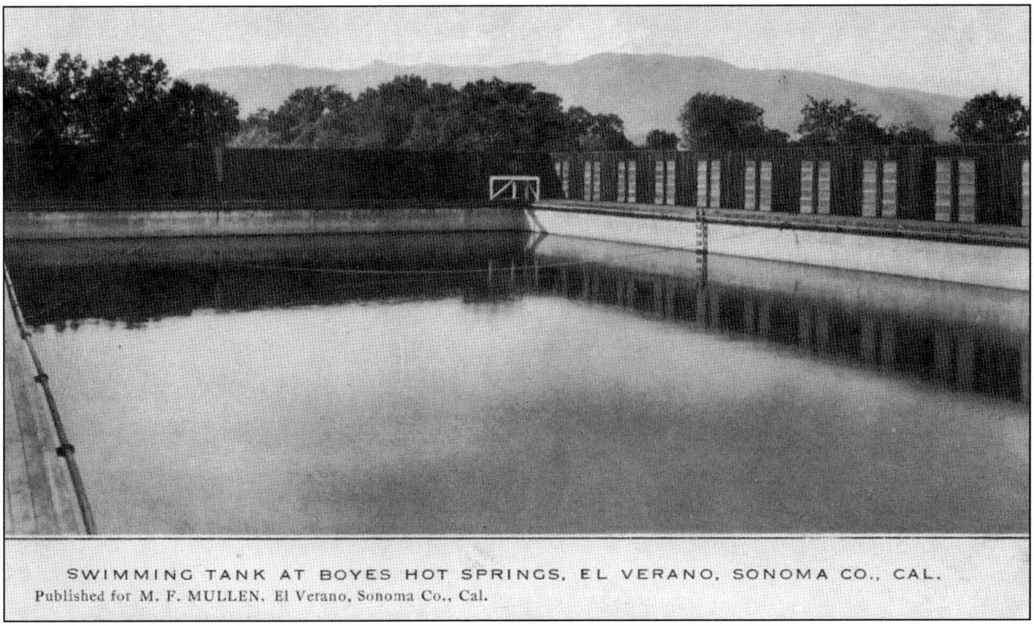

An earlier version of the Boyes swimming tank was not covered. Note that the card says that Boyes Hot Springs is in El Verano, possibly because the card was published for M.F. Mullen, a prominent El Verano pioneer.

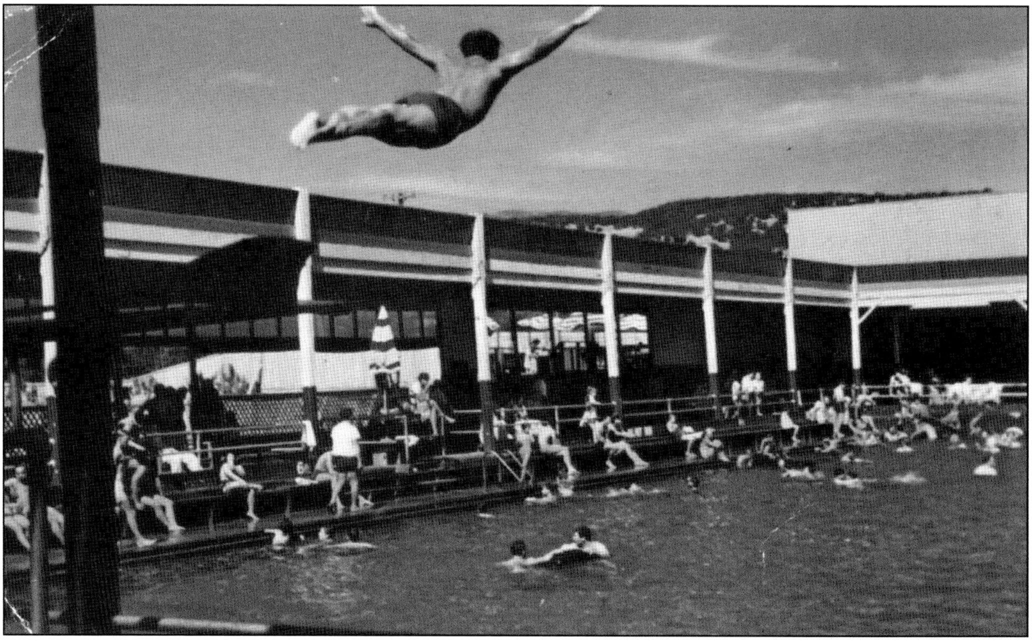

What better way to capture the pure joy of the swimming pool than an image of a diver in mid-flight?

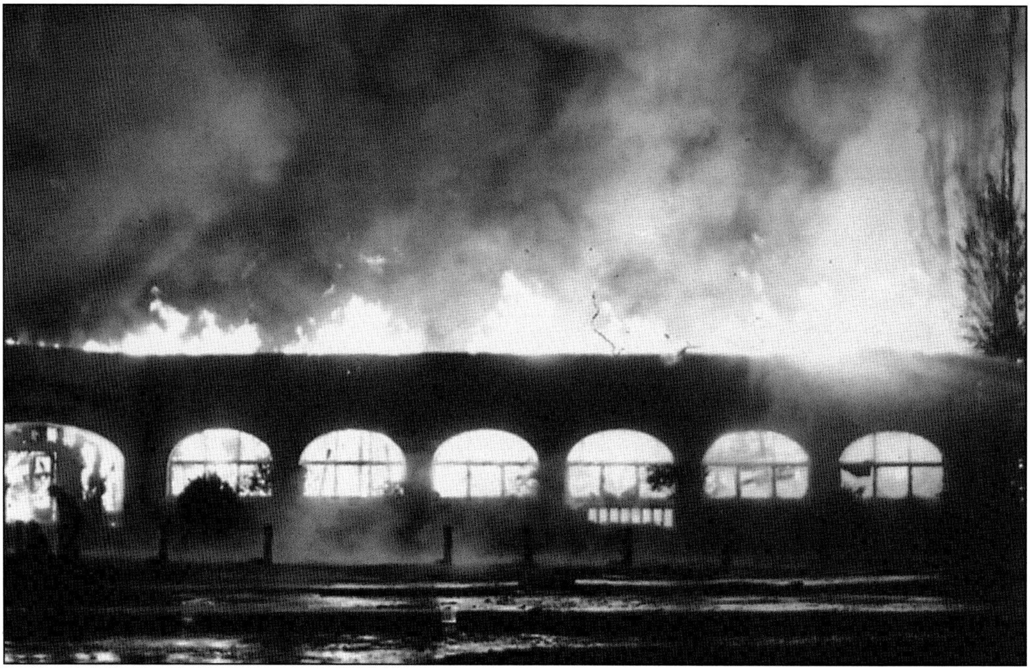

On April 17, 1969, the Boyes Bath House suffered a disastrous fire that destroyed most of the 24,000-square-foot complex. Not all the buildings suffered, however, and guests were still using parts of the resort the next day. The owner, Luis Vela, vowed to rebuild and continue operation. Unfortunately, he could not carry out his plans, and the site was abandoned for a number of years. In the 1980s, housing was built on the former resort property. (Courtesy of the Sonoma Valley Historical Society.)

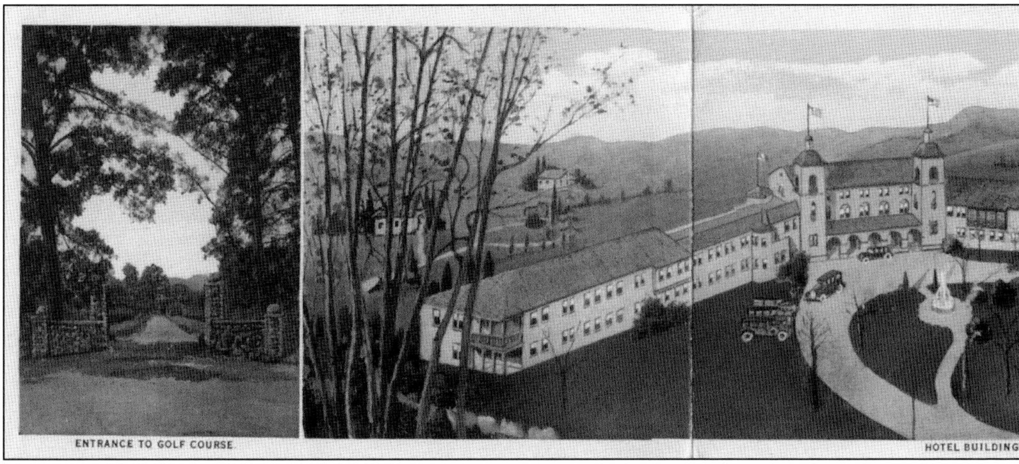

This fold-out card (split into two images) is not a photograph but a naively rendered painting portraying the Elysian fields of the Boyes Hot Springs golf club, hotel, and baths. The resort is located along Highway 12 at Boyes Boulevard.

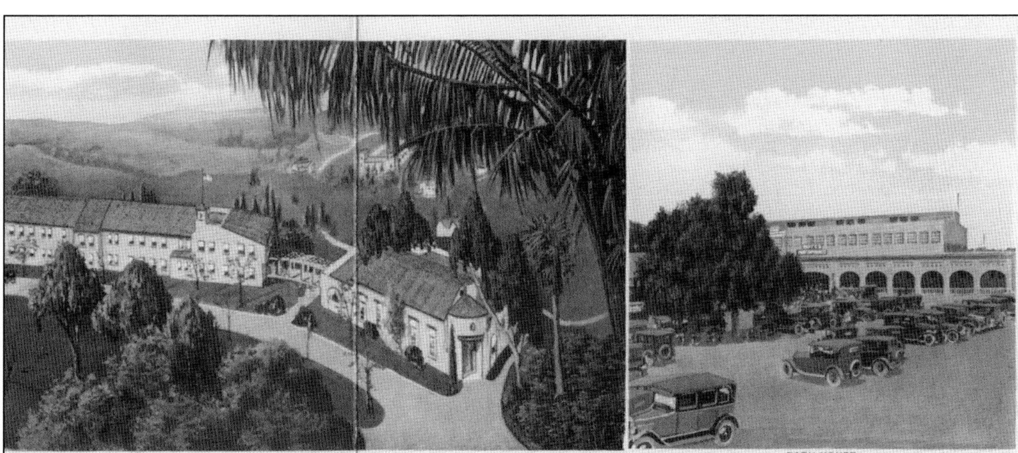

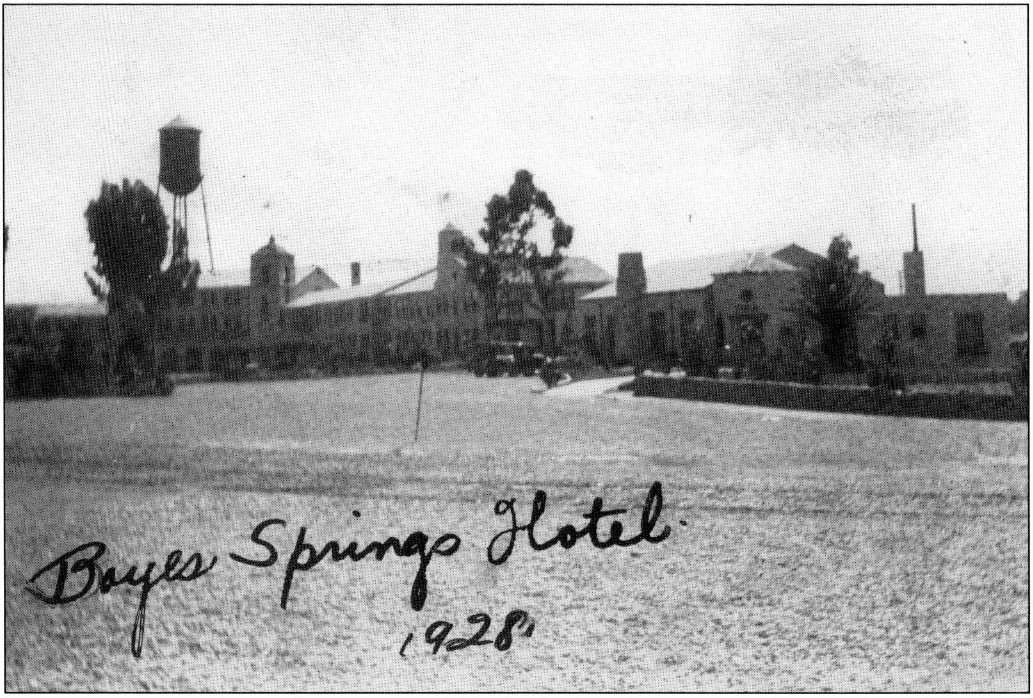

In 1928, the Boyes Hot Springs Hotel was renamed Sonoma Mission Inn "in recognition of its historic and romantic background," as reported in the *Sonoma Index-Tribune*. An association with Sonoma rather than Boyes Hot Springs was considered better for marketing, as is the case today.

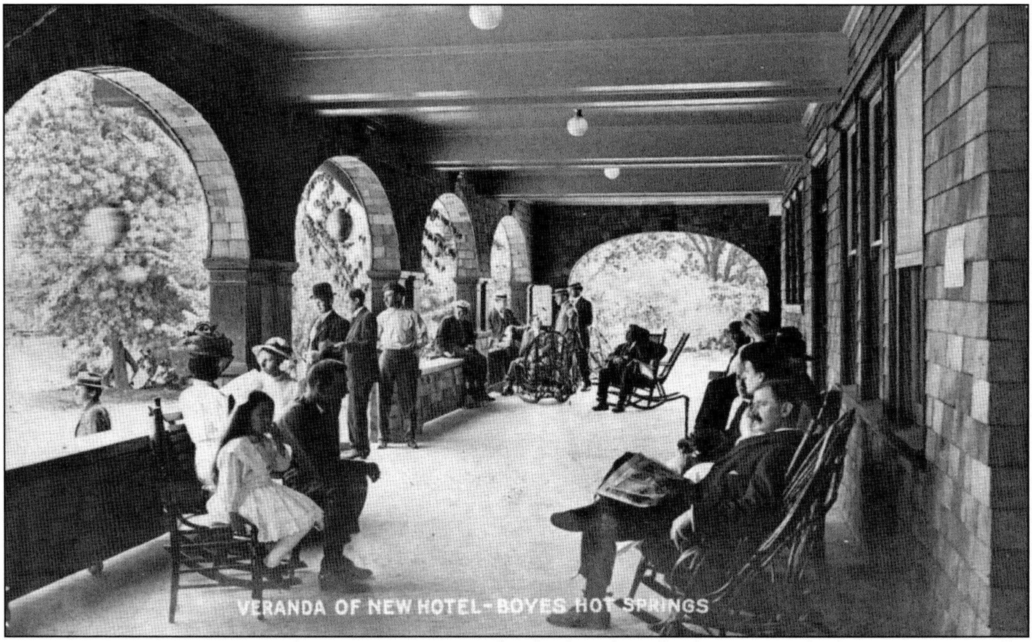

In 1889, Capt. Henry E. and Antoinette Boyes built their hotel adjacent to the hot springs on the land they purchased from Thaddeus M. Leavenworth. It became the center of the burgeoning resort communities of the Valley of the Moon.

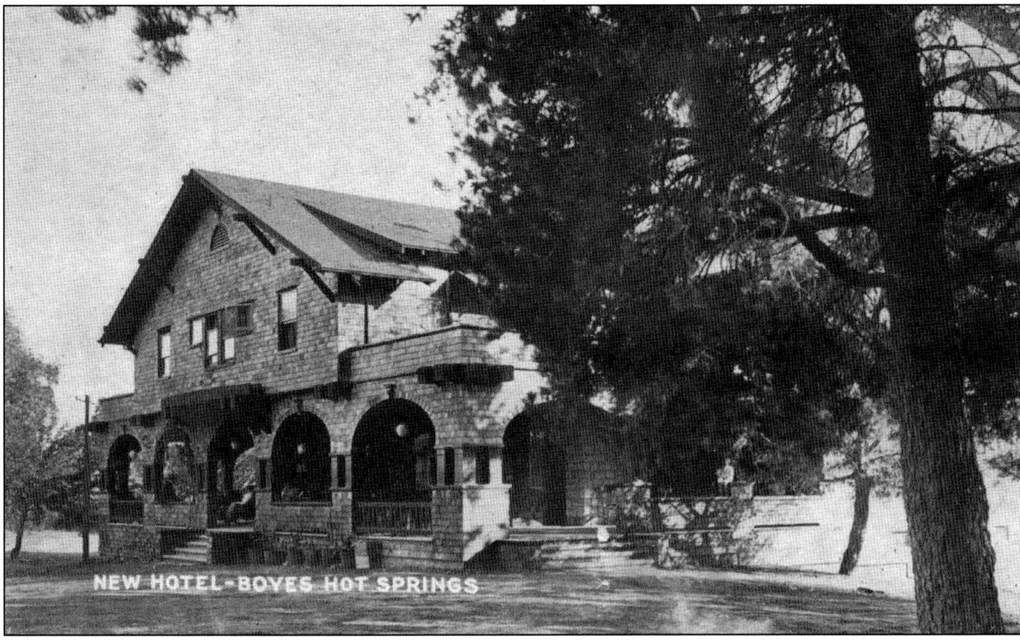

The old hotel at Boyes Hot Springs was a stately wood-framed and shingled structure suggesting a rustic manor house. There was no hint of association with the Mission or Mexican/Spanish heritage until the new hotel was built in 1925. (Below, courtesy of the Sonoma Valley Historical Society.)

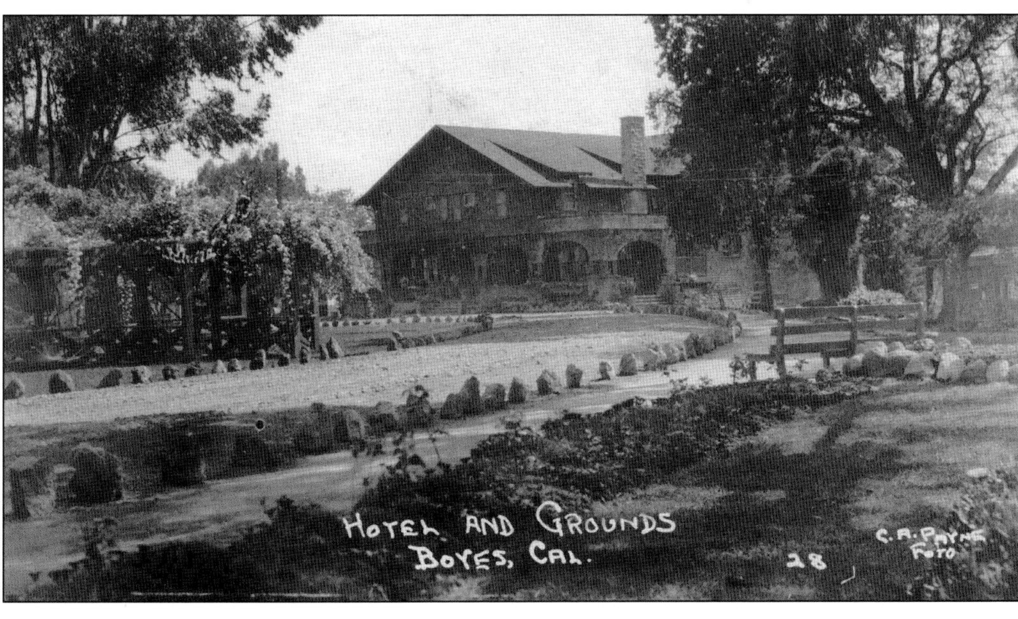

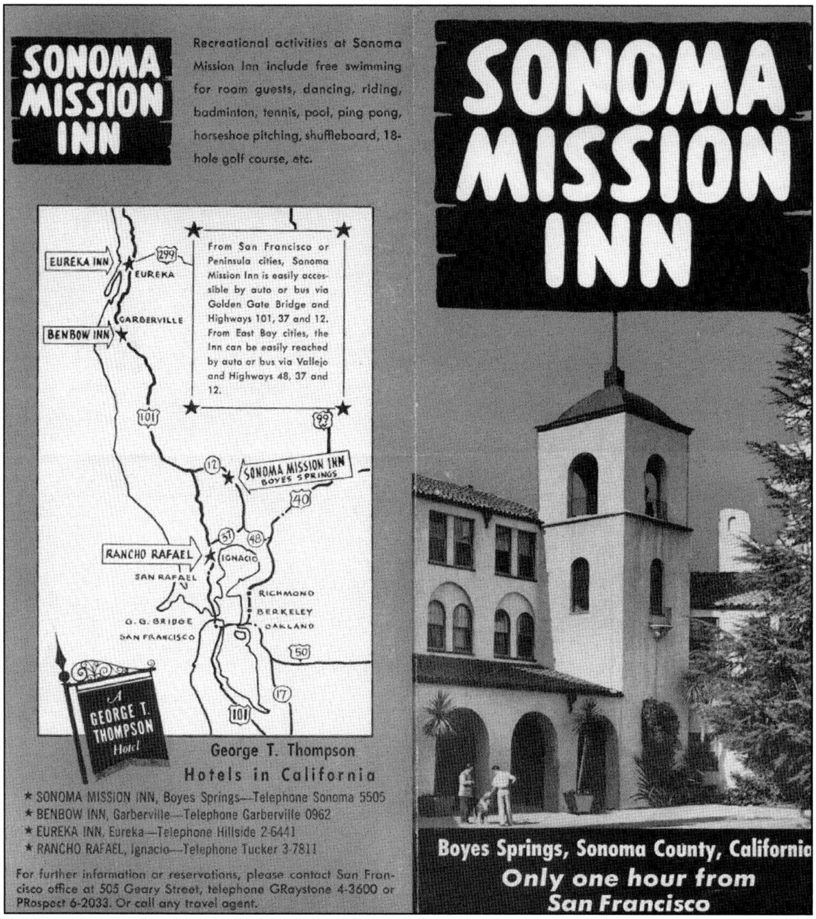

This brochure was produced when George Thompson was the owner of the inn. Thompson bought the hotel in 1945. The price list inside the brochure includes "double beds, $8.00, suites, $15." For $6 per day under the American Plan, guests could get three meals.

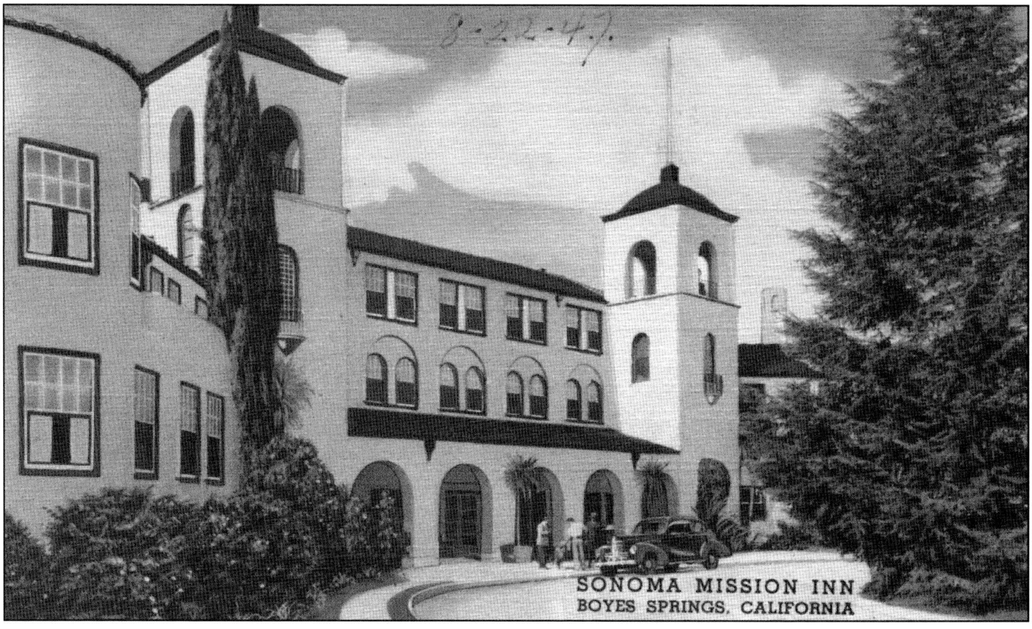

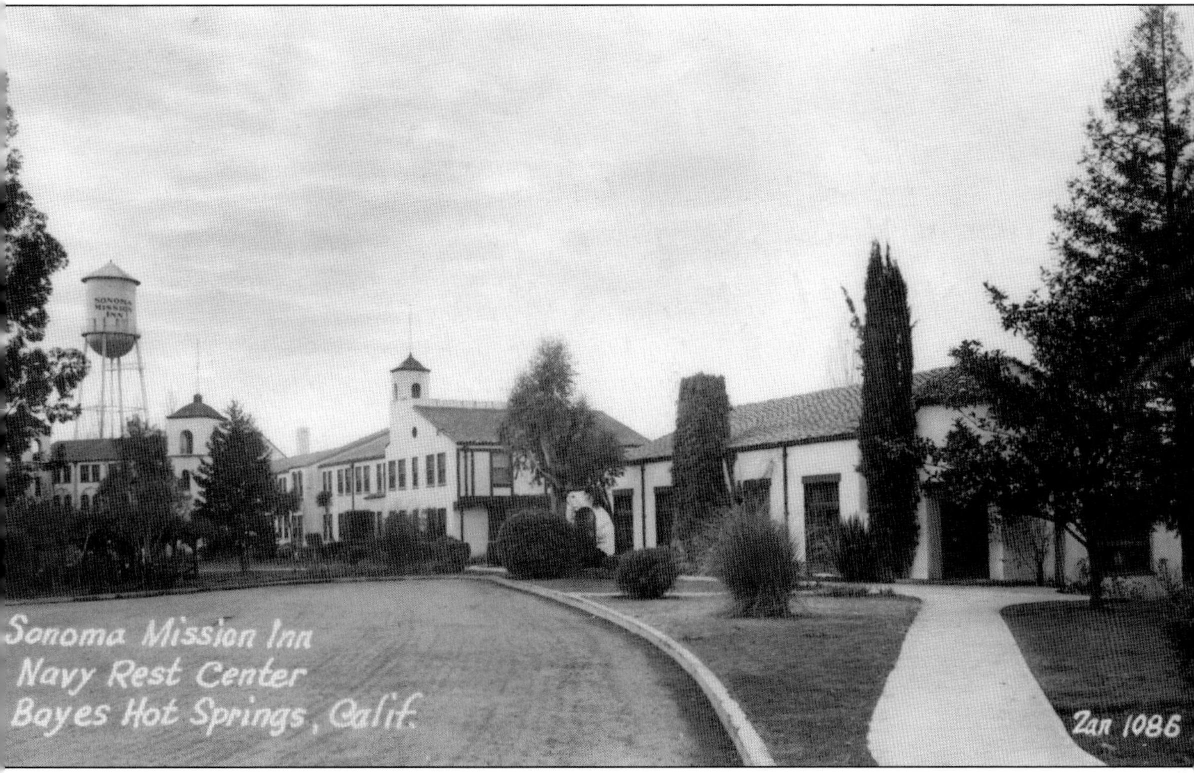

On January 15, 1943, the US Navy commenced its lease of the Sonoma Mission Inn and began to run it as a rest and recreation center. The inn remained in use by the Navy for the duration of World War II. The inn reopened in 1945 under the ownership of George Thompson.

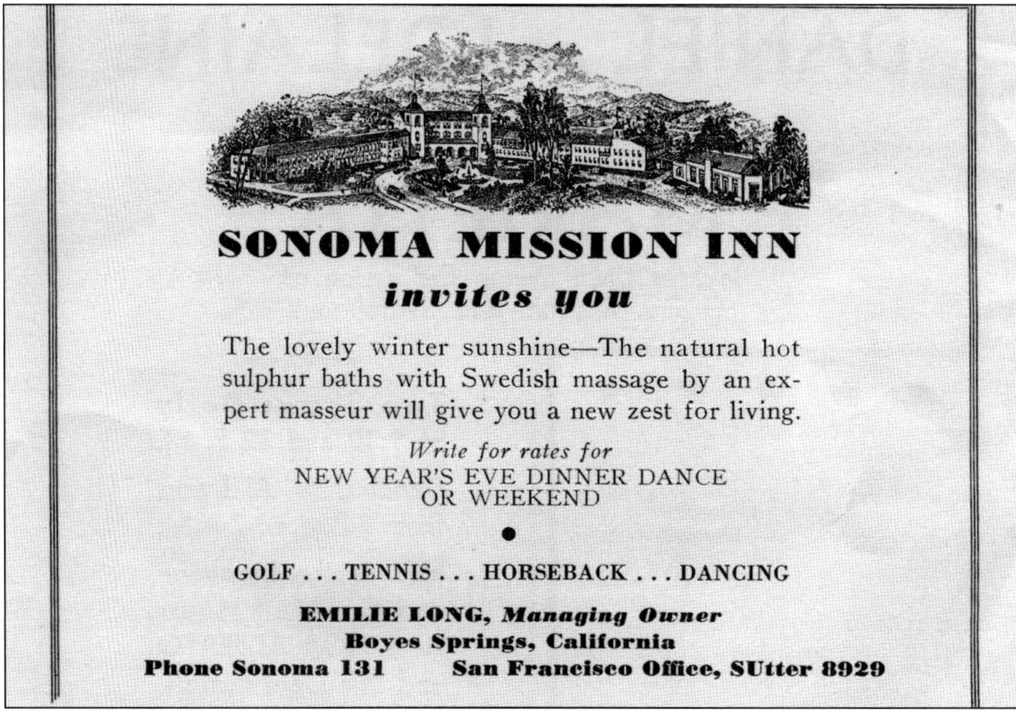

Emilie Long, "prominent S.F. hotel woman," bought the Sonoma Mission Inn in 1933. She ran the hotel until the Navy took over in 1943. She became a bright light in the social scene of the Springs, giving many parties and hosting many out-of-town guests, all of which was reported in the *Sonoma Index-Tribune*.

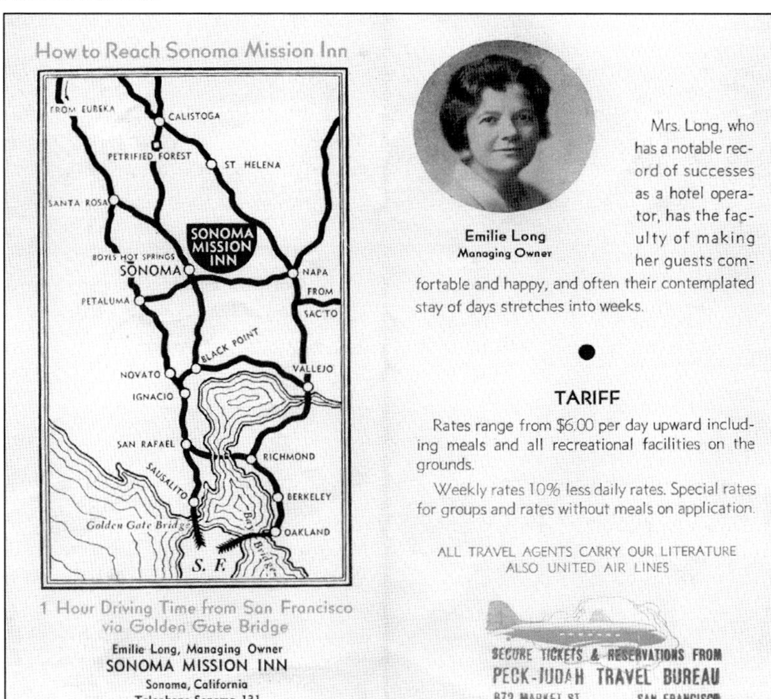

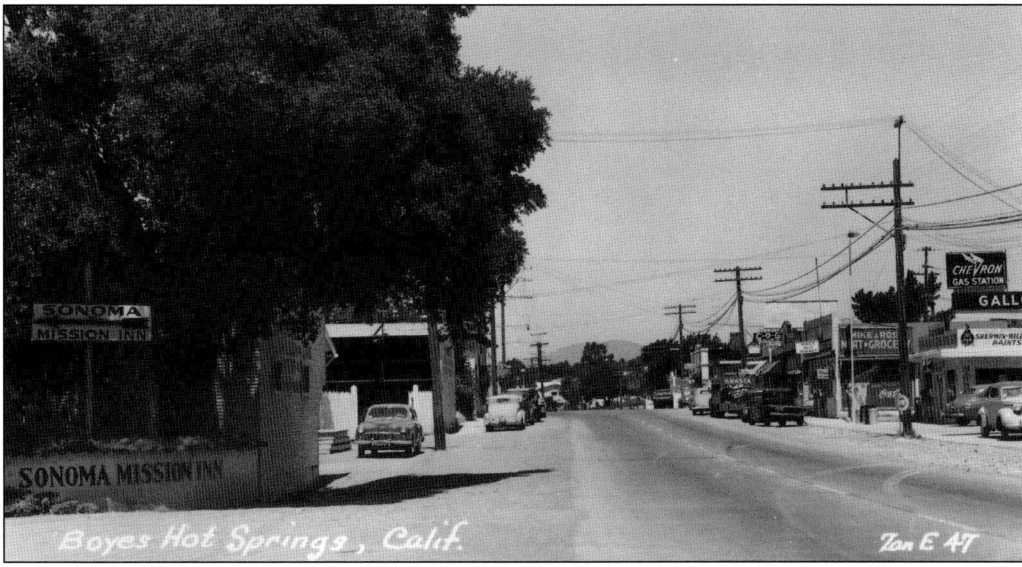

In the 1950s, the world of Boyes Hot Springs just outside the gates of the Sonoma Mission Inn included Gallo's Chevron station, Mike and Rose's Grocery, Valley Hardware, and Denny's COG Club. In the background, Sonoma Mountain looms over the bend in the highway. (Courtesy of Stanford University Library, Special Collections.)

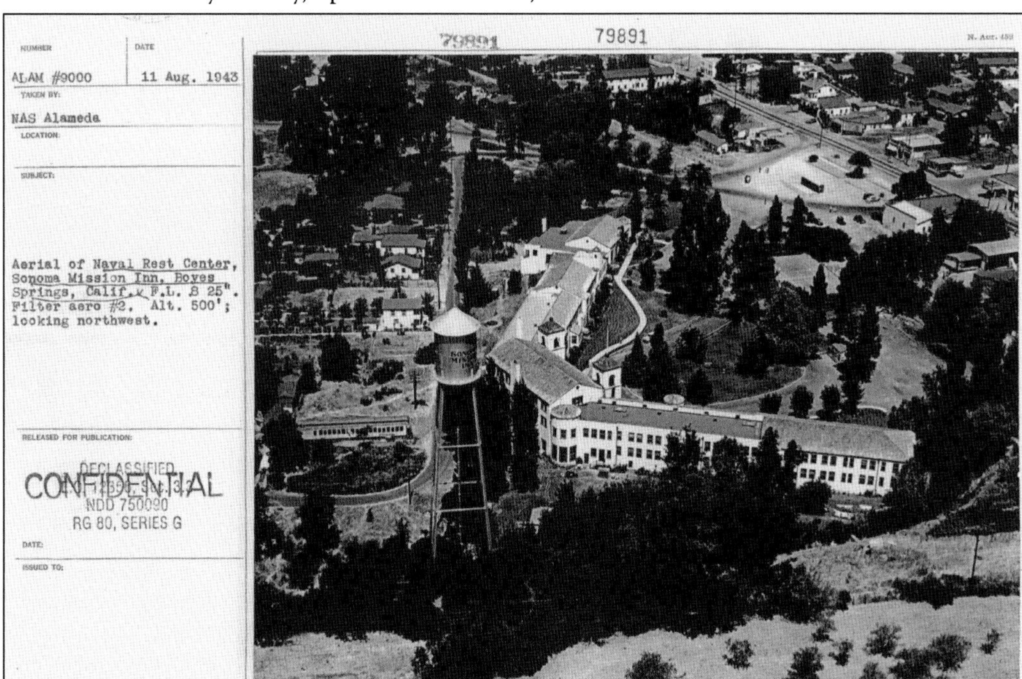

On August 11, 1943, the US Navy shot aerial photographs of the Sonoma Mission Inn that now provide historians with interesting and valuable information about the area at that time. Toward the upper right is the plaza with its palm tree and the little depot building. The railroad tracks had been pulled up the year before for the war effort. (Courtesy of Robert Parmelee and the National Archives.)

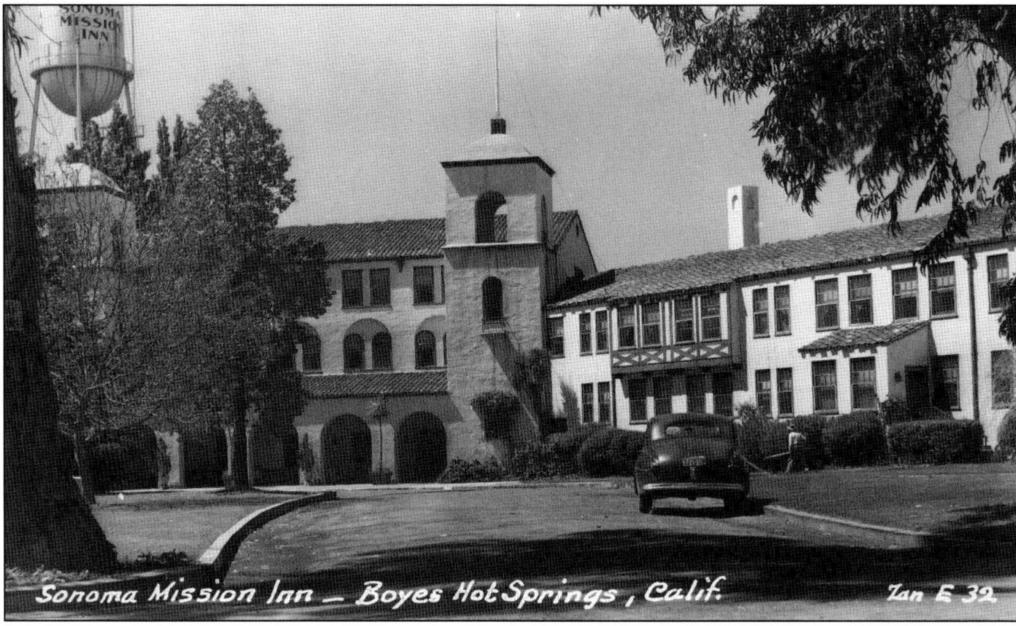

A lone automobile graces the foreground of this Alexander Stark photograph from the 1950s. The view from this spot in 2016 would be much the same.

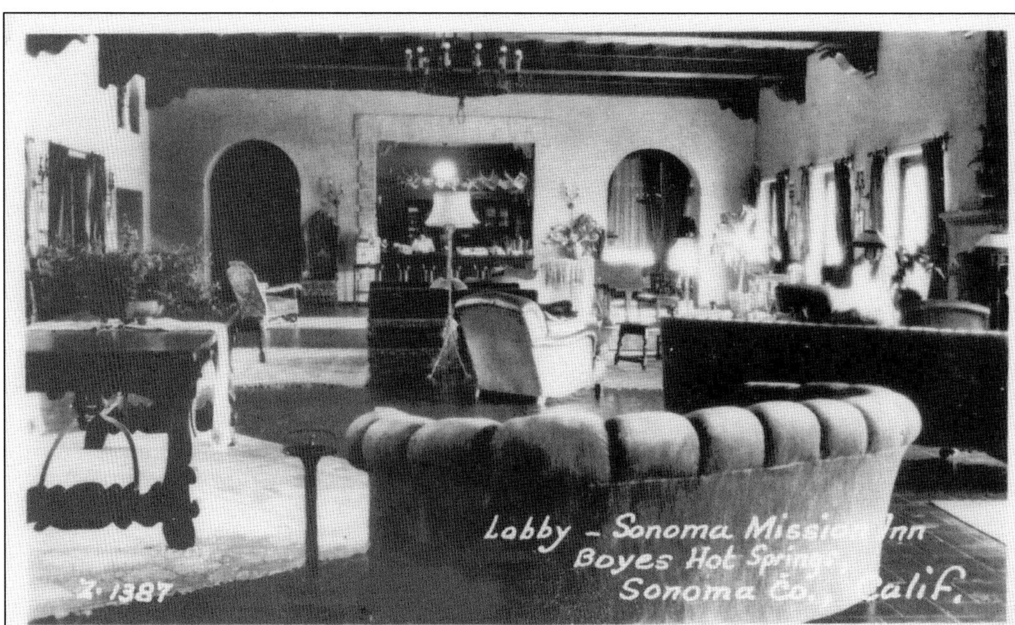

The lobby of the Sonoma Mission Inn in the 1950s, like the exterior, is not that different from what exists today.

Four

Mid-Century Prosperity

On May 5, 1955, the *Sonoma Index-Tribune* reported on a meeting of the new Boyes Hot Springs Merchants' Association. Tom Polidori, of Polidori's Store, was president of the association. Among those attending were pharmacist Pine Wagner, postmaster Marie Shane, car dealer Babe Gallo, *Valley of the Moon Daily Review* publisher Zan Stark Jr., and postcard photographer Zan Stark Sr. Mary Fazio opened her original Pizza Shack four years later.

By mid-century, the resort business was still vital, but the area had a core of small businesses that served both tourists and locals. With the railroad gone and the car ascendant, gas stations proliferated, as did drinking establishments. A 1951 full-page list of businesses in the *Index-Tribune* featured fifteen bars and taverns and five service stations.

The Boyes Bath House got new owners and was completely remodeled in 1953.

A major addition to the commercial building stock of Boyes Hot Springs was the Plaza Center building, constructed starting in 1951 by A.B. Peluffo. His first tenants were Dr. Michael Makita, Valley Drug Store, and the post office.

In the mid-1950s, three food markets in Boyes alone were advertising in the *Index-Tribune*: the Food Center, the Woodleaf Store, and Mike and Rose Gitti's Boyes Hot Springs Store.

In 1966, the Boyes Hot Springs Library was remodeled and featured a new children's section.

Boyes Hot Springs celebrated its centennial in 1949—apparently this was dating from the arrival of Thaddeus Leavenworth, although the name "Boyes" was not used in the valley until 1882. The celebration included a street dance, a barbecue, and a baseball game.

The Gallo brothers founded their DeSoto-Plymouth agency on the highway in Boyes in 1955.

A committee to consider incorporation for Boyes Hot Springs was formed in 1959.

In 1964, a devastating fire swept through the area, reminiscent of the 1923 conflagration. By that time, firefighting was much advanced, and the damage, terrible as it was (19 homes burned), was relatively limited.

As happened in many places across the country, as the 1950s became the 1960s and 1970s, prosperity waned, and the Springs took a downturn. The Boyes Bath House burned down in 1969, as did Fetters Hotel in 1975.

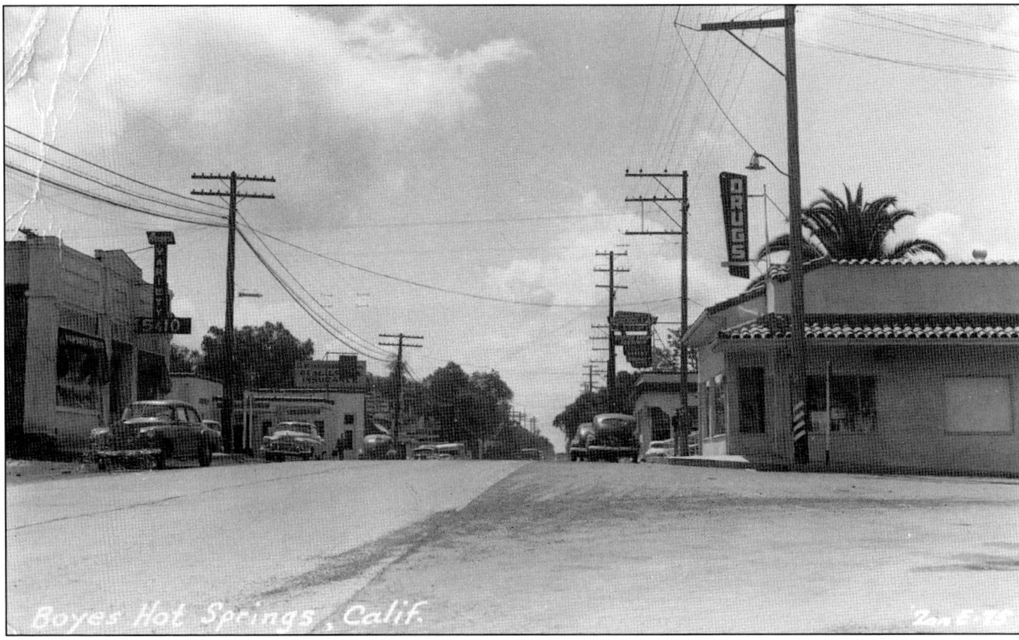

Zan Stark took these two wonderful photographs in the early 1950s near the intersection of Boyes Boulevard and Highway 12, where the Plaza Center building is located. The above image shows the first addition to the Plaza Center building with Pine Wagner's sign. At right is the Liaros building, which housed the Boyes Variety Store. (Both, courtesy of Stanford University Library, Special Collections.)

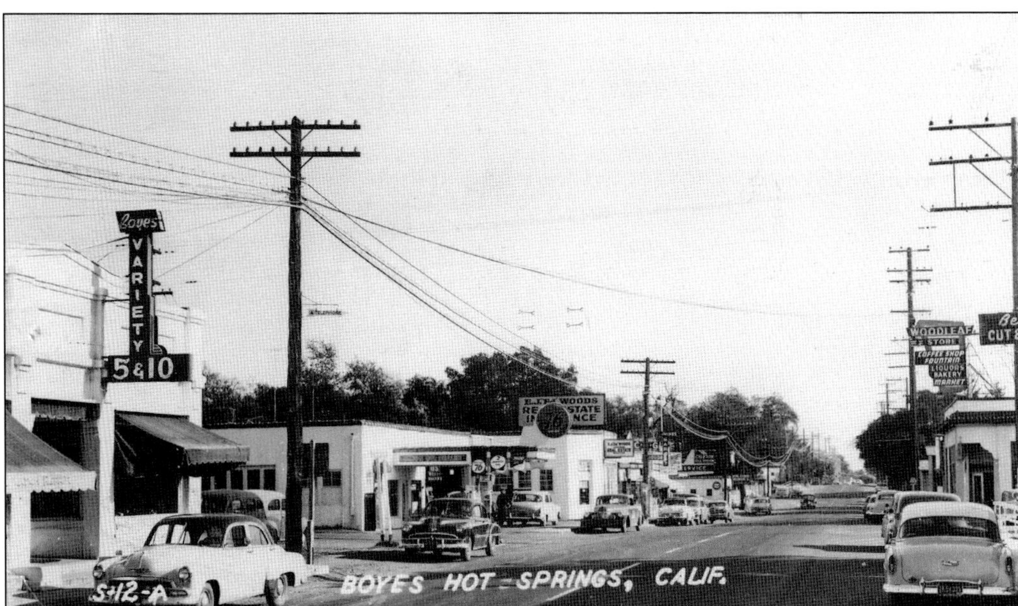

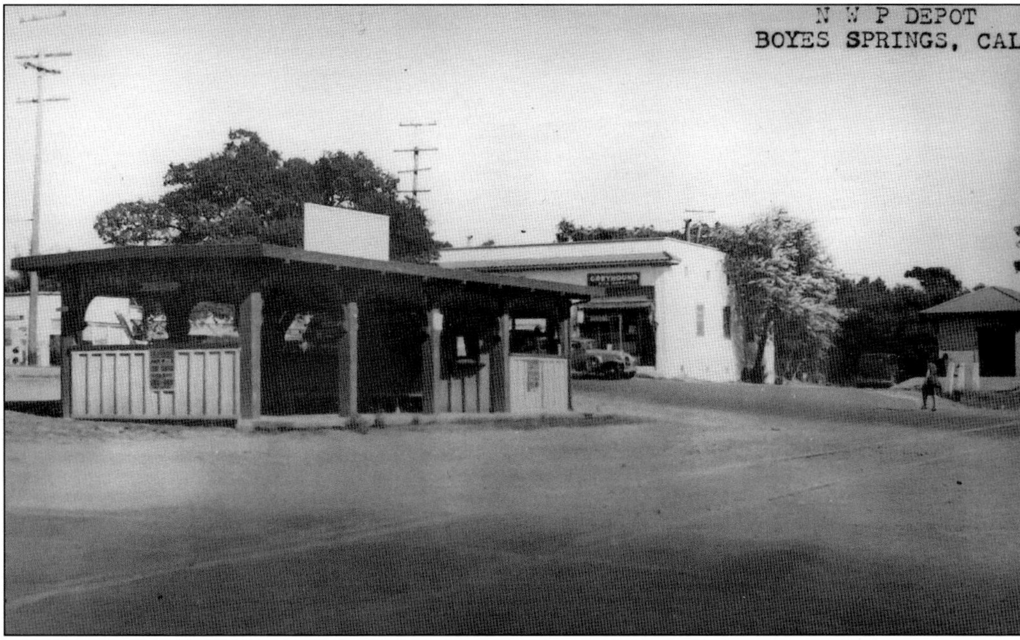

The Northwestern Pacific Railroad rebuilt its station in Boyes Hot Springs in 1925. In 1935, facing a decline in ridership due to competition with drivers using the new Golden Gate Bridge, the railroad discontinued passenger service. Limited freight service continued until 1942, when, despite much popular opposition, the tracks were torn up for the war effort, and the railroad era ended for the Springs. (Courtesy of the Sonoma Valley Historical Society.)

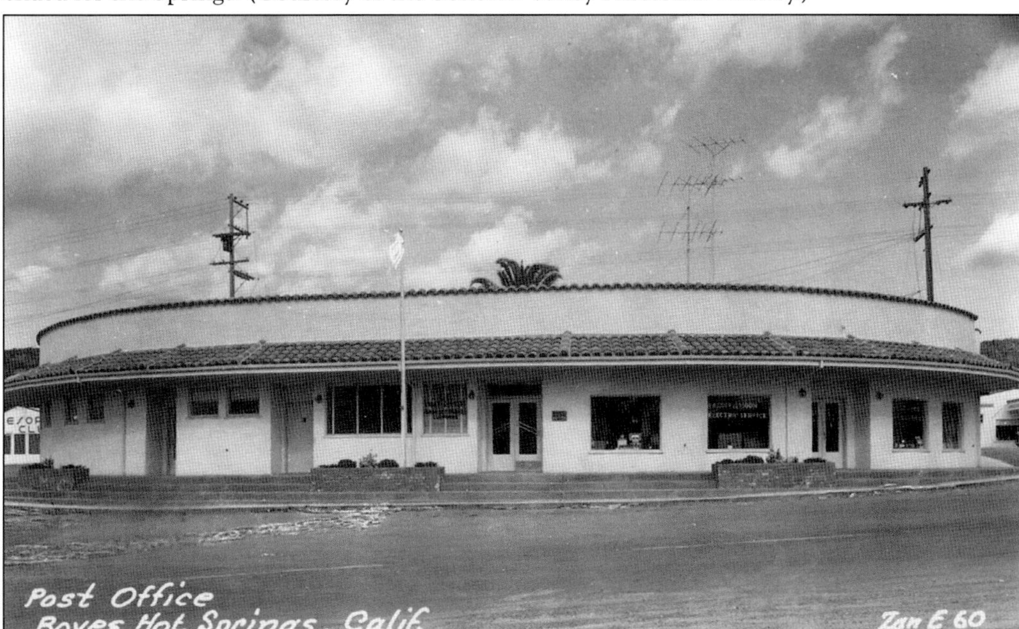

The Plaza Center—so named because it sits on the site of the old Boyes Plaza—was built between 1951 and 1955 by A.B. Peluffo. The first tenants were Pine Wagner's Valley Drug Store, Dr. Michael Makita, and the post office. The old plaza was originally laid out by the Northwestern Pacific Railroad for its Boyes Hot Springs depot. (Courtesy of the Sonoma Valley Historical Society.)

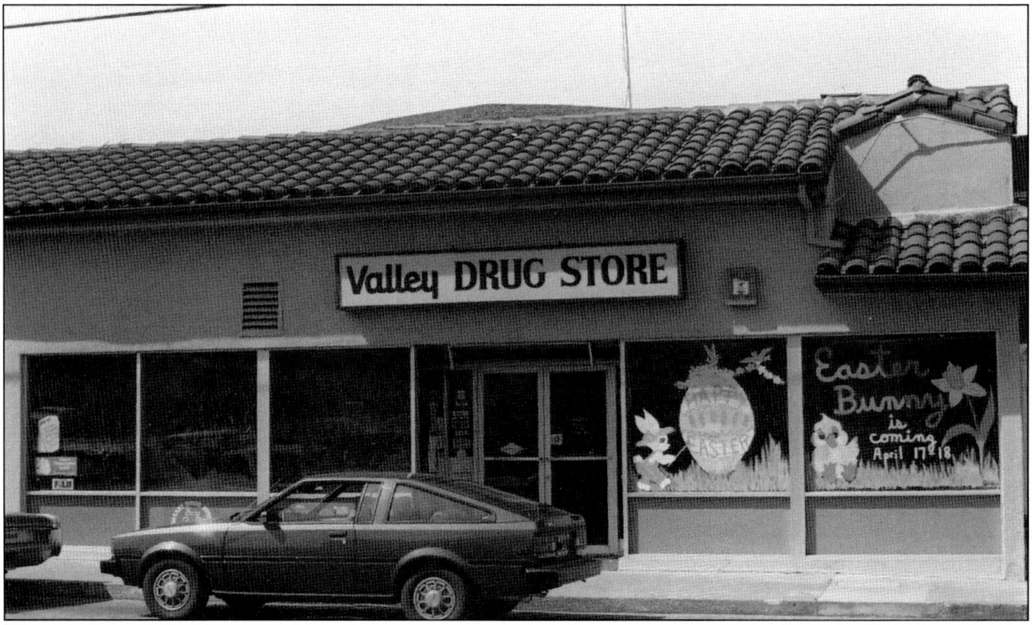

Pine Wagner, a female pharmacist, opened Valley Drug Store in 1942 on Highway 12 in a building owned by Bud Castner. When the first part of the Plaza Center building was finished in 1951, she moved her pharmacy there. Wagner graduated from pharmacy school in 1917 and practiced until 1962. She sold the store that year, and it carried on for many years afterward. (Courtesy of the Sonoma Valley Historical Society.)

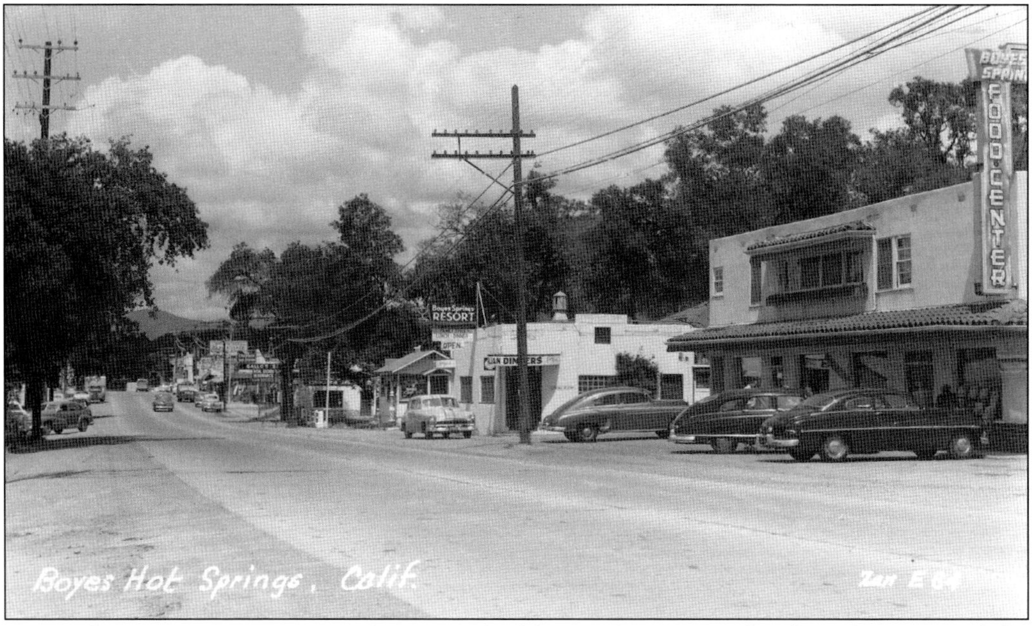

In March 1949, a new store opened in a new building at the corner of Calle Del Monte and the Sonoma Highway: the Boyes Hot Springs Food Center. The store's owner was A. Schubmacher, and the builder and owner was L. Saccato. The architect was Hugh Duffy. That same year, Horace Smario and Frank Del Rosso took over the store. (Courtesy of Stanford University Library, Special Collections.)

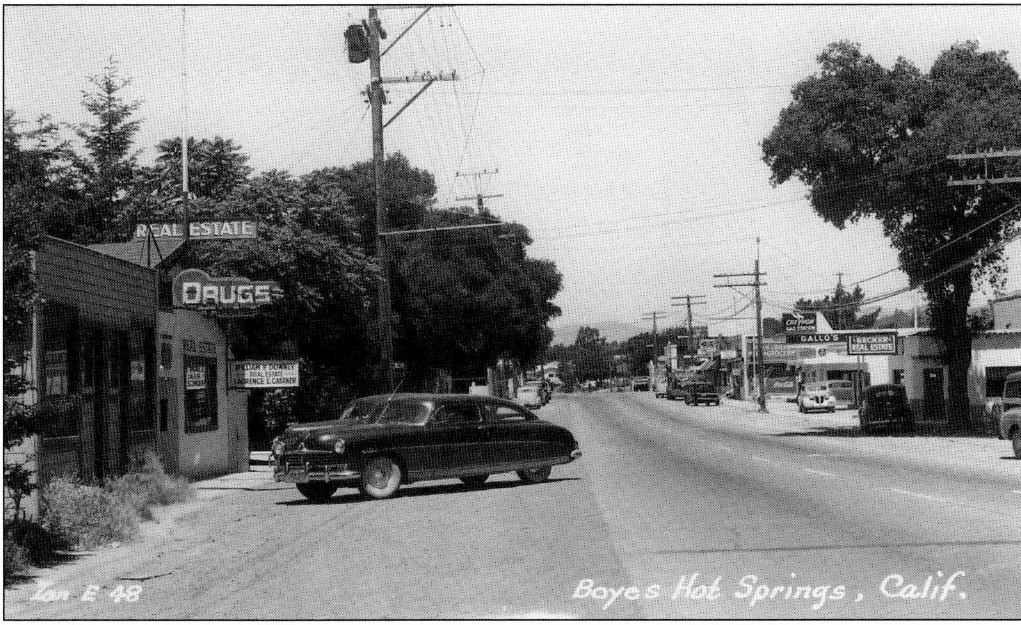

In this photograph taken on Highway 12 near Arroyo Road, at left is the original location of Pine Wagner's Valley Drug Store, along with the real estate offices of L.E. "Bud" Castner and William P. Downey, in buildings owned by Castner. Across the highway is the real estate office of Saul Becker, with Gallo's service station beyond. Most of these buildings still exist in 2016. (Courtesy of the Sonoma Valley Historical Society.)

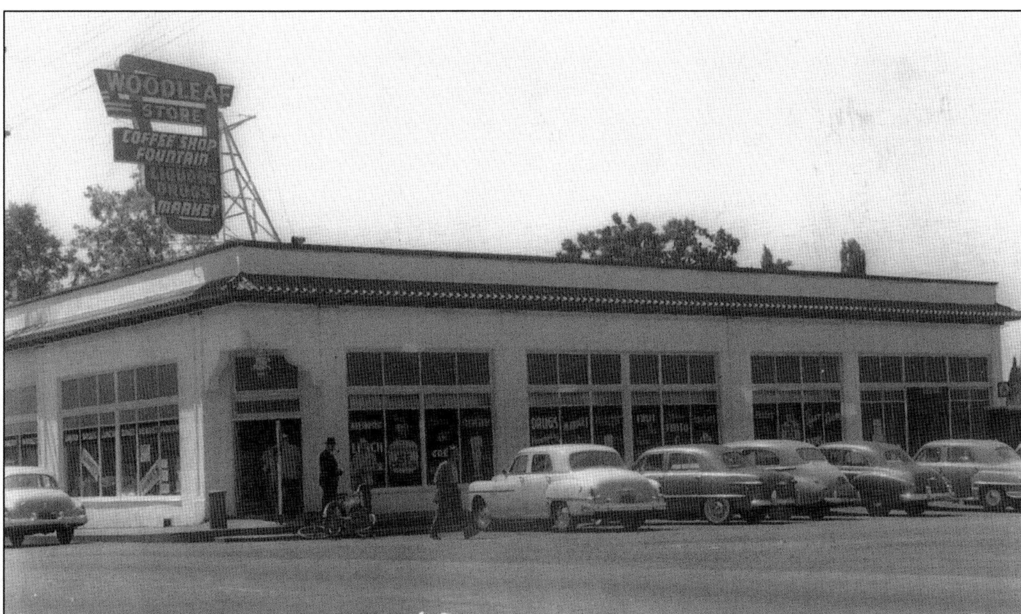

The Woodleaf Store is one of the businesses that spanned the eras. It was founded in the 1920s and remained in business into the late 1950s. (Courtesy of Stanford University Library, Special Collections.)

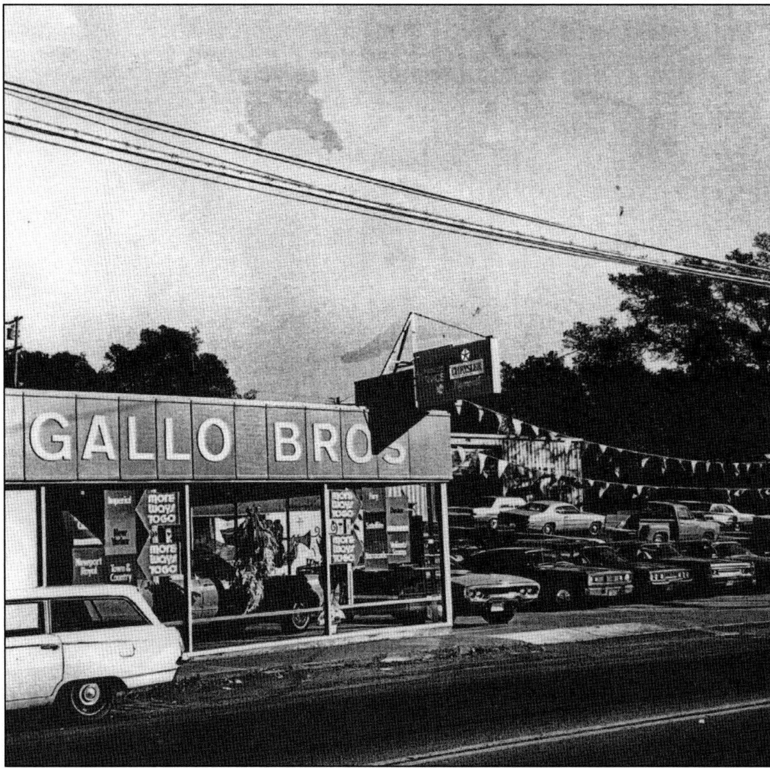

In 1949, Enrico and Guido "Babe" Gallo bought this property on the highway in Boyes Hot Springs, which included a gas station, a hardware store, and apartments. In 1955, it became Gallo Brothers Desoto-Plymouth. The brothers retired in 1979 and sold the business, which continued as Sonoma Valley Motors. Today, the building on Sonoma Highway between Arroyo Road and Vallejo Street houses Golden West Glass. (Courtesy of Robert Parmelee.)

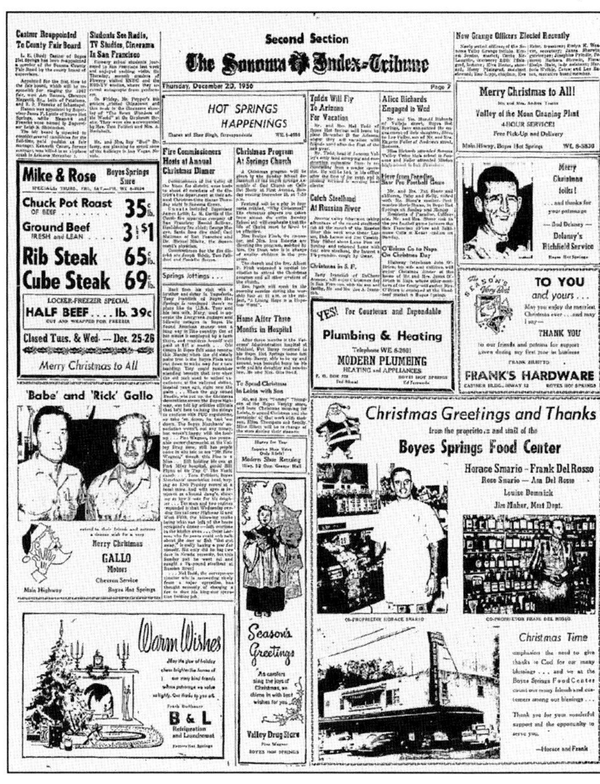

Second Section

The Sonoma Index-Tribune

Thursday, December 20, 1956 — Page 7

Castner Reappointed To County Fair Board

Students See Radio, TV Studios, Cinerama In San Francisco

New Grange Officers Elected Recently

HOT SPRINGS HAPPENINGS

Merry Christmas to All! Valley of the Moon Cleaning Plant. 4-HOUR SERVICE! Free Pick-Up and Delivery. Main Hiway, Boyes Hot Springs. WE 6-3830

Fire Commissioners Hosts at Annual Christmas Dinner

Christmas Program At Springs Church

Todds Will Fly To Arizona For Vacation

Alice Richards Engaged to Wed

Catch Steelhead At Russian River

Here from Paradise, Saw Pro Football Game

O'Briens Go to Napa On Christmas Day

Christmas in S. F.

Mike & Rose — Boyes Springs Store. Chuck Pot Roast of Beef 35c lb. Ground Beef Fresh and Lean 3 lbs. $1. Rib Steak 65c lb. Cube Steak 69c lb. Locker-Freezer Special: Half Beef . . . . lb. 39c. Cut and wrapped for freezer. Closed Tues. & Wed. — Dec. 25-26. Merry Christmas to All

Merry Christmas folks! . . . and thanks for your patronage. — Bud Delaney — Delaney's Richfield Service, Boyes Hot Springs

Springs Jottings . . .

Home After Three Months in Hospital

To Spend Christmas In Lolita with Son

YES! For Courteous and Dependable Plumbing & Heating. Telephone WE 6-2001. MODERN PLUMBING, HEATING and APPLIANCES. Boyes Hot Springs

The Season's Very Best TO YOU and yours . . . May you enjoy the merriest Christmas ever . . . and may I say — THANK YOU to our friends and patrons for support given during my first year in business. FRANK'S HARDWARE, Boyes Hot Springs

'Babe' and 'Rick' Gallo . . . Merry Christmas. GALLO Motors, Chevron Service. Main Highway, Boyes Hot Springs

Modern Shoe Rebuilding

Christmas Greetings and Thanks from the proprietors and staff of the Boyes Springs Food Center. Horace Smario – Frank DelRosso. Rose Smario — Ann Del Rosso. Louise Dominick. Jim Maher, Meat Dept.

Co-Proprietor Horace Smario. Co-Proprietor Frank Del Rosso

Warm Wishes. May the glow of holiday cheer brighten the homes of our many kind friends whose patronage we value so highly. Our thanks to you all. B & L Refrigeration and Laundromat

Season's Greetings. As carolers sing the joys of Christmas, we chime in with best wishes for you. Valley Drug Store, Pine Wagner, Boyes Hot Springs

Christmas Time emphasizes the need to give thanks to God for our many blessings . . . and we at the Boyes Springs Food Center count our many friends and customers among our blessings . . . Thank you for your wonderful support and the opportunity to serve you. —Horace and Frank

The front page of the second section of the *Sonoma Index-Tribune* was the place to discover what was happening in the Springs. Here, it provides Christmas greetings from Enrico and Babe Gallo, Horace Smario and Frank del Rosso at the Food Center, Pine Wagner of Valley Drug Store, and a host of others. In the upper right corner, a notice announces that Bud Castner has been reappointed to the county fair board. The new Grange officers are listed at upper left. (Courtesy of the Sonoma Valley Historical Society.)

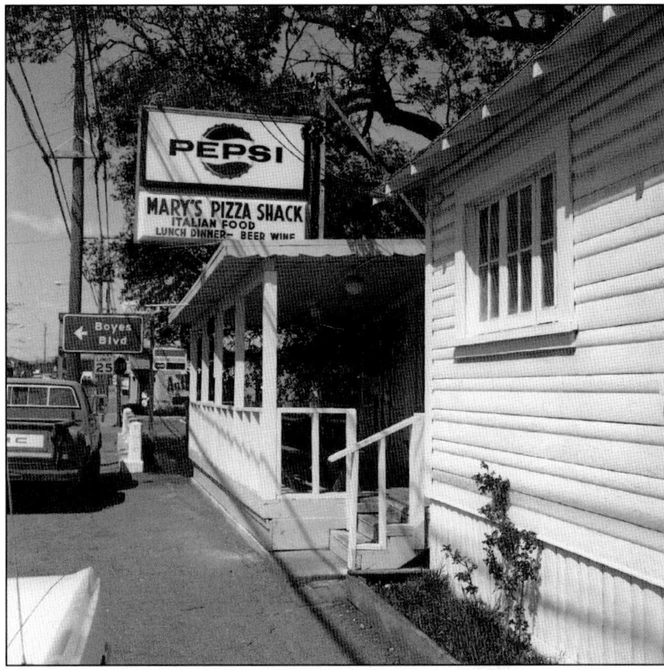

In 1959, Mary Fazio opened her first Pizza Shack on the highway at Arroyo Road. Springs residents have many fond memories of eating pizza on the front porch. (Courtesy of Mary's Pizza Shack.)

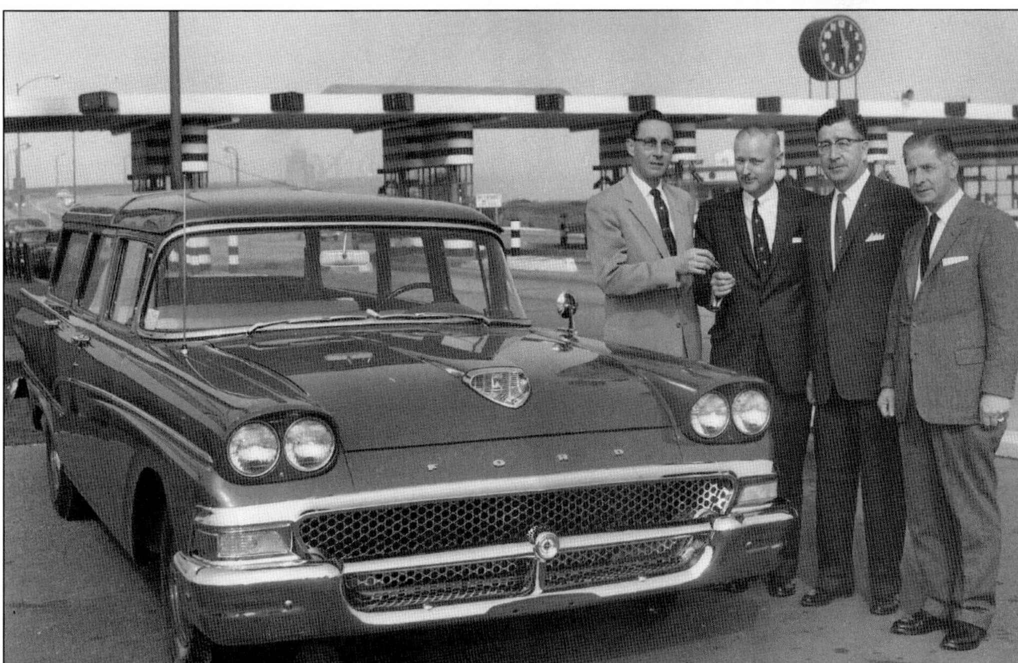

Boyes Hot Springs businessman L.E. "Bud" Castner (second from left) was a Golden Gate Bridge District commissioner from 1952 to 1992 and the district's director for almost 40 years. As a real estate agent and developer in Boyes Hot Springs, he rented space to the first doctor, dentist, and pharmacist in the area. He also founded the first hardware store, Valley Hardware, located next to the building that is now Golden West Glass. (Courtesy of the Sonoma Valley Historical Society.)

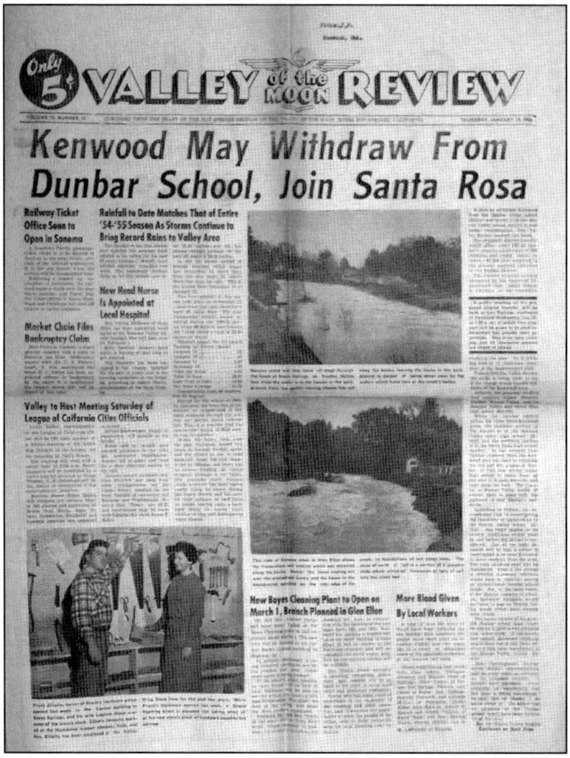

Only 5¢ VALLEY of the MOON REVIEW

Kenwood May Withdraw From Dunbar School, Join Santa Rosa

Railway Ticket Office Seen to Open in Sonoma

Rainfall to Date Matches That of Entire '54-'55 Season As Storms Continue to Bring Record Rains to Valley Area

New Head Nurse Is Appointed at Local Hospital

Market Chain Files Bankruptcy Claim

Valley to Host Meeting Saturday of League of California Cities Officials

New Boyes Cleaning Plant to Open on March 1, Branch Planned in Glen Ellen

More Blood Given By Local Workers

The *Valley of the Moon Daily Review* was published from the late 1940s through the early 1960s. The owners and publishers for the last 10 years of its existence were Zan Stark Jr. and Zan Stark Sr. The senior Stark was a photographer and publisher of postcards. He recorded some of the finest images of the Springs in the mid-20th century. (Courtesy of the Sonoma Valley Historical Society.)

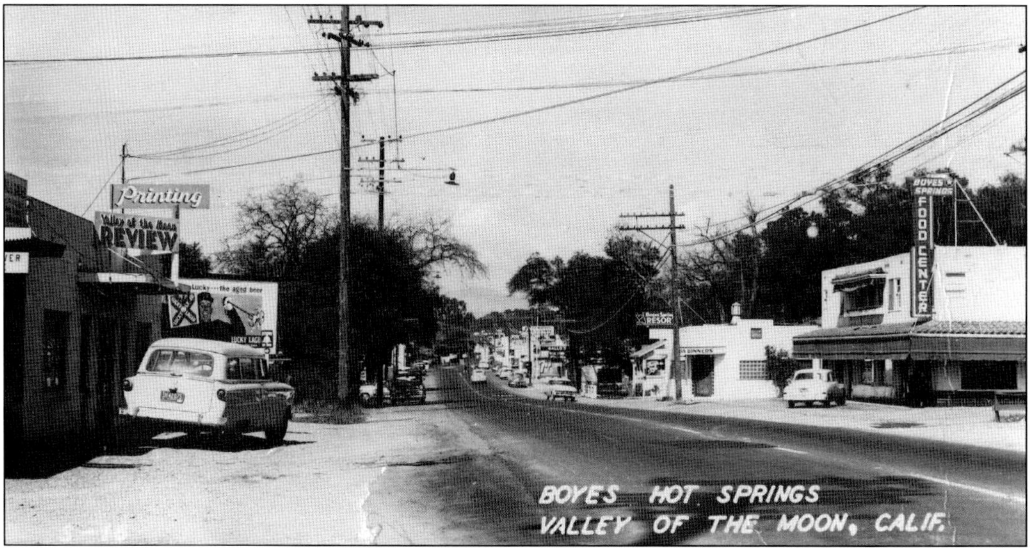

This view of Sonoma Highway looking north in Boyes Hot Springs features two businesses that were important to the community in the 1950s, and the photograph itself was taken by the proprietor of one of them. At left is the office of the *Valley of the Moon Daily Review*, which was edited by photographer Alexander Stark, better known as Zan. At right is the Boyes Hot Springs Food Center. Stark took this photograph of the *Valley of the Moon Daily Review* building, the highway, and the Boyes Food Center sometime in the early 1950s. Just beyond the Food Center is the Boyes Hot Springs resort, which is now a parking lot. The sign for Gallo's car lot is in the distance. The *Daily Review* building still stands in 2016. (Courtesy of Stanford University Library, Special Collections.)

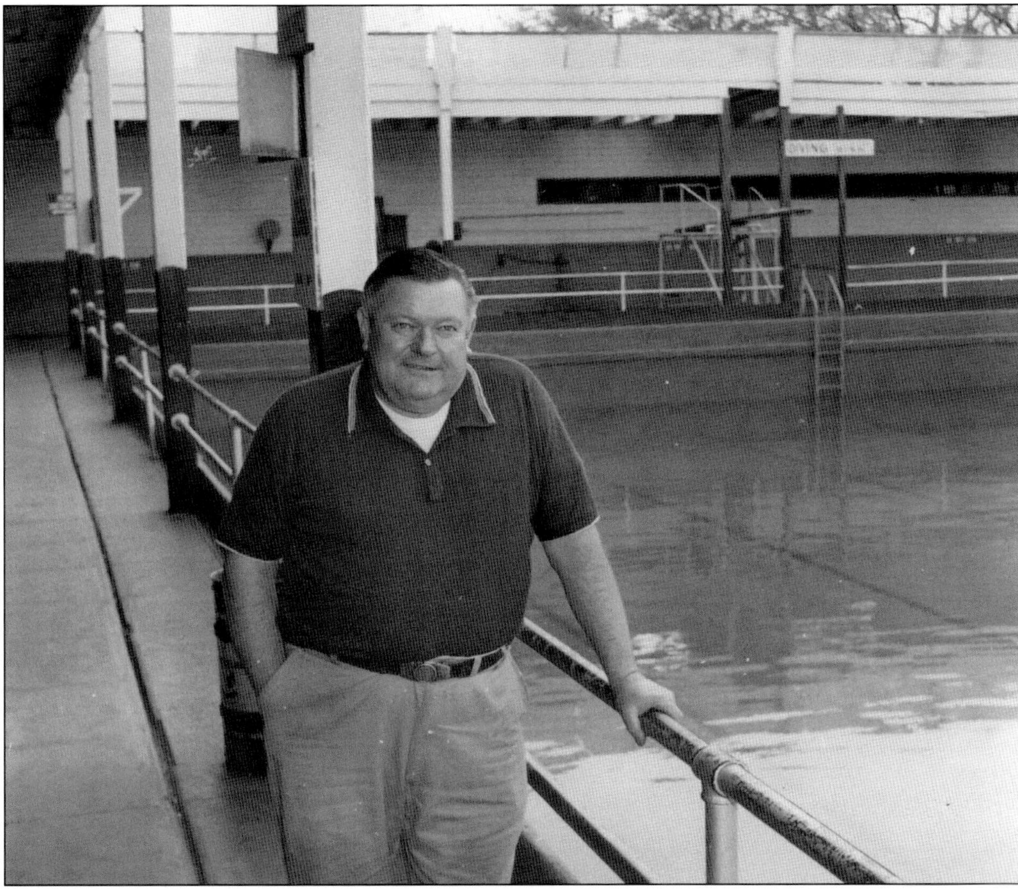

"Confident of another successful season, Bill Johnson, manager of the Boyes Hot Springs Bath House stands by the big pool, which will be officially opened tomorrow, April 1. The 145'x72', 586,000 gallon heated pool was filling as this photo was taken. Other renovated attractions await Bath House visitors, including lawn picnic area, amusement arcade, restaurant, lunch counter massage parlor, bar and hot plunge," reported the *Sonoma Index-Tribune* on March 31, 1960. (Courtesy of the Sonoma Valley Historical Society.)

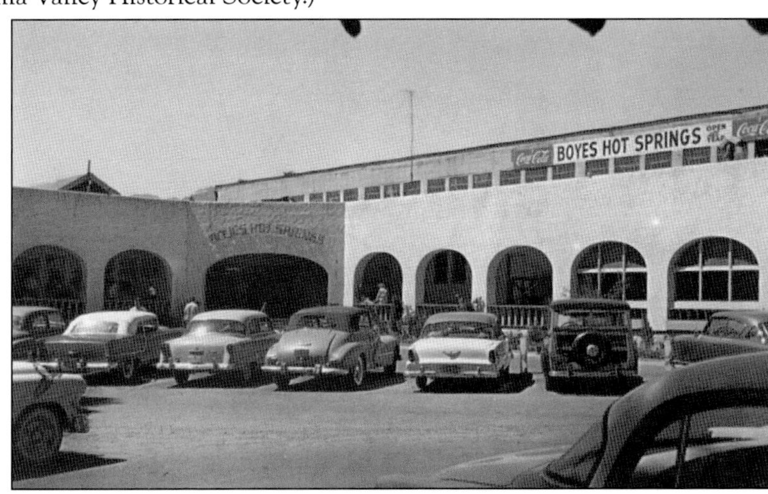

By the 1950s, the Boyes Bath House was looking perhaps a little less stately and magical with all the cars parked directly in front of the entrance. They are great cars, though.

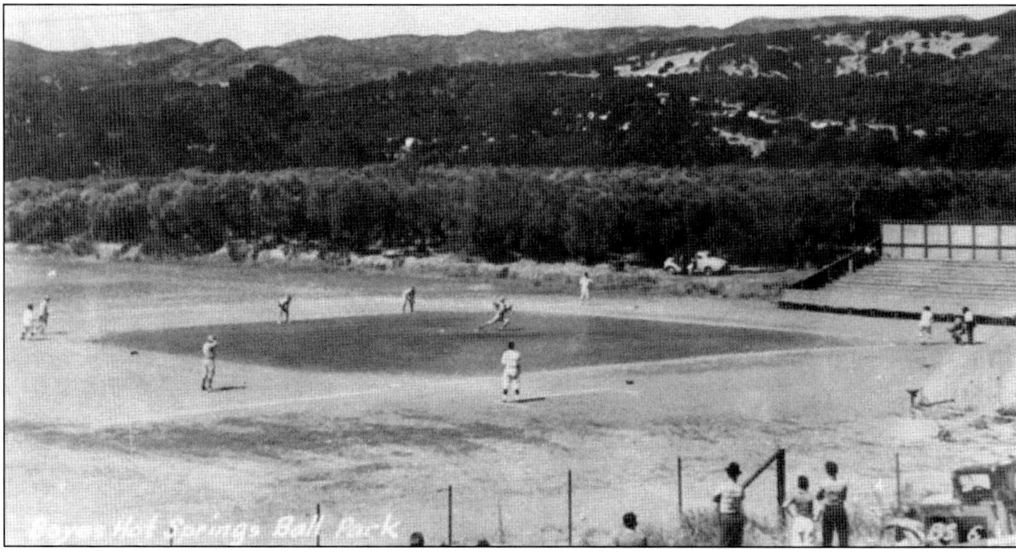

In this photograph looking east over the Boyes Hot Springs ballpark, the Mayacamas Mountains are visible in the background. In 1912, the *San Francisco Chronicle* reported that an eight-acre ballpark was being constructed in Boyes Hot Springs and that the San Francisco Seals would train there. Professional baseball and football teams trained in the valley until the early 1950s. (Courtesy of Stanford University Library, Special Collections.)

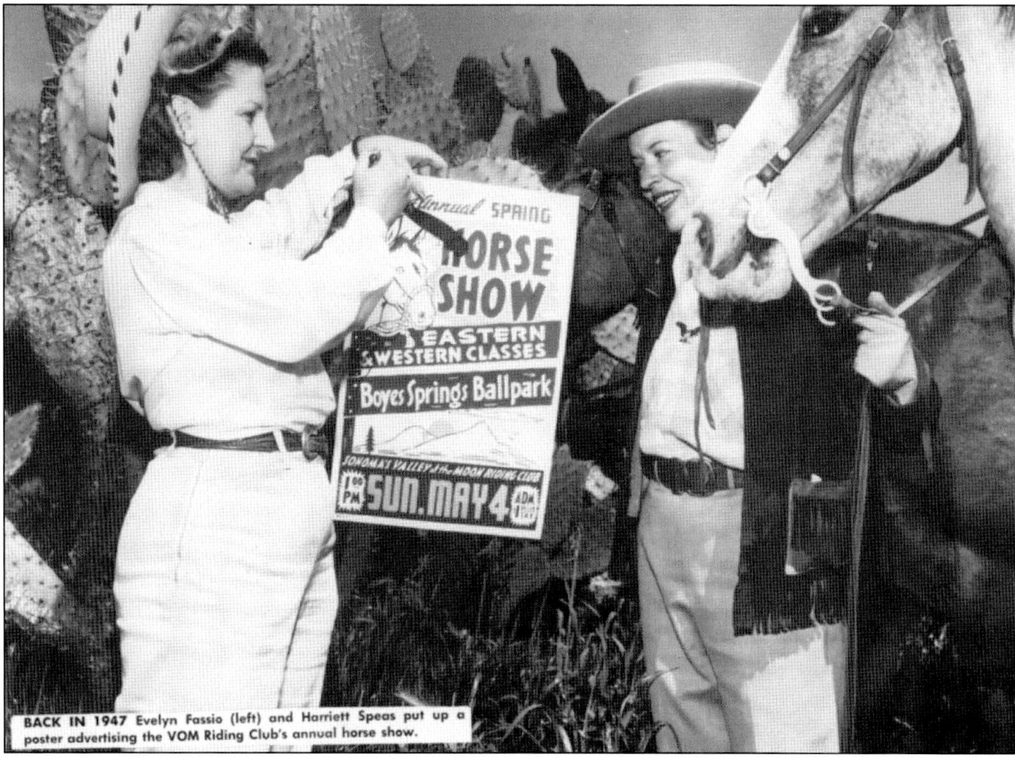

The Valley of the Moon Riding Club was established in 1939. The ballpark was a popular venue for more than just baseball games. Rodeos, Easter egg hunts, and folk dance festivals were also held there. (Courtesy of the Sonoma Valley Historical Society.)

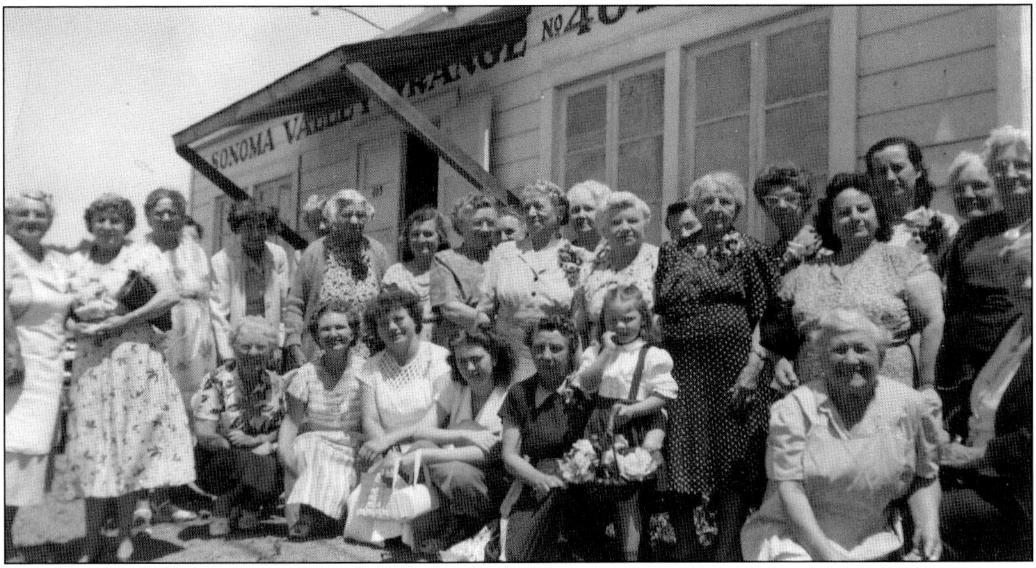

The Sonoma Valley Grange was founded in 1924 but did not have its own building until 10 years later. In 1934, the organization bought this building from Selig Rosenthal of Rosenthal's Resort. Since its founding, the Grange has served the community as a meeting place and polling place, as well as serving as a venue for the organization's own events. The National Grange of The Order of Patrons of Husbandry was founded in 1867 for the benefit of farmers. As farms have been lost to urbanization, many Granges have become general public service groups. (Both, courtesy of the Sonoma Valley Grange.)

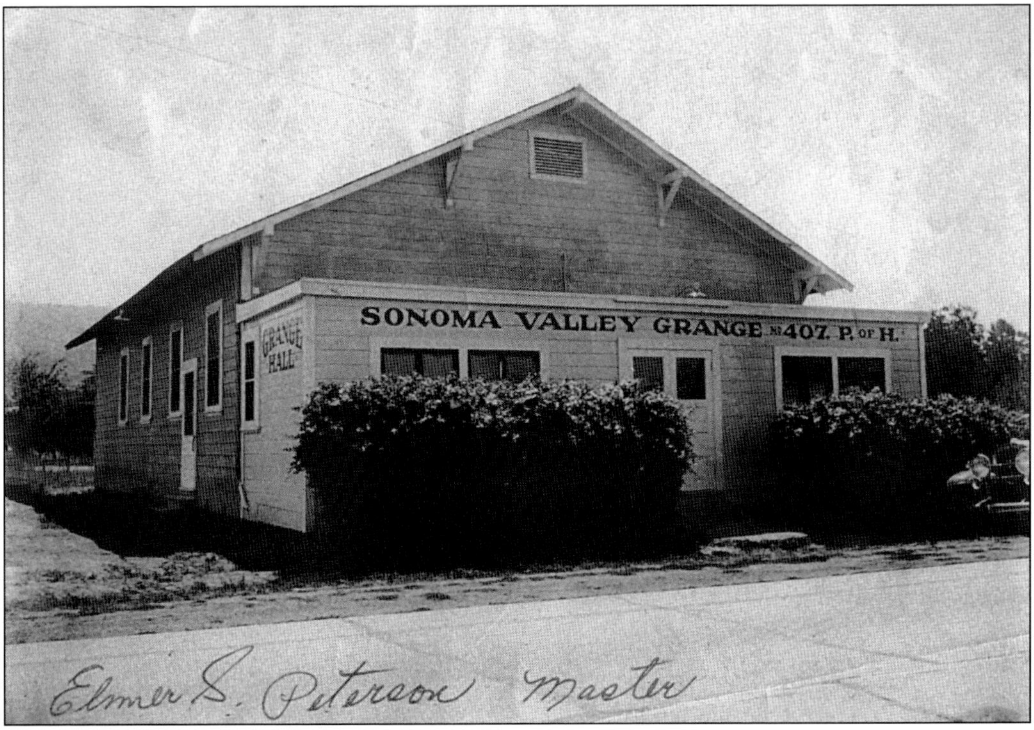

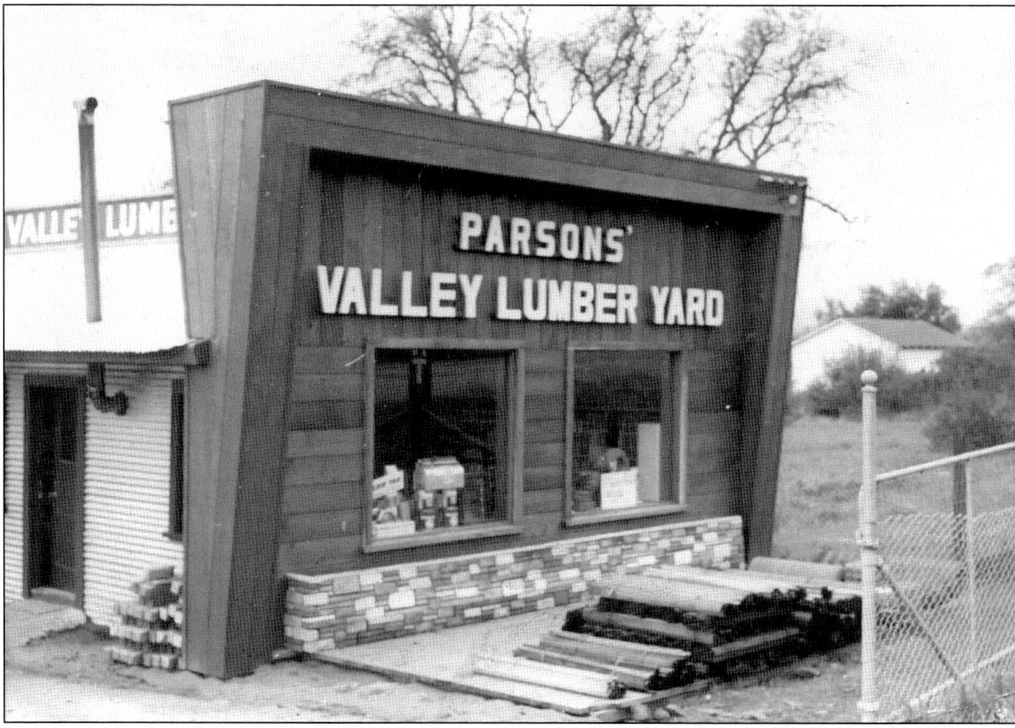

In 1950, Vernon Parson came from Walnut Creek and bought the Valley Lumber company. His sons Don and Bob helped run it. In 1988, Alan and Helen Medina became owners and have been running Parsons Lumber & Hardware ever since. (Courtesy of Don Parsons.)

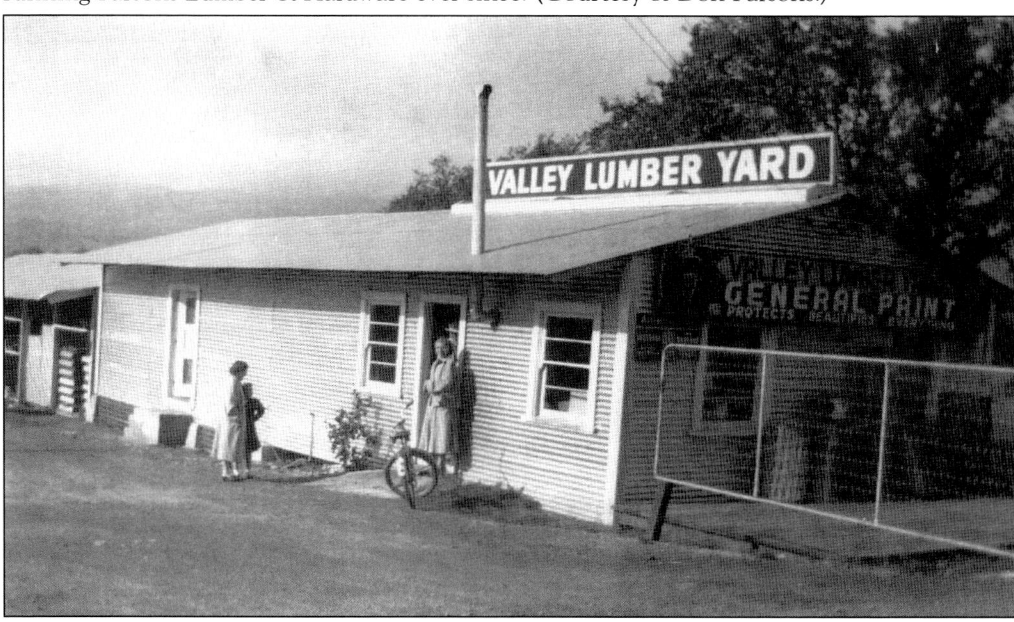

The Sonoma Valley Lumber Company was in business by 1918 on this main highway site. That year, an advertisement in the *Sonoma Index-Tribune* stated that the proprietor, C.A. Bergstrom, was in France, but "the manager of the yard will be glad to give you figures and will guarantee satisfaction."

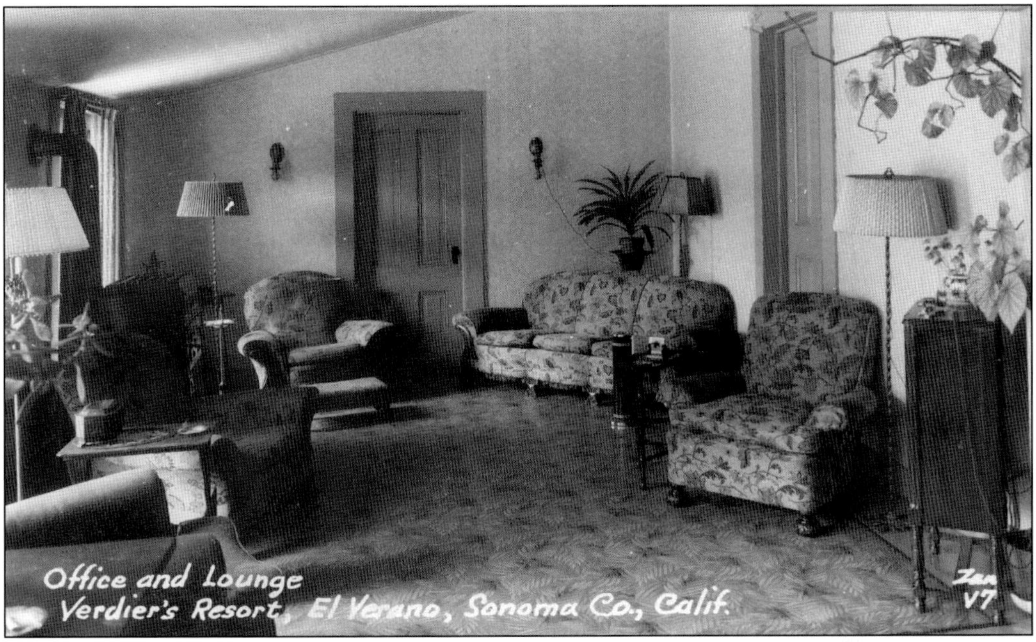

Verdier's was located at Linden and Oak Streets in El Verano. It advertised: "Only 40 miles north of San Francisco over the Golden Gate Bridge. A vacation spent at Verdier's will leave an indelible impression. . . . Swim in our colorful pool with soft velvet waters. . . . Dance to an orchestra or the juke box. . . . Cocktail Lounge, a unique bar where you'll meet old and new friends. Excellent mixologists."

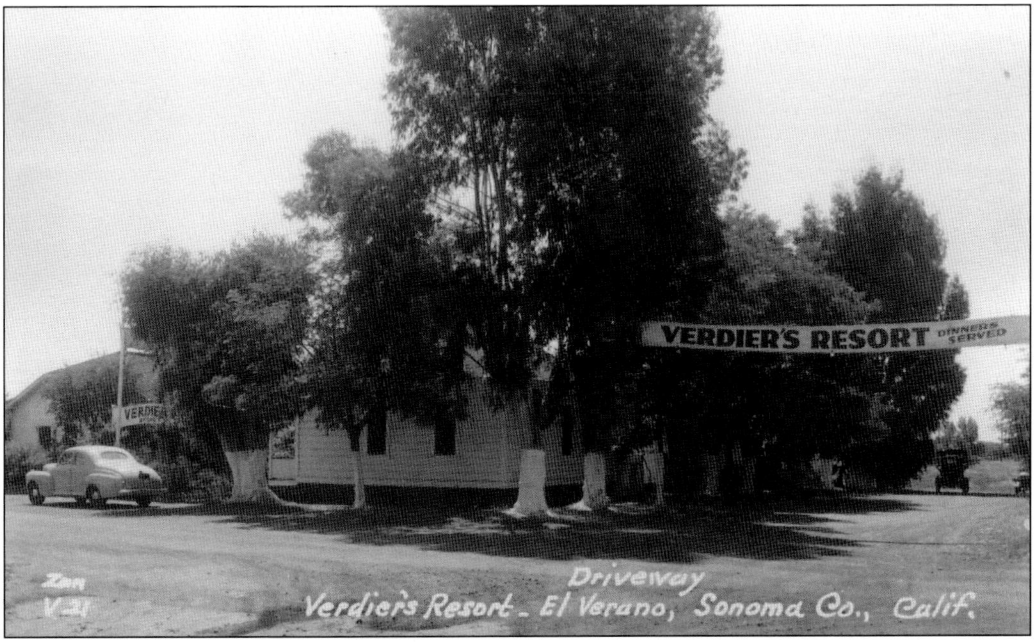

The Dutil family ran a boardinghouse in El Verano as early as 1900. Around 1902, they opened their French Cottage resort. In the 1920s, it became Verdier's Resort. The Verdier family made many improvements, including landscaping and new buildings. On July 4, 1931, the resort celebrated the nation's birthday with a masquerade ball.

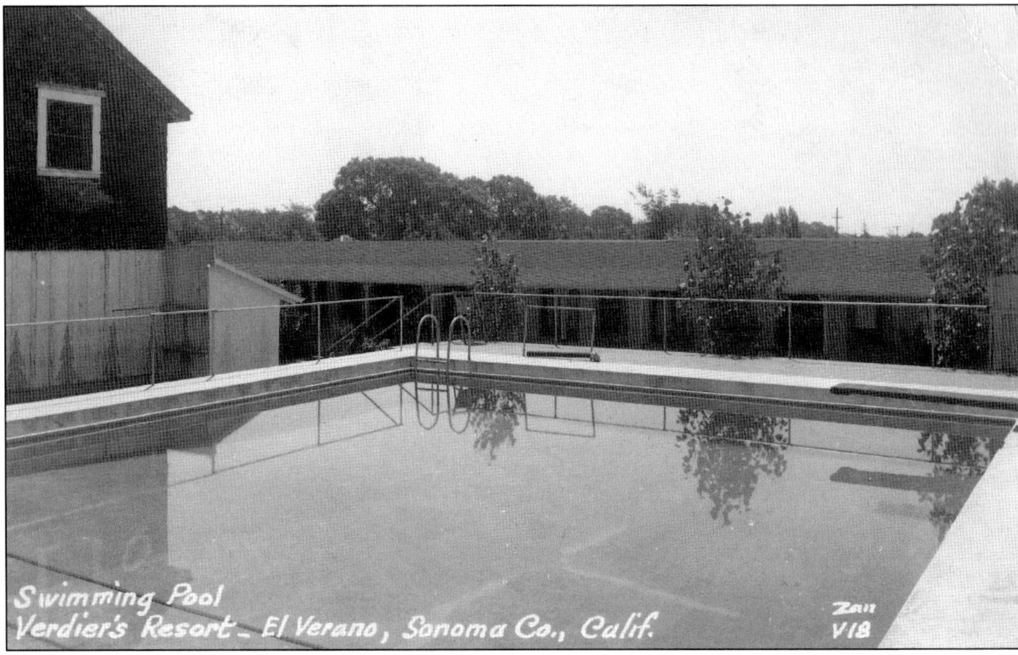

In 1951, the *Sonoma Index-Tribune* noted that there were 10 public swimming pools in the Valley of the Moon (including this one at Verdier's Resort).

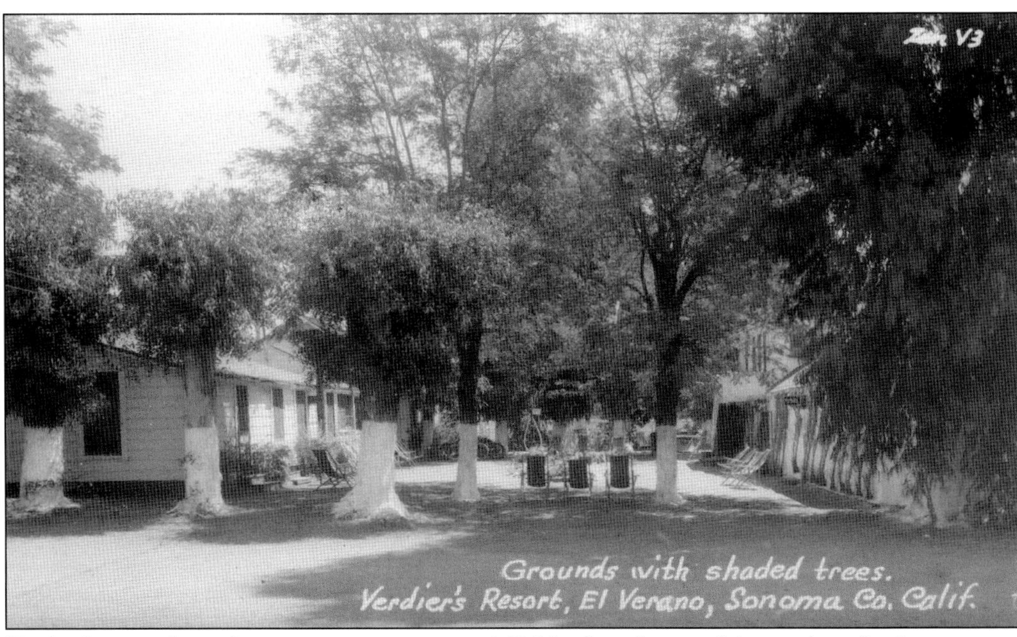

Verdier's went through numerous owners until 1964, when Juanita Musson bought the property. In March 1969, Juanita's was destroyed by fire.

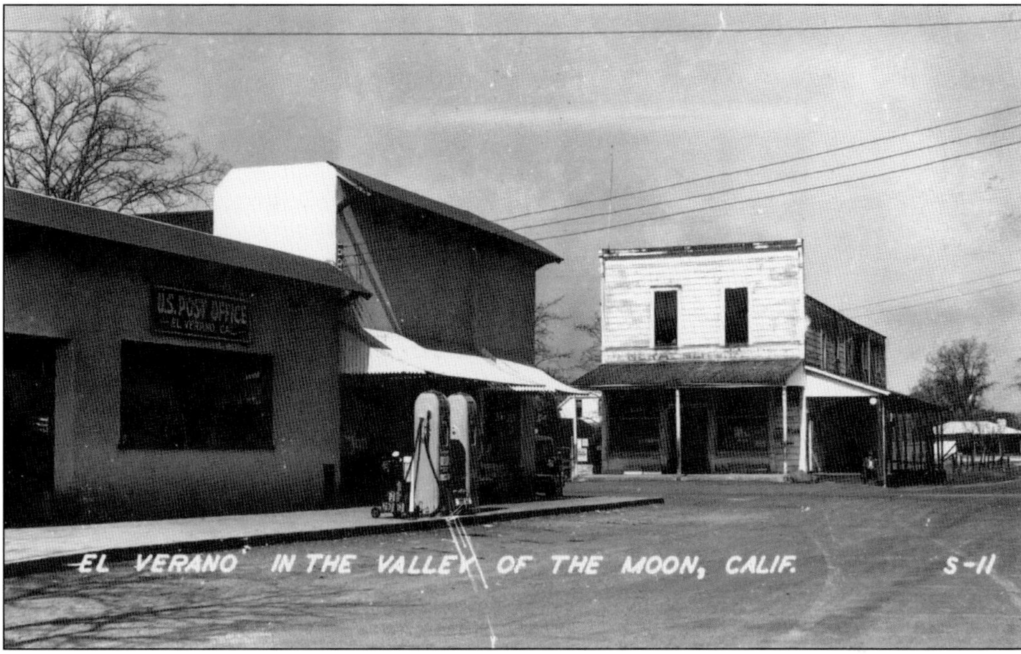

Since 1889, the El Verano Post Office has either been in Mullen's General Store (visible in the background of this 1950s postcard), or in the building in the foreground, which was then Danieli's Store. They are located at the intersection of Laurel and Bay Streets. The Mullens and the Danielis were prominent pioneer families in El Verano. See page 33 for an earlier photograph of Mullen's. (Courtesy of Stanford University Library, Special Collections.)

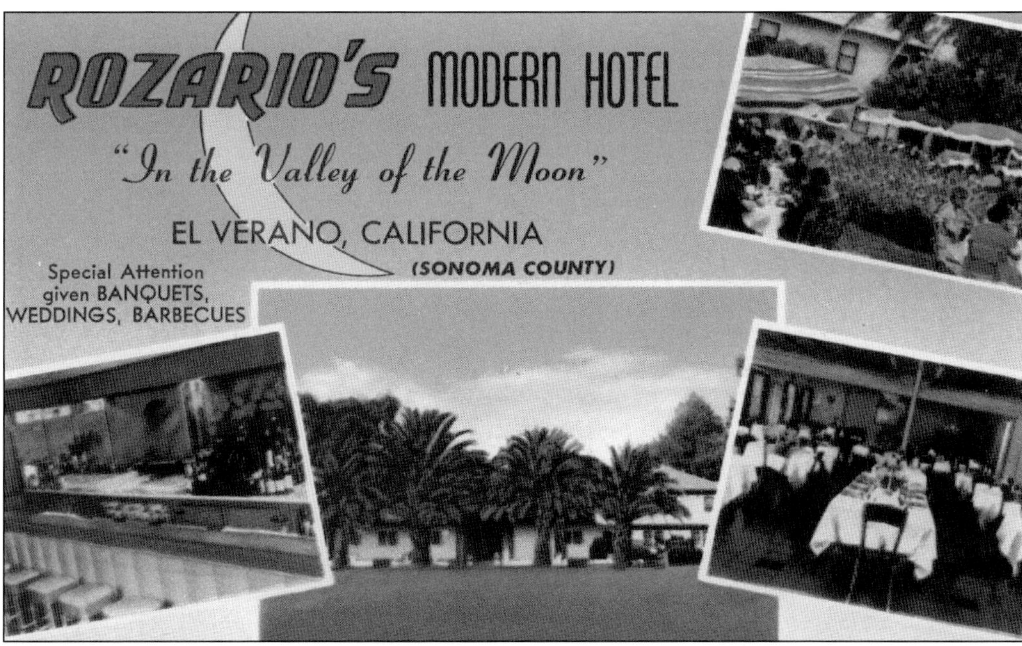

The Rozario family bought Parente's Resort, located on Verano Avenue, in 1943. They ran the resort for 11 years, making many improvements to the property. In 1955, they sold to Carl Innskeep and Joe LaRango, newcomers from Montana.

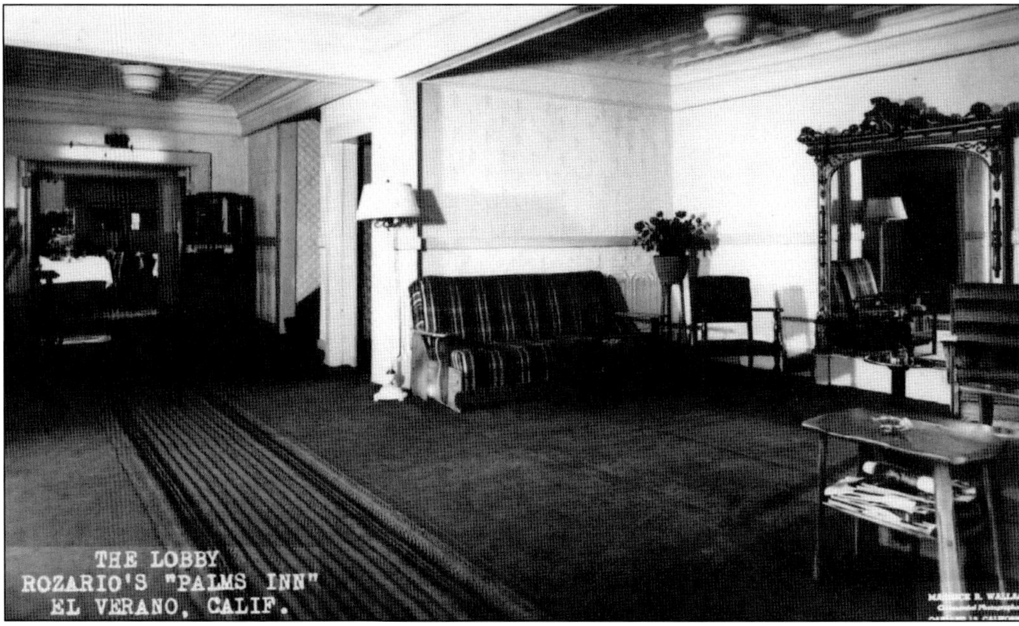

The former Rozario's "Palms Inn" (pictured in both of these images) was open under the names Innskeep's and El Verano Inn until the 1980s. In 1985, it was torn down to make room for an addition to the Finnish American Home Association complex. (Both, courtesy of the Sonoma Valley Historical Society.)

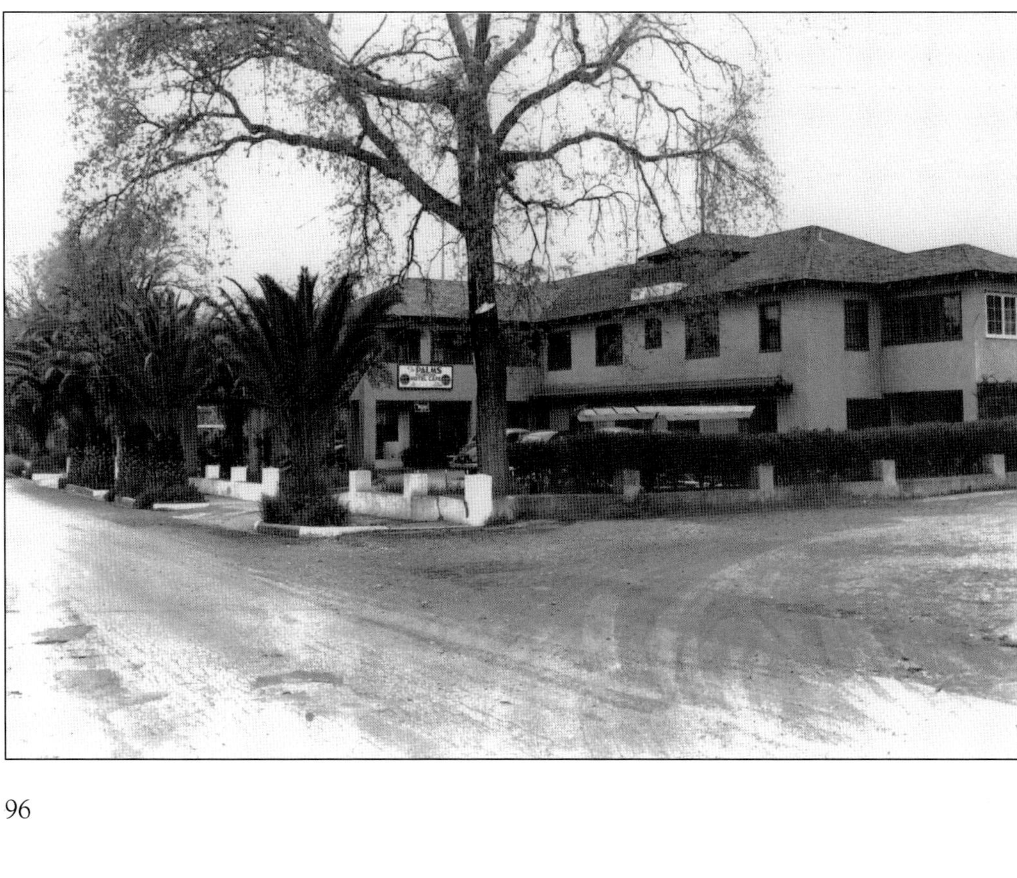

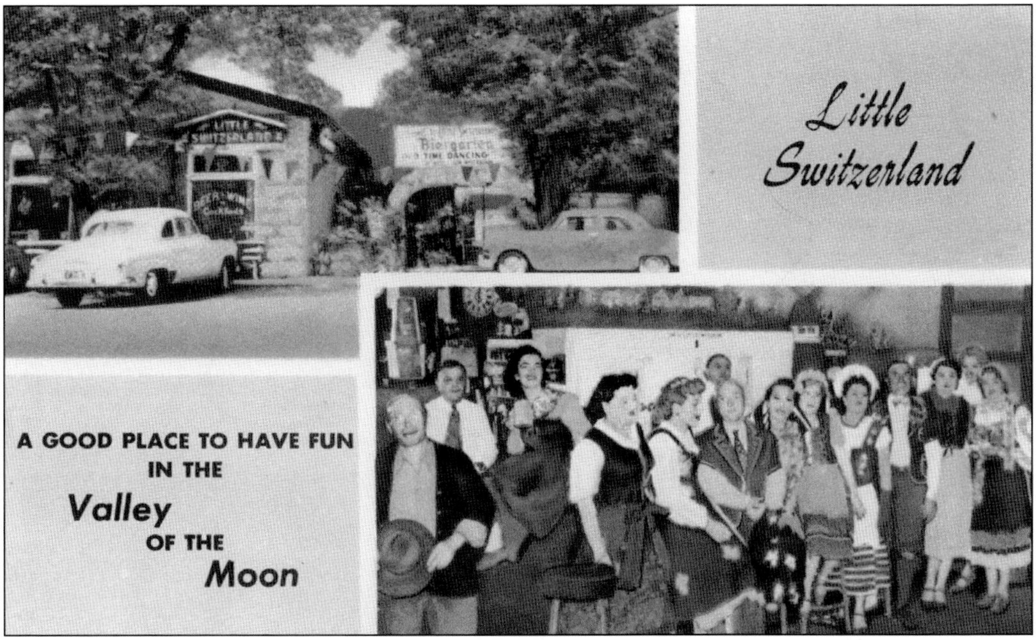

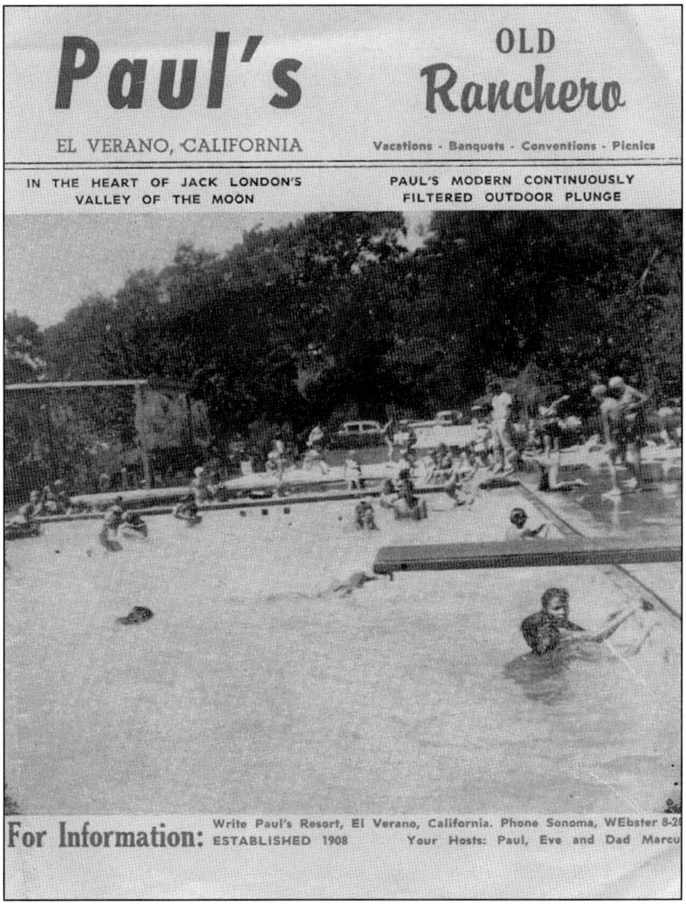

The Villa Savoy Resort, located at Grove and Riverside Streets in El Verano, was founded in 1906. In 1919, the resort was taken over by Phil Rossi and his wife. They sold it to Walter Reichmuth in 1945, and he renamed it Little Switzerland. The longstanding polka-dance venue was also known for an occasional punk rock show. In 2013, new owner Max Young renamed the place Rossi's 1906.

Paul Vannucci was operating Paul's Resort on Verano Avenue in El Verano by 1924. In 1943, Paul Marcucci Jr. and Eve Marcucci bought it from him (and they did not need to change the name, obviously). Under the Marcuccis, Paul's Resort was a roaring success. Large banquets and lavish parties were common. (Courtesy of Eve Marcucci and Yvonne Marcucci Thibault.)

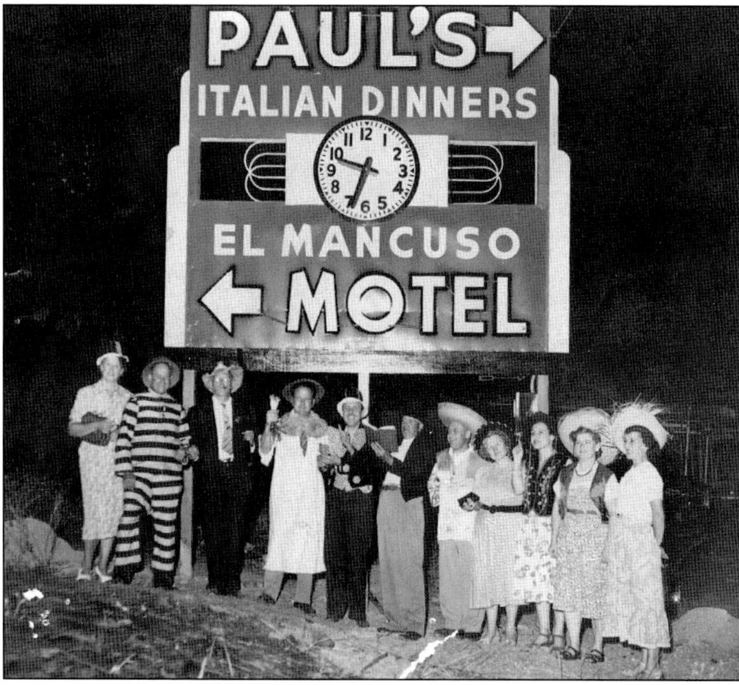

This Paul's Resort and El Mancuso Motel sign is from 1950. (Courtesy of Eve Marcucci and Yvonne Marcucci Thibault.)

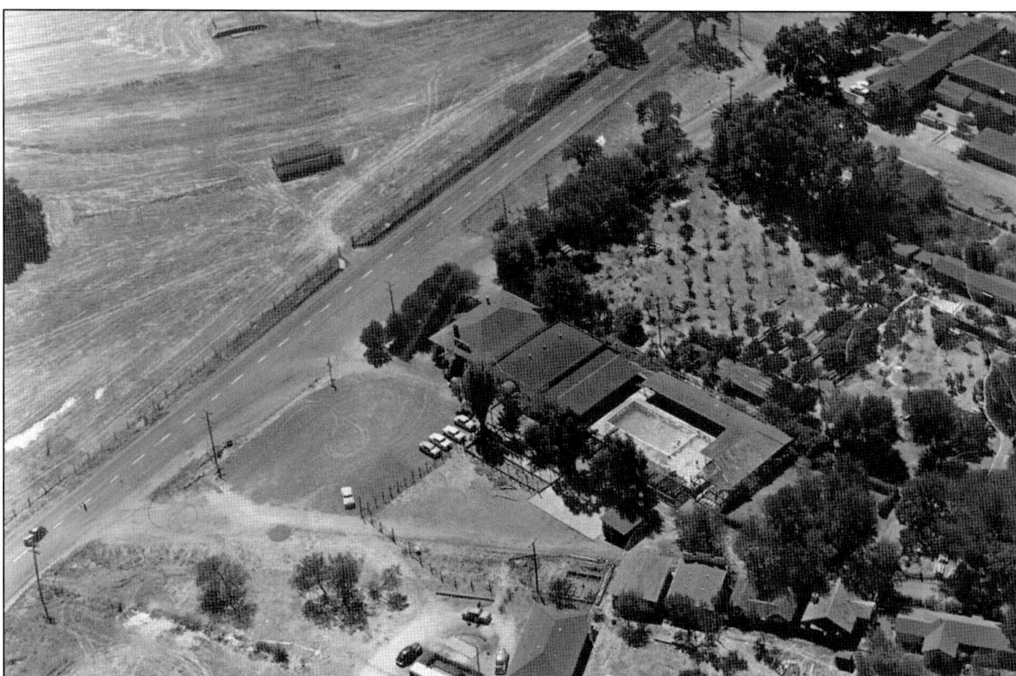

Paul Marcucci was a constant builder, even getting a contractor's license in order to expedite his projects. In 1953, the *Sonoma Index-Tribune* reported that "a four bedroom cottage is now being completed at Paul's . . . with ten more similar units to be constructed. . . . A new, private 2-bedroom dwelling is also under construction and five new garages have been recently completed." (Courtesy of Eve Marcucci and Yvonne Marcucci Thibault.)

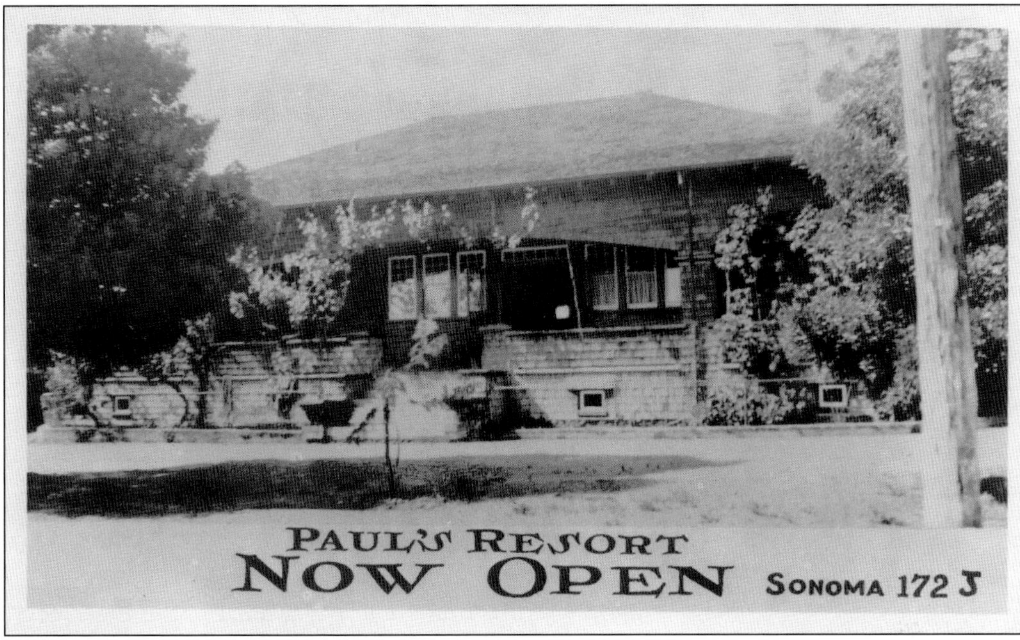

Although it has now been closed for decades, the main building at Paul's Resort housed many memories. Recently, there was some hope that it could be reopened for public use, but on the morning of March 10, 2013, it became the latest of the old resorts to succumb to fire. (Courtesy of Eve Marcucci and Yvonne Marcucci Thibault.)

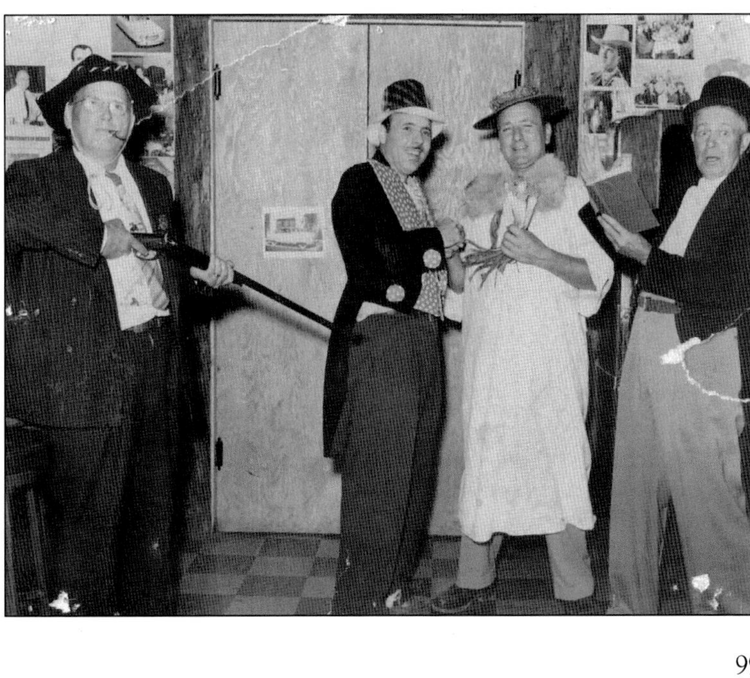

From left to right, Paul Marcucci Sr., Paul Marcucci Jr. (owner of Paul's Resort), Pete Mancuso (owner of the El Mancuso Motel), and Curtis Rich are pictured at Paul's Resort in 1950 celebrating the "shotgun wedding" of Paul's Resort and the El Mancuso Motel. (Courtesy of Eve Marcucci and Yvonne Marcucci Thibault.)

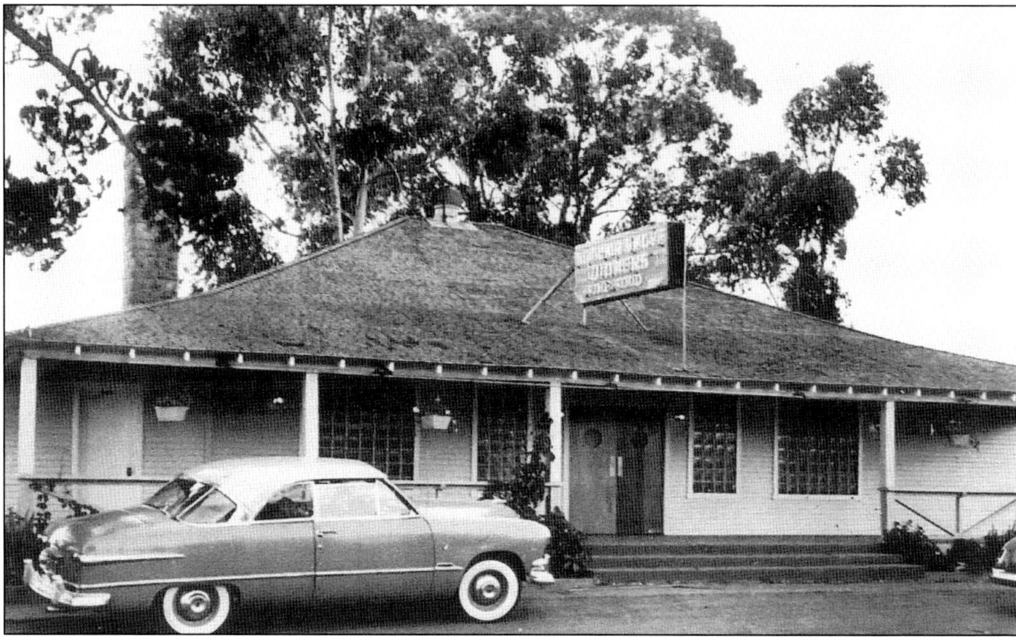

In 1923, the *Sonoma Index-Tribune* called Sonoma Grove the leading resort of the valley. "Situated in a beautiful natural park between here [Sonoma] and Boyes Hot Springs, Sonoma Grove is ideally located. . . . The service under the personal direction of Mrs. Rose Bianchini is hard to excel." (Courtesy of the Sonoma Valley Historical Society.)

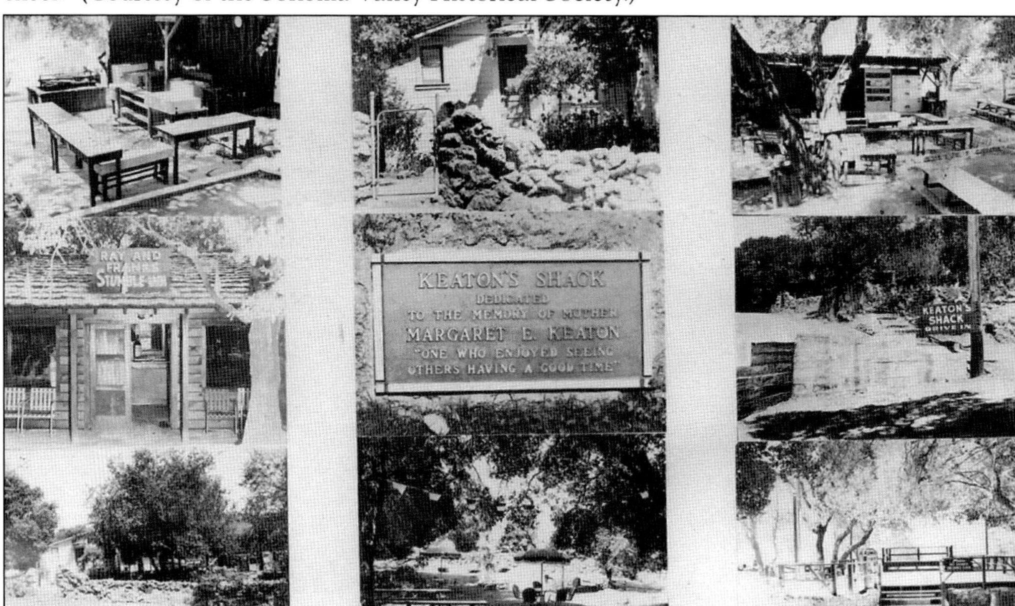

Sitting high on the cliff overlooking Sonoma Valley, Keaton's Shack had the best view of any resort in the area. The bucolic grounds featured an outdoor dance floor, extensive picnic grounds, and a bar called the Stumble Inn. Keaton's was started in 1945 by returning veteran Frank Keaton as a weekend retreat, and he opened his place to the public. Keaton's once hosted a barbecue for 1,500 people. Keaton later became coroner of Marin County.

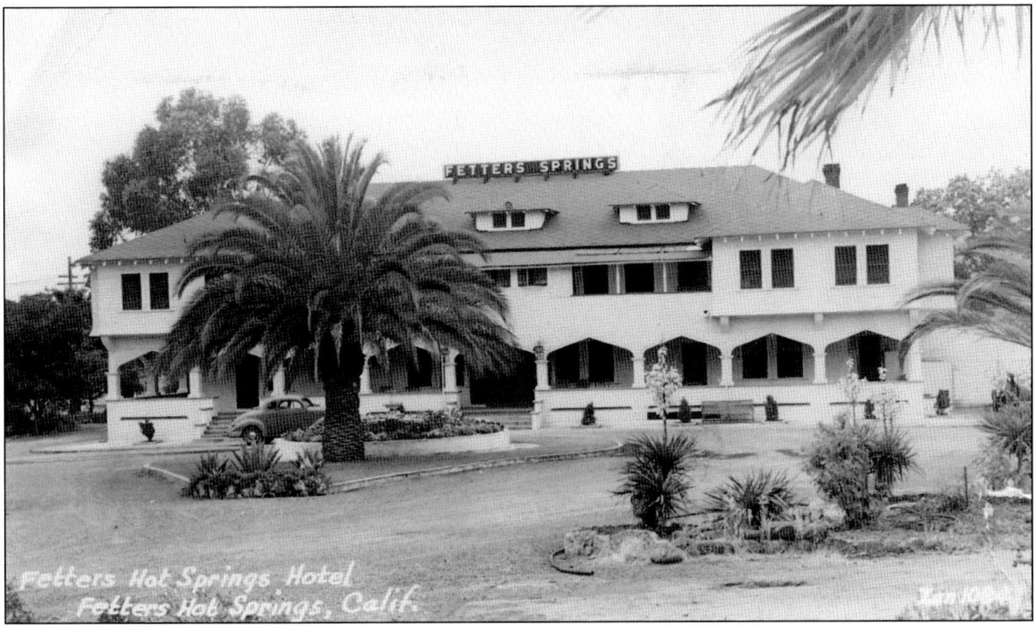

The largest resorts, such as Fetters, spanned the eras. Established in 1908, Fetters Springs Resort flourished well into the 1950s.

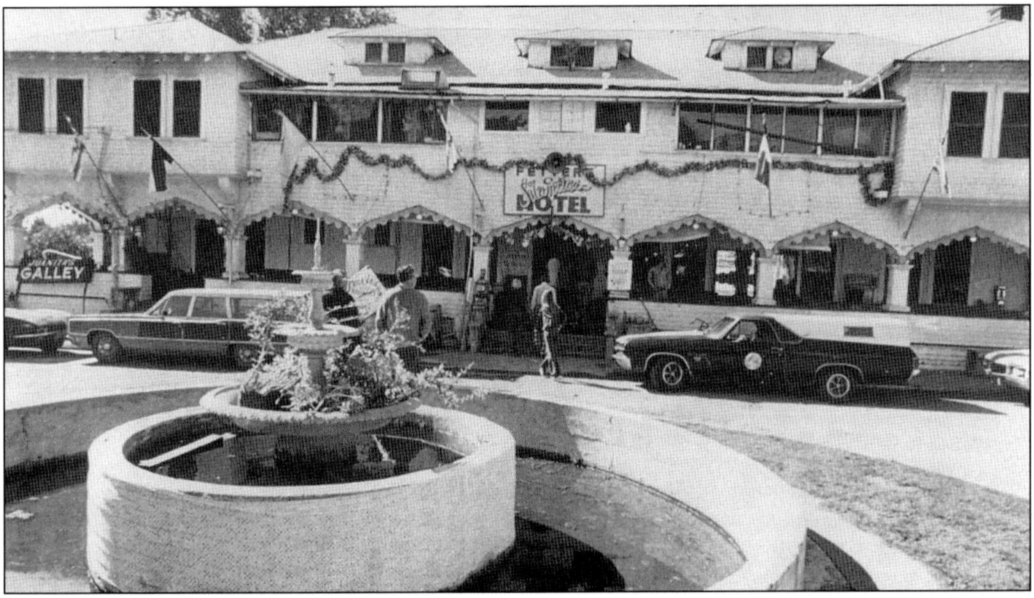

Juanita's restaurant at the Fetters Hotel was a popular spot. Juanita Musson's establishments were known for her assortment of pets that roamed at will. Most people loved and admired her; some feared her wrath. (Courtesy of the Sonoma Valley Historical Society.)

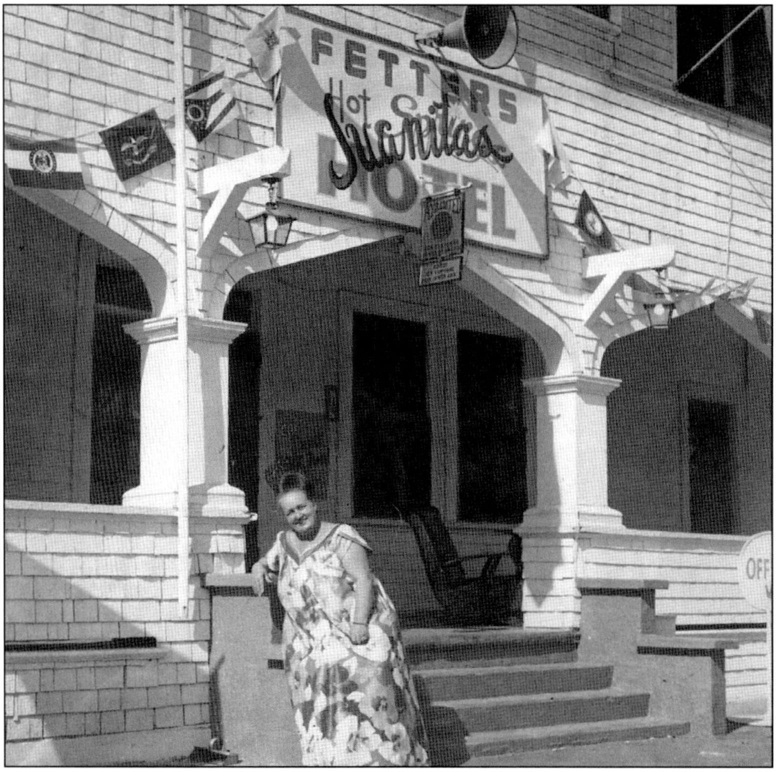

Juanita Musson was perhaps the most famous and notorious figure in Sonoma Valley for 26 years starting in 1964. Her first restaurant was at the old Verdier's Resort in El Verano. After a fire there, she moved to the Fetters Hotel, where she ran her establishment until that building was destroyed in a blaze in 1975. According to Tommy Smothers, "there was a naturalness. There was no pretense about [her]." (Courtesy of the Sonoma Valley Historical Society.)

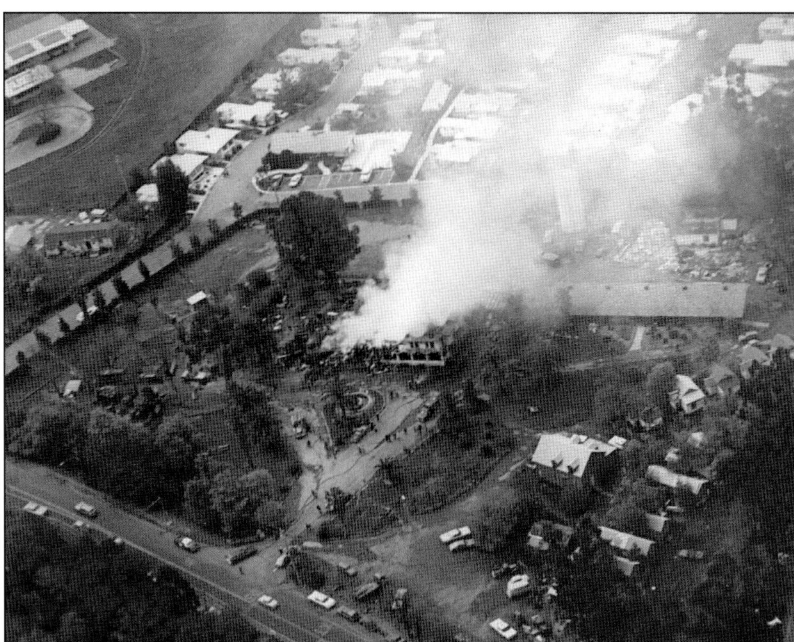

On a Sunday in April 1975, a tragic fire consumed the Fetters Hotel. One life was lost, and fire chief Angelo Pedroncelli noted that the Fetters building had been of concern to the fire department for some years. They had trained specifically on how to fight a fire at the site. (Courtesy of Jeff Gilbert.)

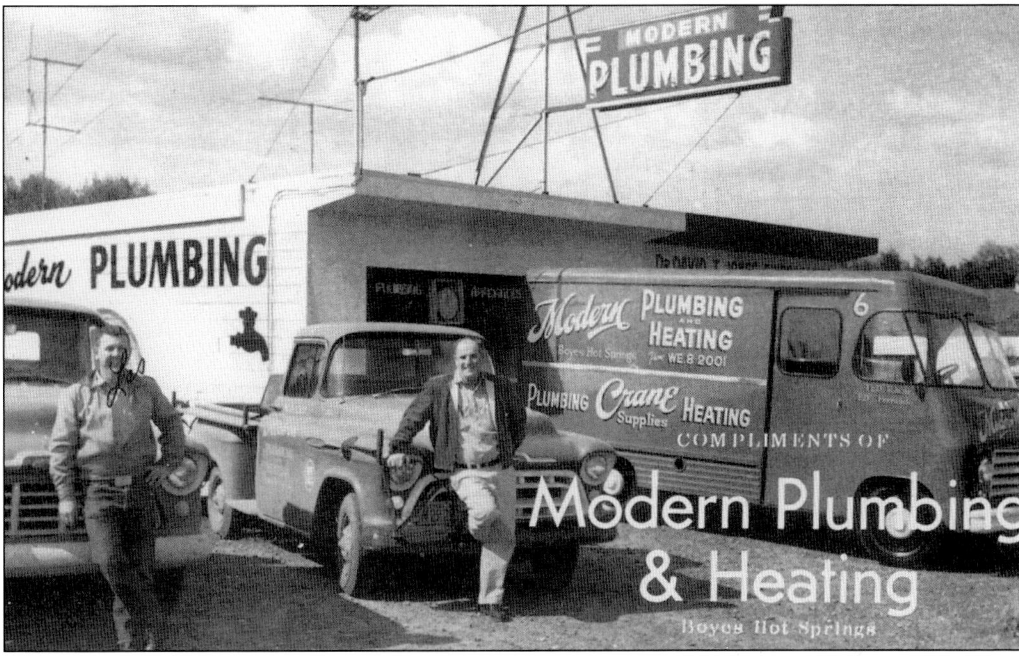

Ted Riboni and Ed Ferrando went into business together, opening Modern Plumbing in the early 1950s. In the mid-1960s, they went their separate ways but continued to locate their businesses in various buildings along the highway. This building, located on the highway near Bernhard Avenue, housed Johnny's Classic Ranges for many years. (Courtesy of the Sonoma Valley Historical Society.)

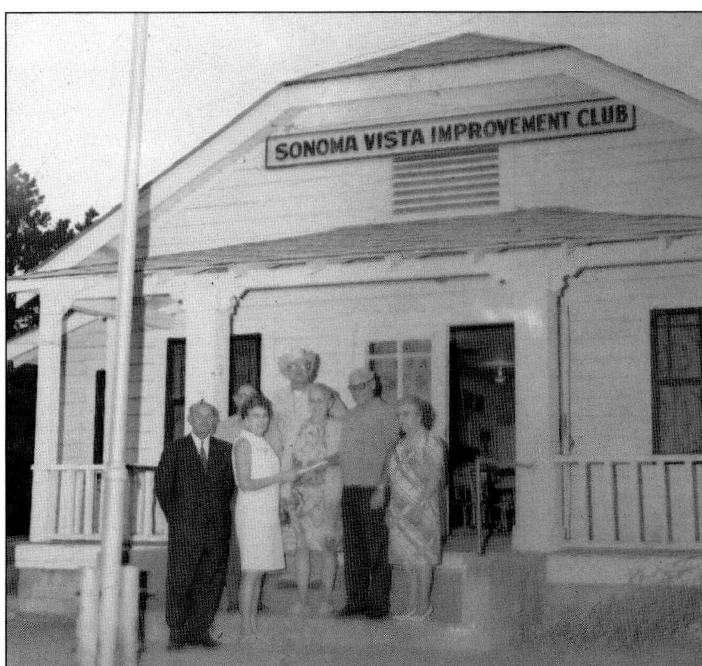

The Sonoma Vista Improvement Club built its clubhouse at Comstock Street and Sonoma Avenue (now Riverside Drive) in 1921. The purpose of the club was to "promote the interest of this neighborhood . . . and to create a friendly feeling generally." In this 1969 photograph, the club secretary, Julie Finchum, presents the deed to the building to Cliff Erickkson, chairman of the Valley of the Moon Recreation District, to whom the club donated its property. The building still stood in 2016. (Courtesy of the Sonoma Valley Historical Society.)

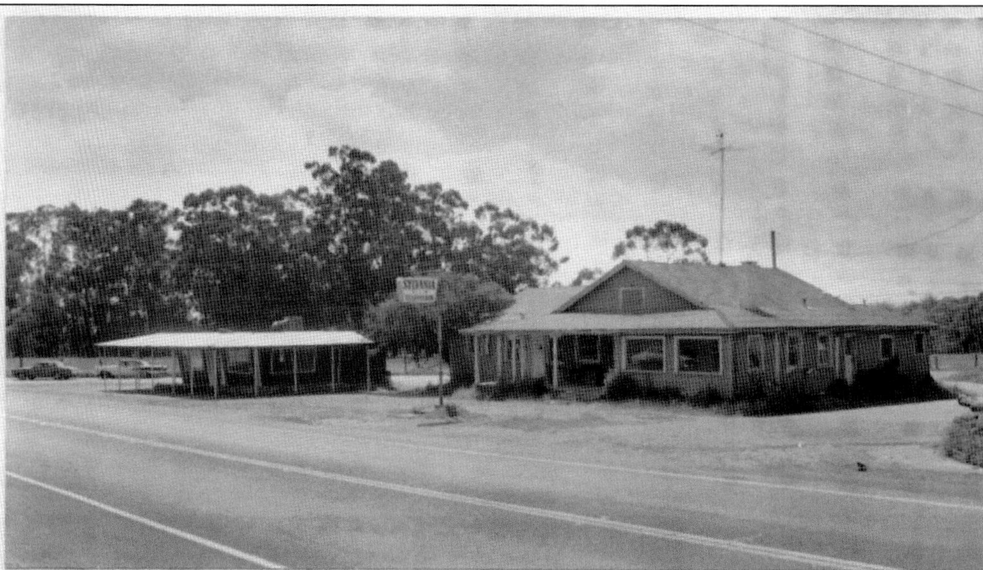

THE GOLDEN ARCHES of a McDonald's restaurant will occupy this site at the northwest corner of Highway 12 and Verano avenue if the international fast-food chain secures the use permit it seeks this week from Sonoma County Planning Department officials. The area is already zoned for commercial use. The two old business buildings pictured on the 35,000-square-foot site, owned by local businessman Jerry Marino, would be torn down. In addition to a 3500-square-foot restaurant building, there will be parking for approximately 50 vehicles. McDonald's will enter into a lease agreement with Marino for the property.

In the 1980s, change came to the Springs. In 1983, McDonald's acquired the parcel at the intersection of Verano Avenue and Highway 12. At that time, only a blinking red light and stop signs controlled traffic at the intersection. (Both, courtesy of the Sonoma Valley Historical Society.)

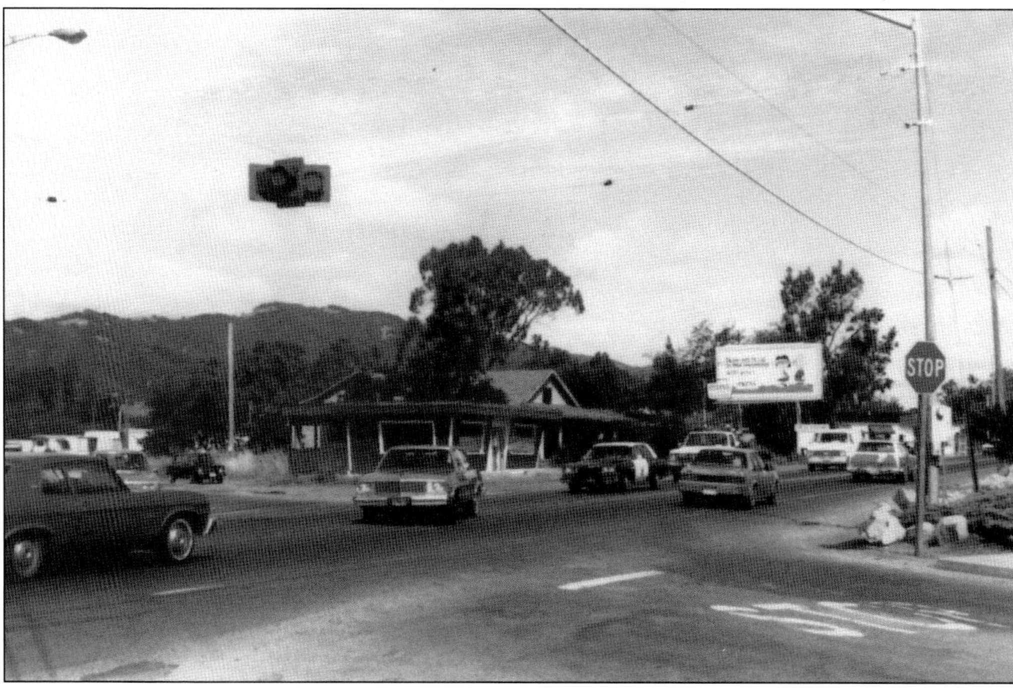

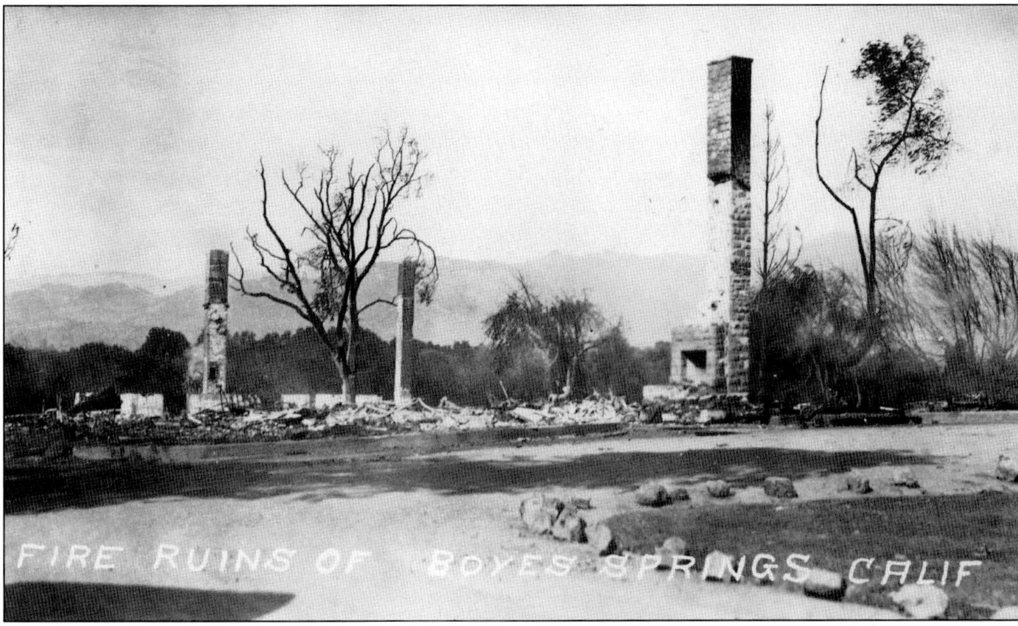

Fire has been a constant issue in the Valley of the Moon. The 1923 conflagration was massive and disastrous, but it was not until September 1964 that another major fire occurred in the area. The 1964 fire, spurred by 80-mph winds, burned for three days and destroyed 19 homes in Agua Caliente, Fetters Springs, and Boyes, as well as many barns and outbuildings further north. (Courtesy of the Sonoma Valley Historical Society.)

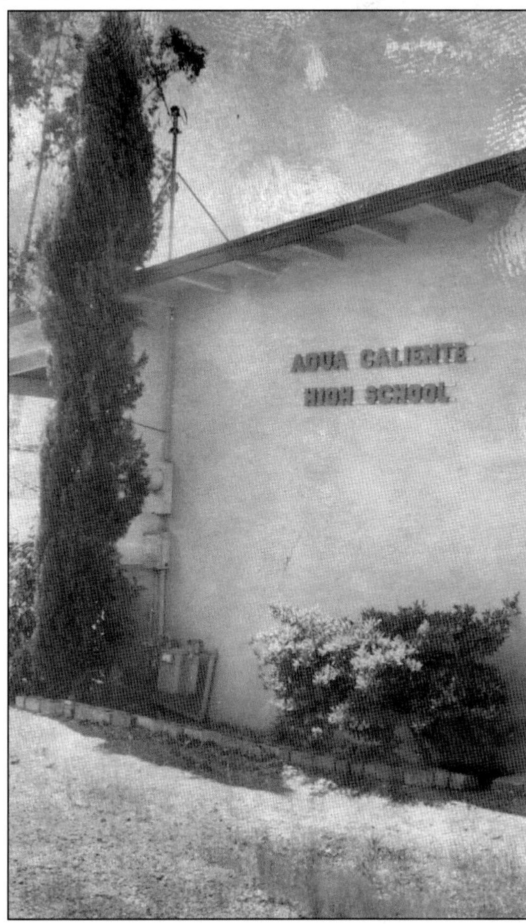

Agua Caliente High School was founded in the late 1960s as a "continuation school." It was fondly nicknamed "Hot Water High." (Courtesy of the Sonoma Valley Historical Society.)

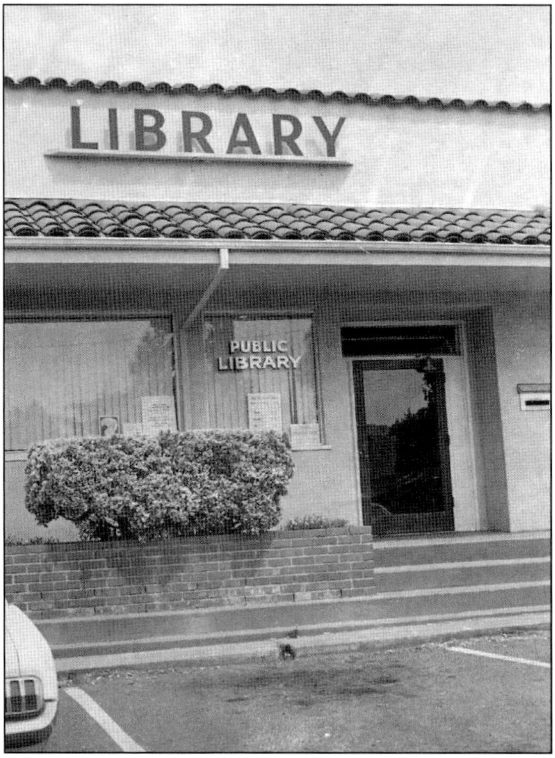

In 1966, the Boyes Hot Springs Library had just been remodeled and featured a special children's section with carpet and pillows for story time. The library closed in 1979. (Courtesy of the Sonoma Valley Historical Society.)

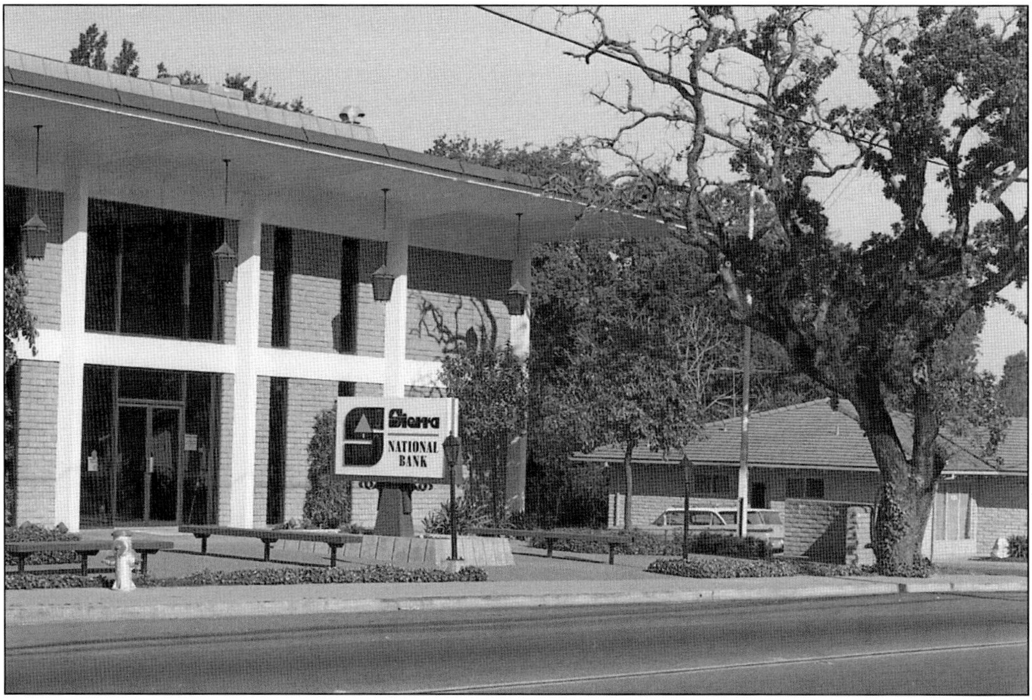

Sierra National Bank opened in a storefront in Boyes Hot Springs in 1964. In 1966, its new building on the corner of the Highway and Sierra Drive opened. In 1979, Sierra was acquired by United California Bank. (Courtesy of the Sonoma Valley Historical Society.)

The new Flowery School, located in a building adjacent to the Fetters depot, opened in 1945. The old school had been in a small building on the highway that became inadequate after the postwar baby boom. "Children were moved into temporary quarters in a former café across the highway and one of the improvement club houses in the area," the *Sonoma Index-Tribune* informed readers. (Courtesy of the Sonoma Valley Historical Society.)

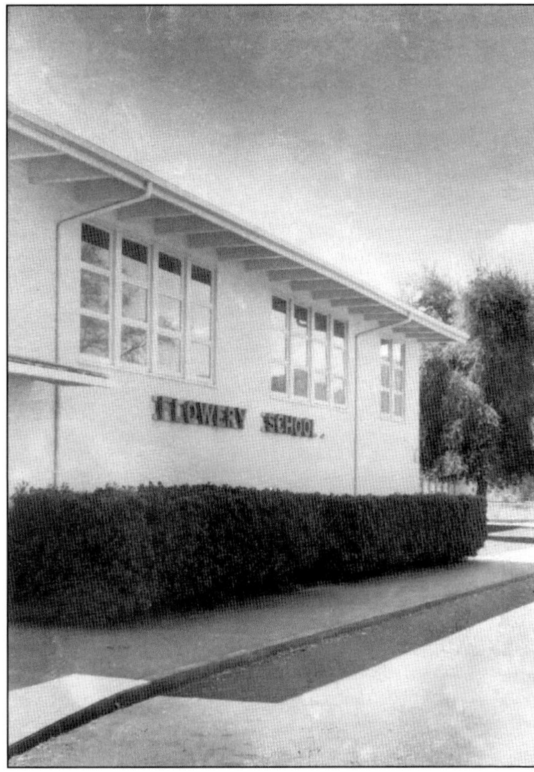

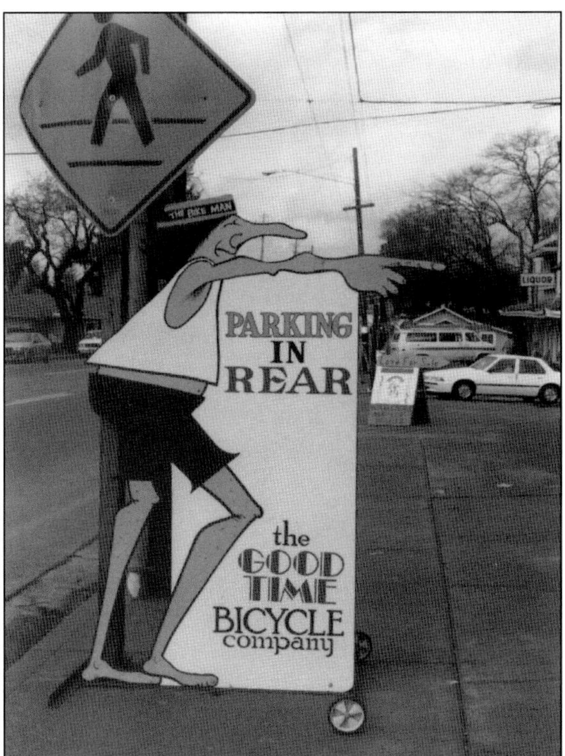

Located just down the street from the Boyes Hot Springs Food Center, near the corner of Calle Del Monte and the Sonoma Highway, Doug McKesson's Good Time Bicycle Company kept the people of the Springs rolling. (Courtesy of Doug McKesson.)

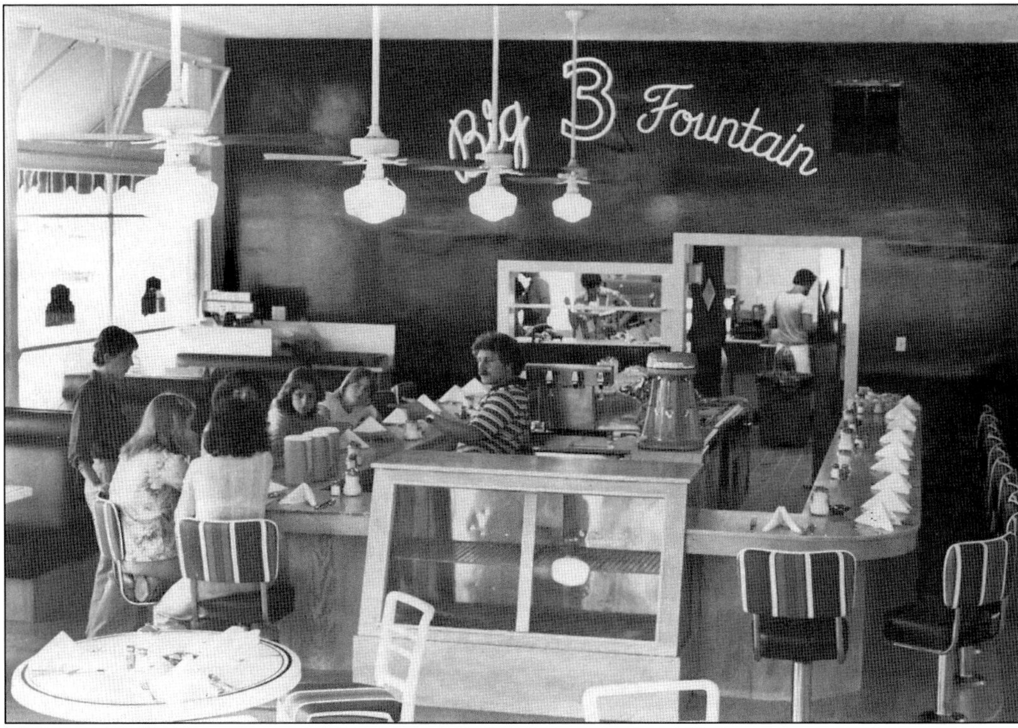

The Woodleaf Store, built at the corner of the Sonoma Highway and Boyes Boulevard in 1924, became the Big 3 in 1959. It remained a store and soda fountain until 1980, when it was purchased by Edward Safdie, the owner of the Sonoma Mission Inn, and turned into a restaurant. Safdie owned the inn from 1979 to 1985, when he sold it to Rahn Properties, a Florida-based real estate developer. (Both, courtesy of the Sonoma Valley Historical Society.)

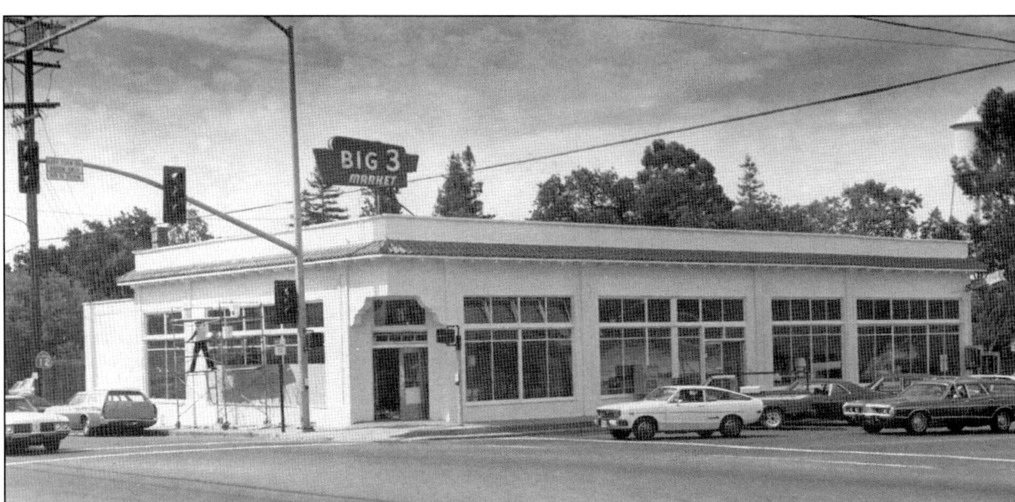

Five

The Springs Today

The upward trend in local real estate values since 1997 (despite the major downslide after 2008) has continued to benefit the Springs. Construction and remodeling of the charming former summer cabins is a common sight in the neighborhoods. In 2014, Sonoma County committed to completing the sidewalk and streetlight project that was started in 2010 by the Sonoma County Redevelopment Agency (which was abolished in 2011, when the project was half-finished, by Gov. Jerry Brown). The entire project was completed in 2016, and the transformation in the streetscape is substantial.

The commercial area on Highway 12 has become home to many new businesses, many of which are occupying and improving buildings that date back to the 1930s and earlier.

Designer Rico Martin's work with the Sonoma County Facade Improvement Program has caused controversy and garnered praise. It certainly is impossible to miss.

In 2015, MidPen Housing started construction on a multi-unit apartment complex on the former site of the Fetters resort. This development will provide affordable housing at a time when rents and real estate values have skyrocketed out of the reach of many.

The people of the Springs are passionate about their home and are actively engaged with maintaining and improving it.

As part of the Environmental Impact Report for the County Redevelopment Project in 1984, the Historic Resource Compliance Report was prepared by architect Dan Peterson. He listed 17 properties that were either eligible for historic listing or contributing to the historic character of the area. A follow-up report was made in 2005; there were no eligible or contributing buildings in it. As of June 2016, five of the original 17 had been destroyed, and four more were threatened. The architectural heritage in the Springs has been poorly preserved.

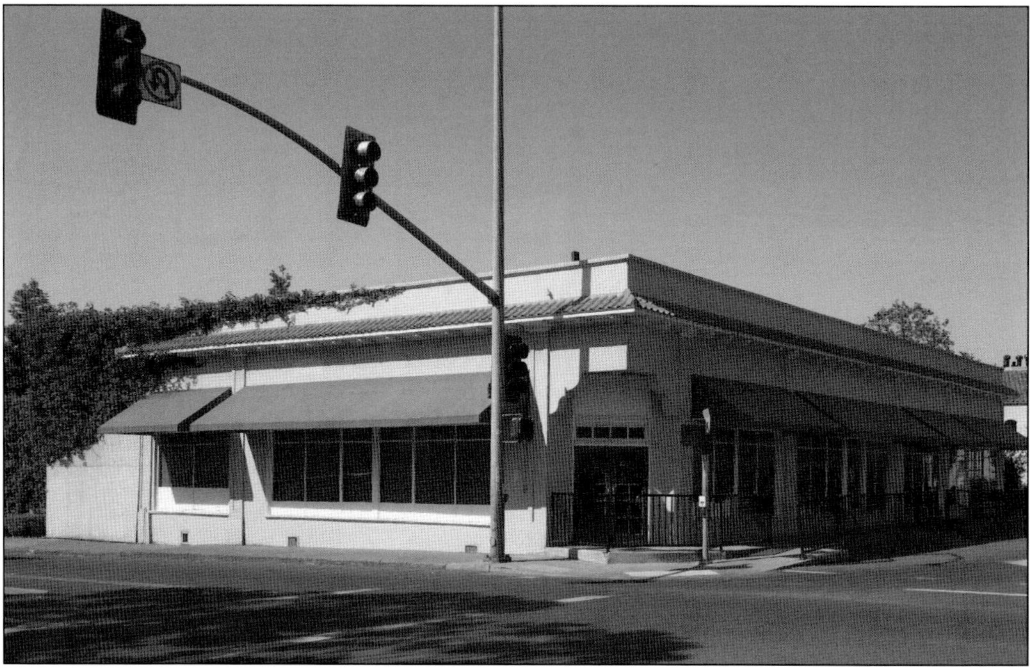

The Sonoma Mission Inn, under the management of Fairmont Hotels & Resorts, operated the Big 3 café until 2016. The café is now closed, and the future of the building is unknown. The bottom image on page 49 shows this building in the 1930s, and the bottom image on page 108 shows it in the 1980s.

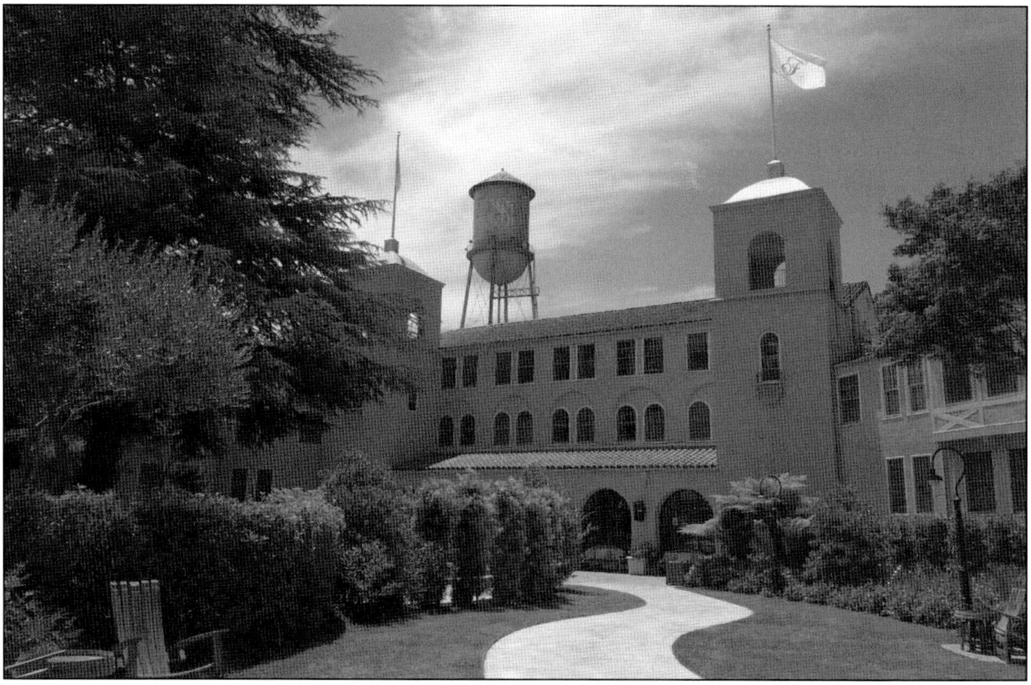

Comparing this photograph of the Sonoma Mission Inn with several from chapter three, there is little difference in 2016 from the 1950s. See page 77.

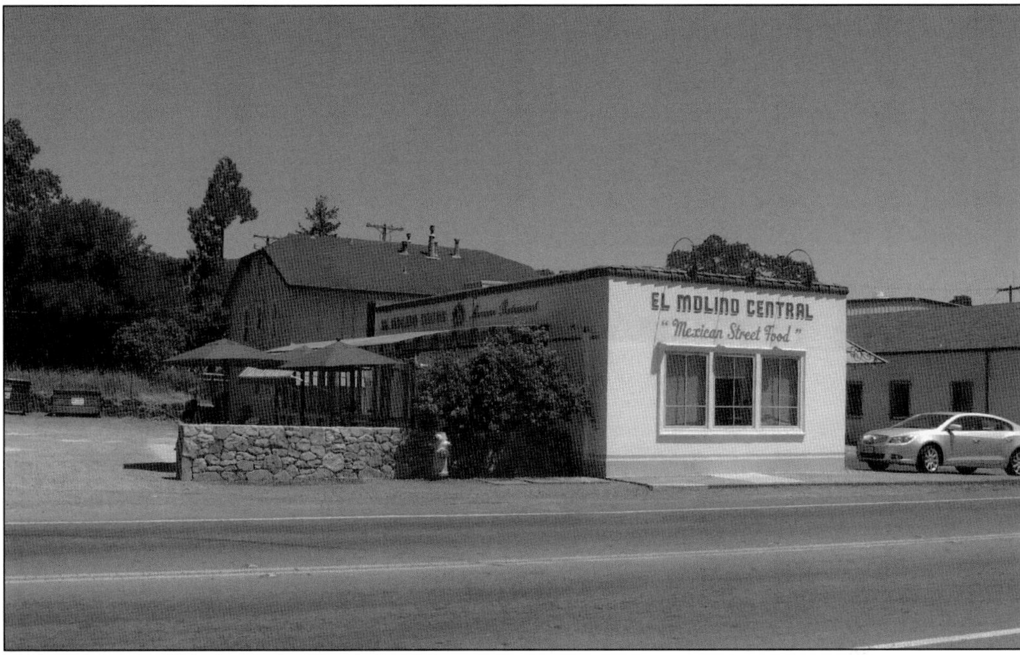

The little concrete-block building on the corner of Central Avenue and Highway 12 started out as a laundromat. After sitting vacant for many years, it was remodeled in the 1990s and became the first Barking Dog coffee shop. After being extensively remolded and beautified, it became the home of El Molino Central in 2010.

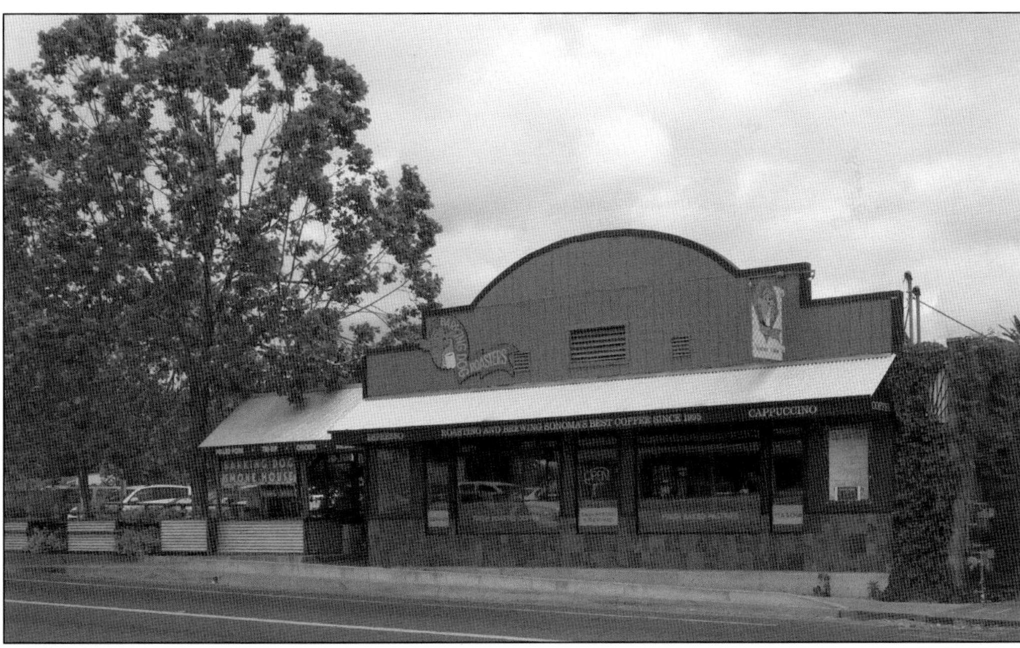

In the image on the bottom of page 52, this building is visible to the left of Kramer's Inn in a 1930s photograph. In that image, a window contains a sign that says "Coffee Shop;" in 2005, Barking Dog Roasters opened in the space. The beautifully redone exterior is a gift to the streetscape.

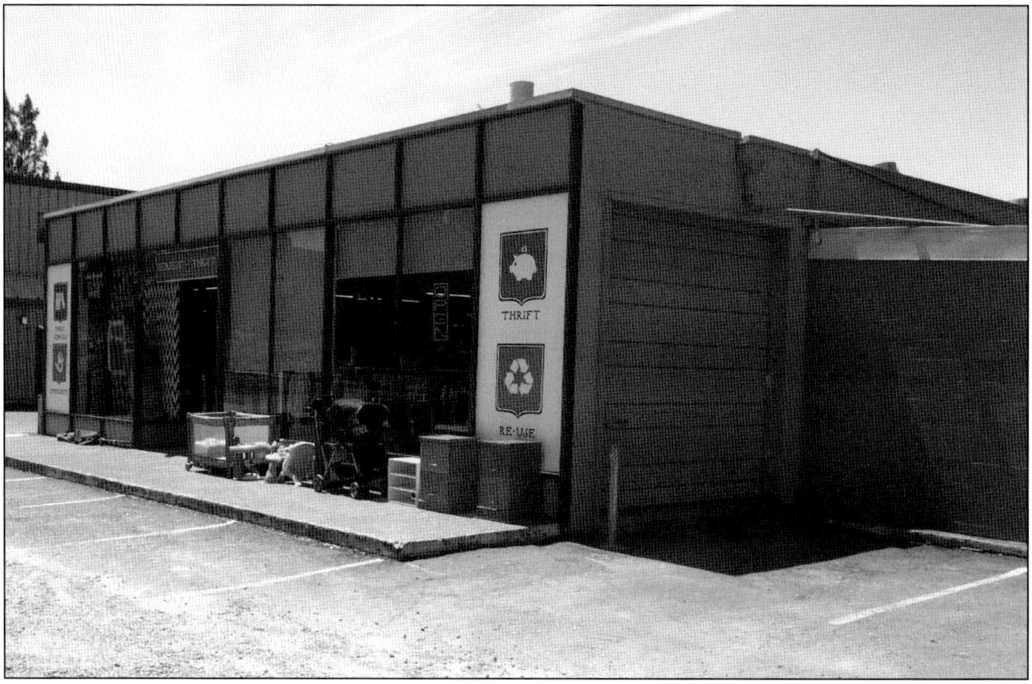

This building housed Modern Plumbing in 1973. In 2012, energetic and public-spirited citizens Jeannette Tomany and Michelle Mammini founded the Republic of Thrift, a nonprofit enterprise that donates considerable amounts of money to Sonoma Valley public schools.

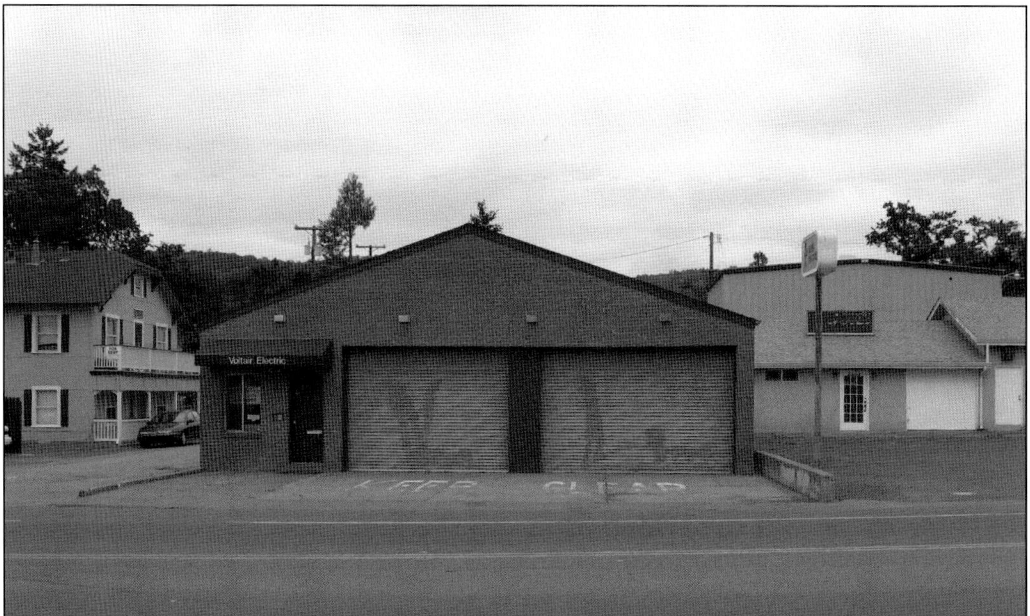

The former Valley of the Moon Fire Department station house (see page 53) had its Mission Revival ornamentation removed sometime in the 1980s. Although Mission Revival is often derided as an architectural cliché, who can argue that the "modern" version of this building is more interesting to the street scene than the original? This building now houses an electrical contractor.

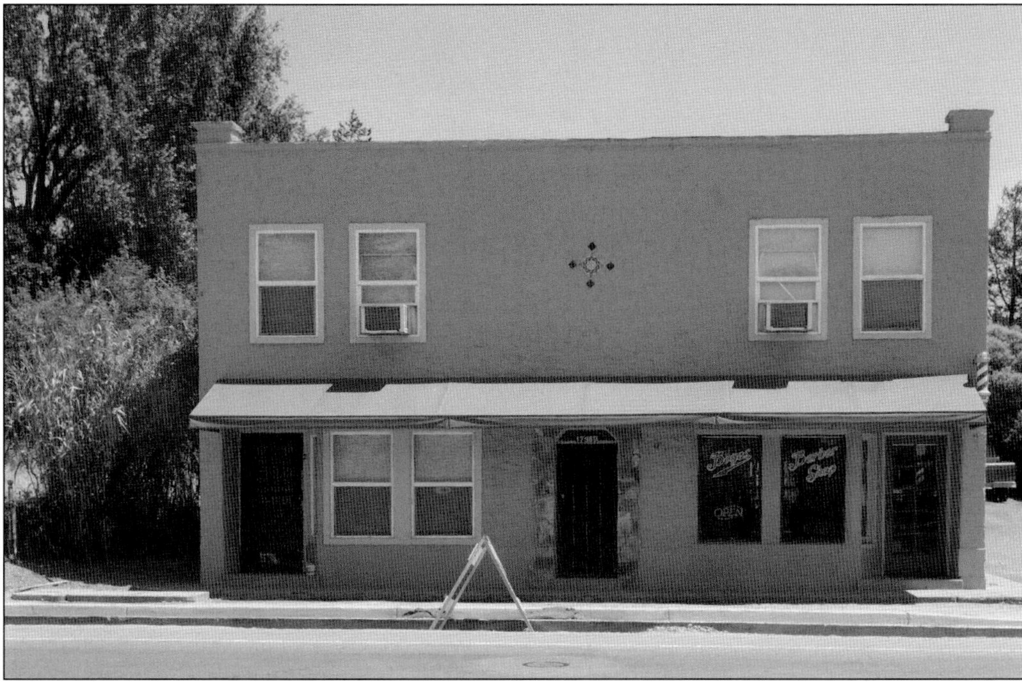

The building that started as the Woodleaf Park Apartments (see page 54) has changed very little since the 1930s. The reason is probably benign neglect, and the structure is quite humble, but its survival should be celebrated nonetheless. (Photograph by the author.)

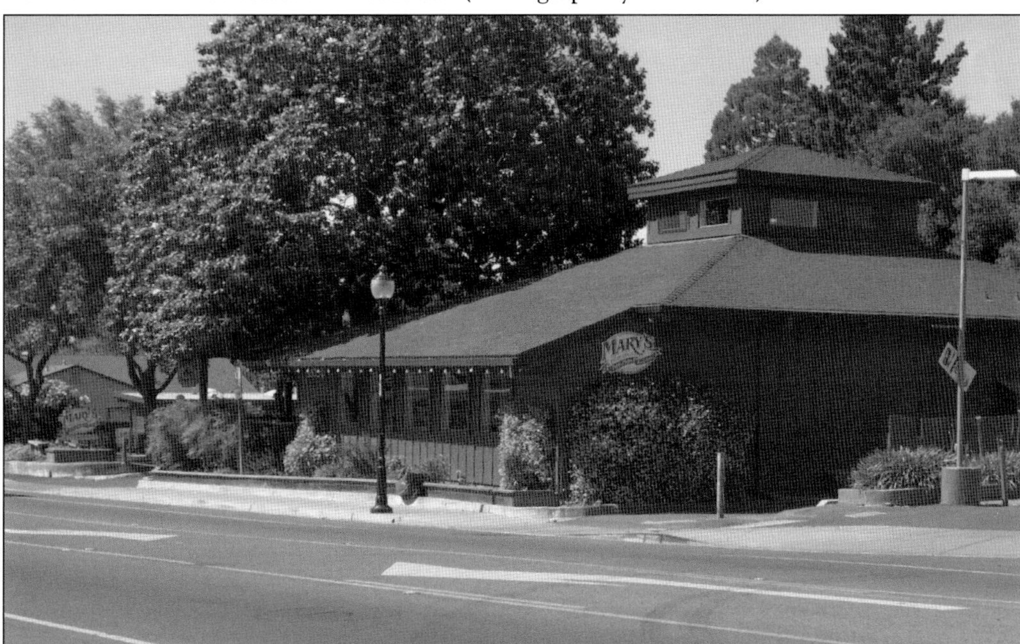

Mary Fazio started her Pizza Shack at the corner of Arroyo Road and Highway 12 in 1959. "Every night seemed like a Saturday at Mary's," said the *Sonoma Index-Tribune*. In 1977, Fazio built her new restaurant just a half-mile from the old one. Mary's Pizza Shack was quite a success, and by 2014, the chain had 20 locations in California.

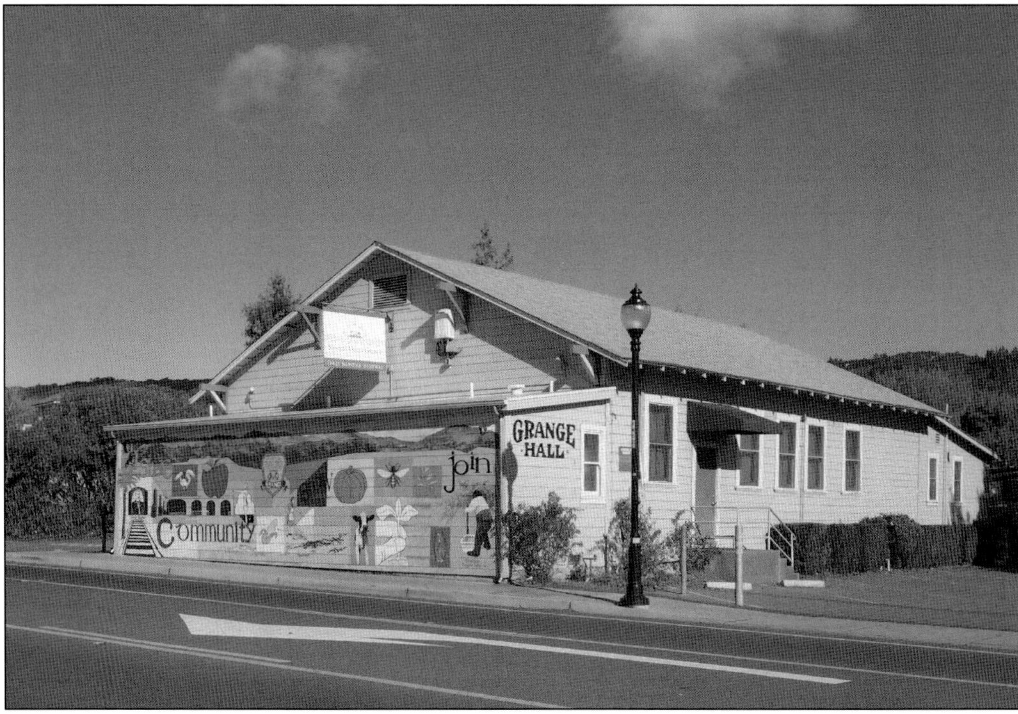

The members of the Sonoma Valley Grange have lovingly maintained the structure over the years and in 2014 started an ambitious program to remodel the restrooms and put in a commercial kitchen. In 2010, through the Facade Improvement Loan Program, this mural, designed by the author and painted by Randy Sue Collins, was installed. The Sonoma Valley Grange is considered to be the community center of the Springs. See page 91 for more photographs of the Grange.

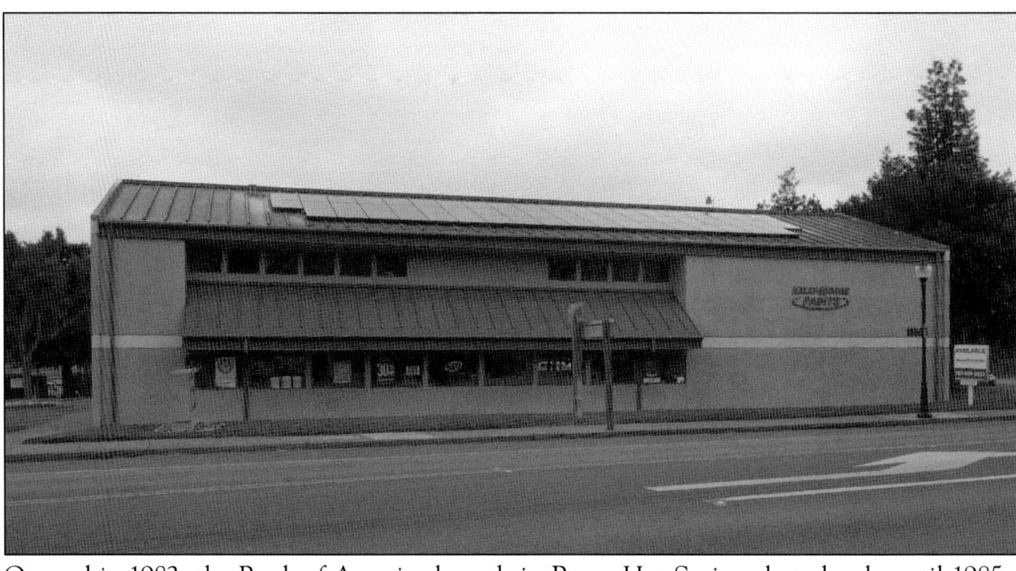

Opened in 1982, the Bank of America branch in Boyes Hot Springs lasted only until 1985, a year in which the bank closed 40 branches in California. In the 1990s, the building housed the Transition Site, an employment-training program sponsored by the Sonoma Developmental Center. Kelly-Moore Paints has occupied the structure since 2010.

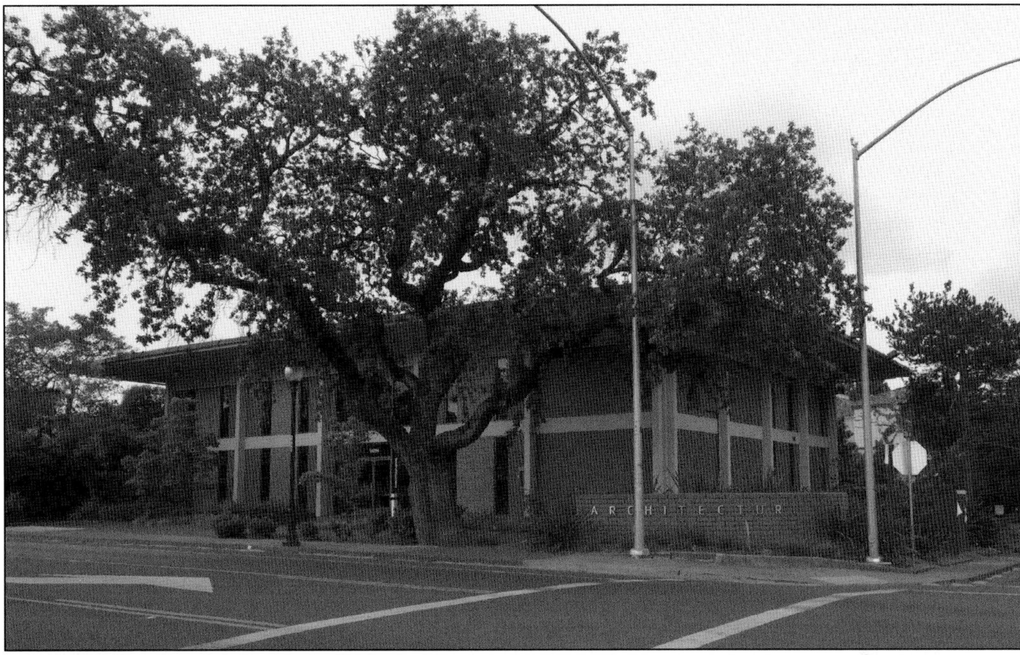

The Sierra National Bank building in Boyes opened in 1966 (see page 106). In 1979, it became United California Bank. In the 1990s, First Interstate Bank took over. The award-winning RossDrulisCusenbery Architecture, Inc., remodeled the building to house its offices in 2004.

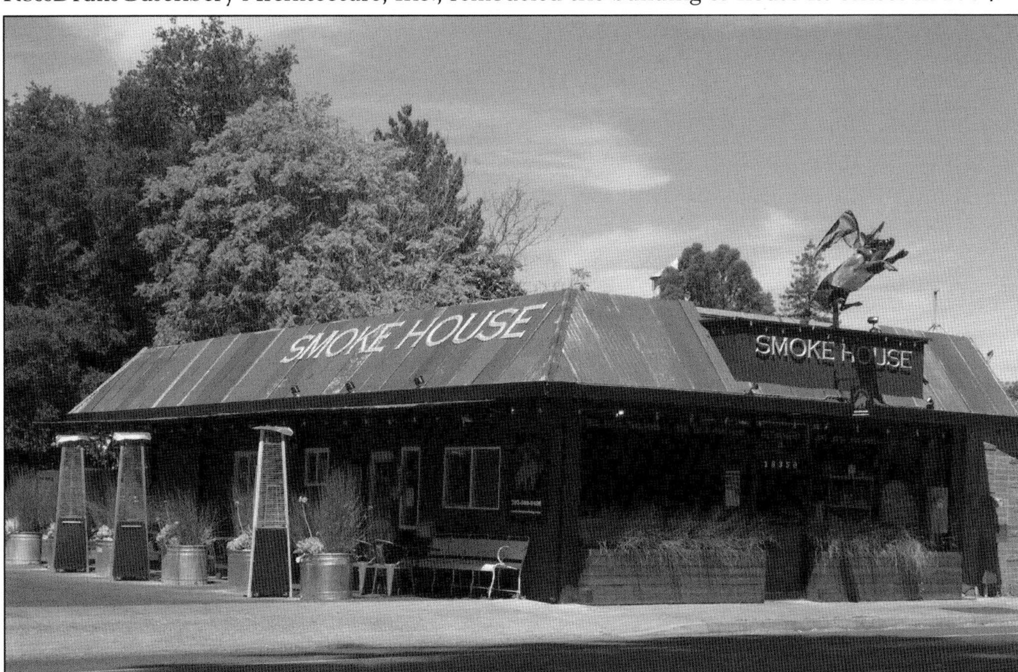

In 2016, the owners of Cochon Volant moved into this building across from Calle Del Monte on Highway 12, extensively remodeling it and installing artist Bryan Tedrick's steel flying-pig sculpture on the roof. This site has been home to many other businesses, including a Thai restaurant, the Hotbox Grill, and a vegetarian Chinese restaurant.

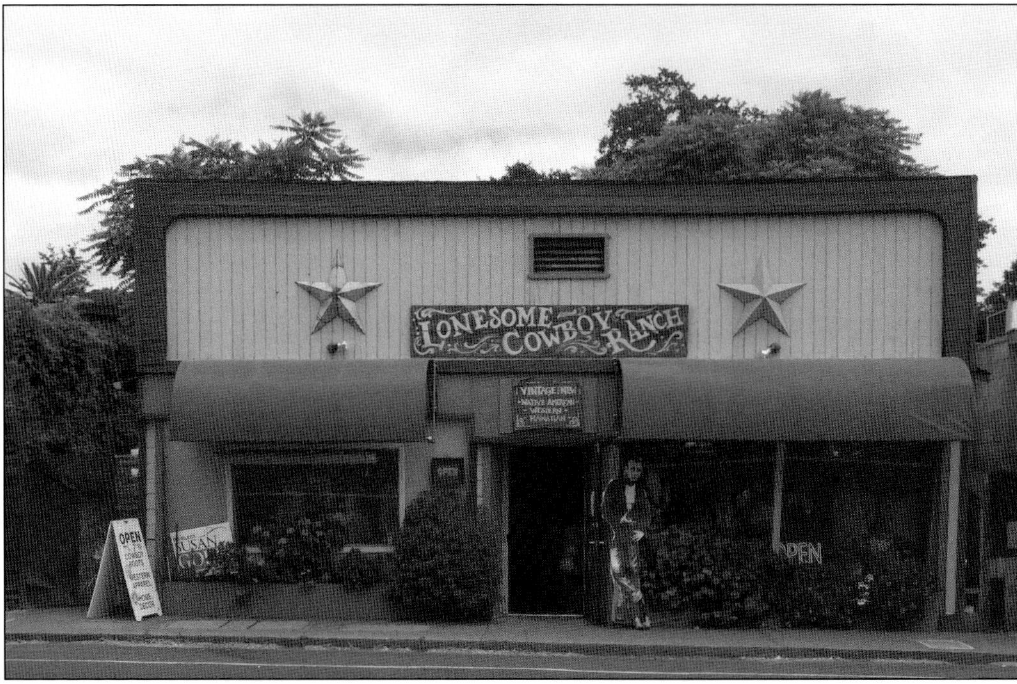

This building is a prime example of reuse over the decades. In the 1920s and 1930s, it was Kramer's Inn (see page 52). In the 1950s, it became Mike and Rose Gitti's grocery store. More recently, it housed the Mas por Menos travel agency, a tattoo parlor, and, as of 2016, the Lonesome Cowboy Ranch Western wear store.

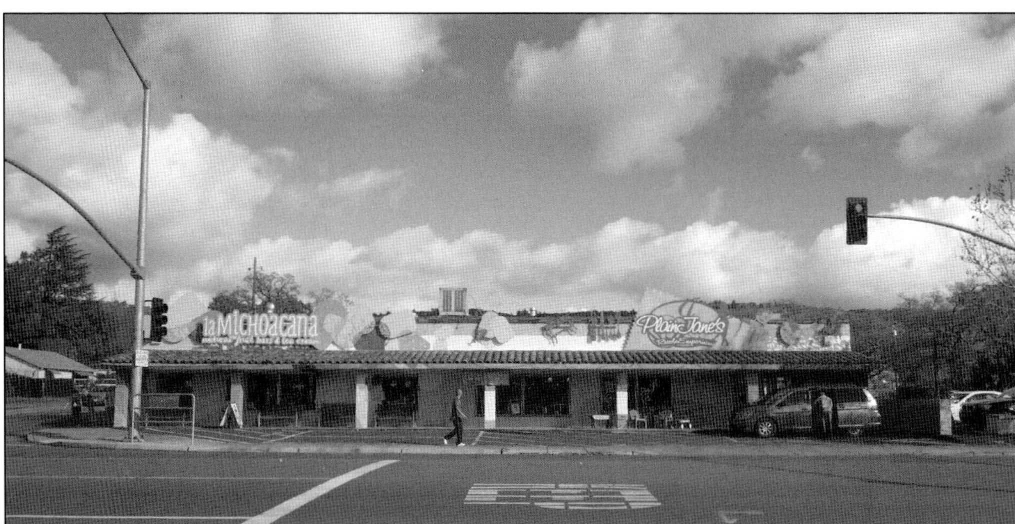

In the 1930s, this building was the home of the Churchill/Questerman Garage (see page 55). In later years, Ferrando's Plumbing was the occupant. Plain Jane's consignment shop celebrated its 25th year there in 2016. La Michoacana ice cream parlor is a more recent tenant. In 2015, designer Rico Martin was hired to do a splashy facade makeover on this and other buildings in the Springs. The result at this location was controversial.

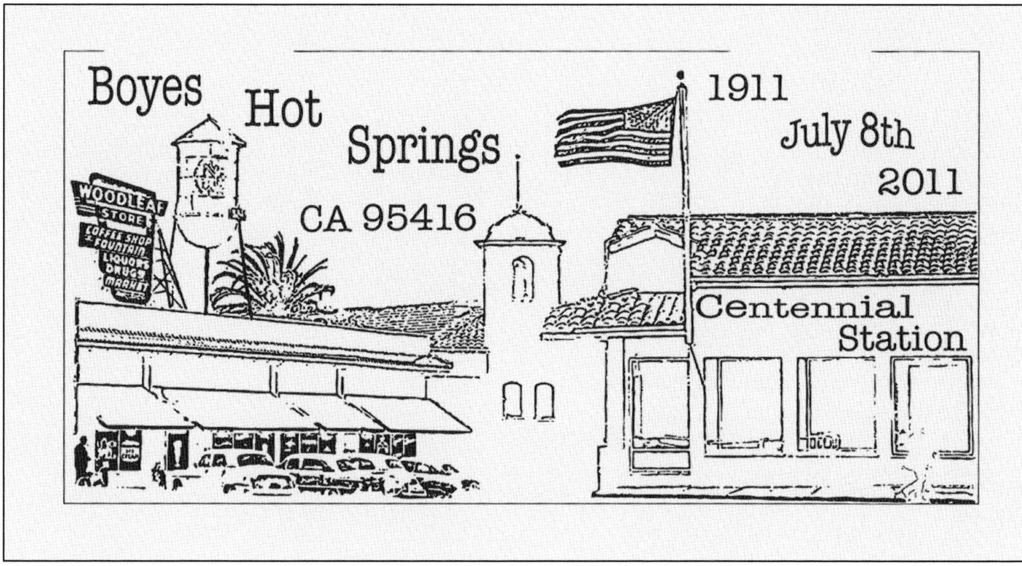

In 2011, the Boyes Hot Springs Post Office celebrated its centennial. In commemoration of this, the author of this book designed a special postmark that was used on July 8, the day of the event.

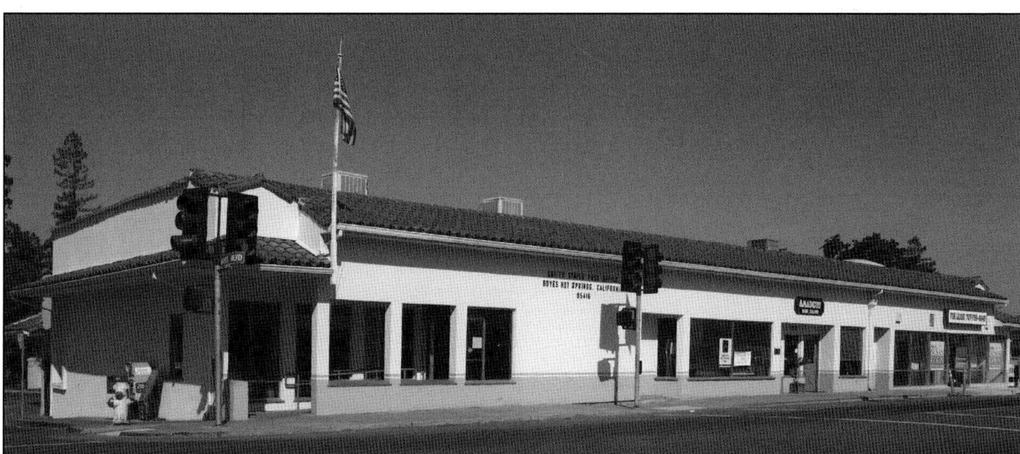

Built by A.B. Peluffo between 1951 and 1955, the Plaza Center building replaced the original Boyes Plaza, which was once the site of the railroad depot and many fiestas. Over the years, the building has housed many businesses, including the offices of Dr. Michael Makita, Valley Drug Store, the post office, and the Church Mouse thrift store.

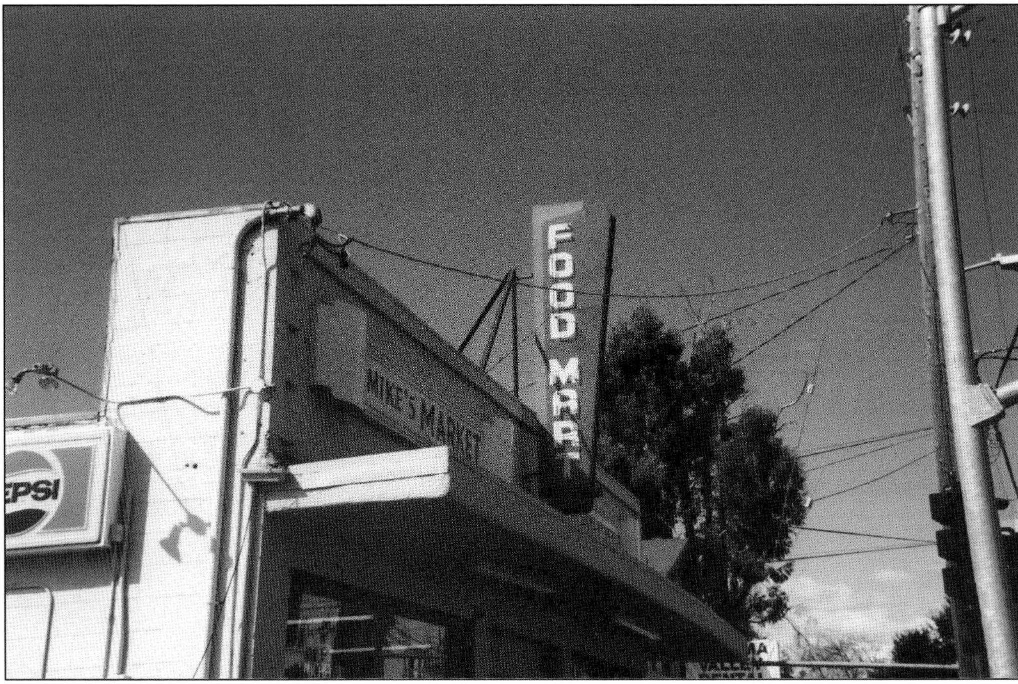

Located at Depot Road and Highway 12, this building has been known through the decades as Tripp's, Mike's Market (above), and El Brinquito (as of 2009). El Brinquito is famous for its barbecued chicken, hence designer Rico Martin's whimsical sculpture and sign (below).

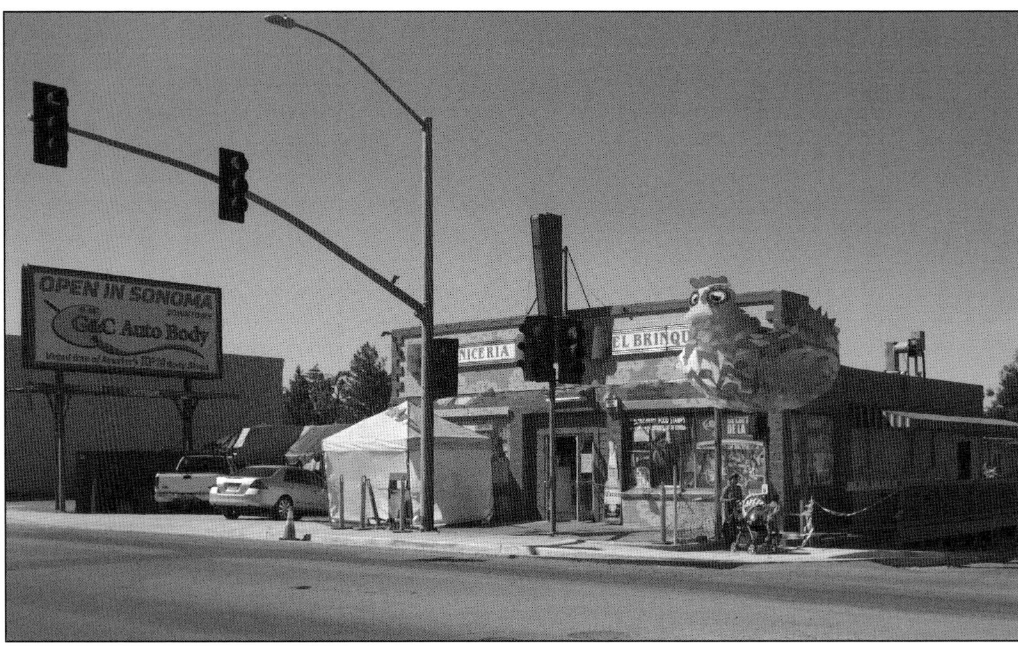

In 2015, the former Sam Ganos building was still going strong as popular restaurant Taqueria La Hacienda. Still recognizable from the 1930s photograph on the top of page 52, the building's later embellishments show how current business owners in the Springs continue to exhibit the vitality of their forebears.

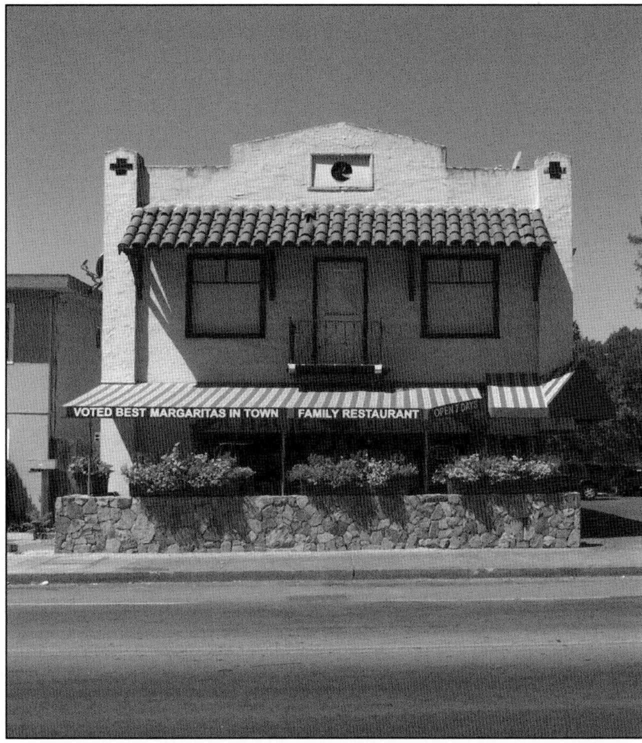

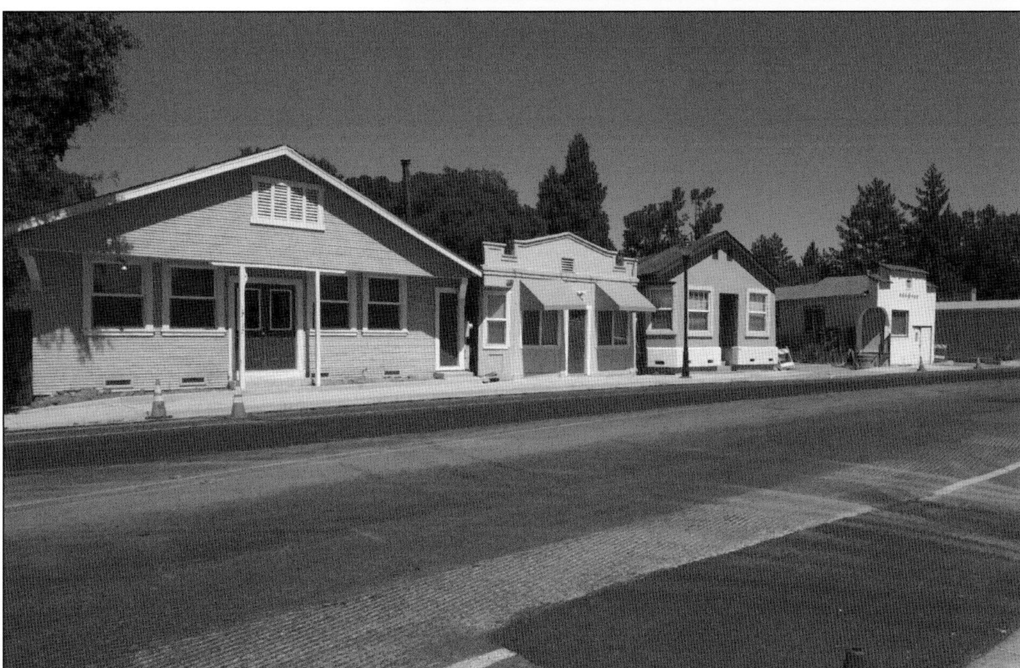

According to the Historic Resource Compliance Report assembled in 2005 for phase two of the sidewalk project, none of these delightful buildings on Highway 12 in Fetters Hot Springs "have sufficient historic integrity to convey" significance. This may be true, but they do represent loving reuse, and their individuality and charm are certainly a gift to the Springs.

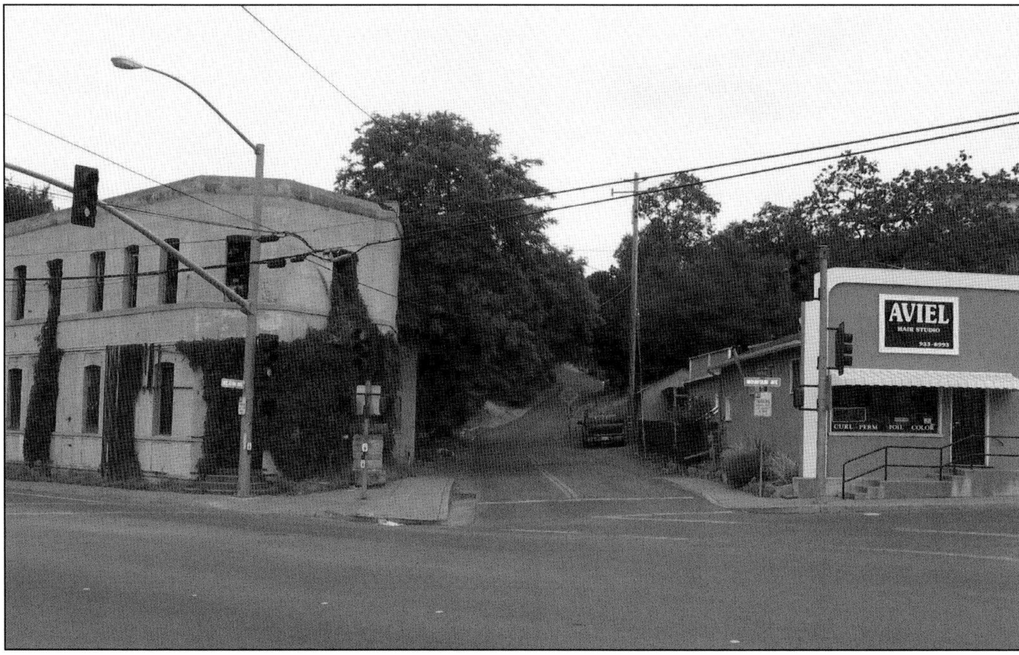

The brick building at the corner of Sonoma Highway and Keaton Avenue was built in 1909 as an inn and resort (see the image at the bottom of page 42) and sat vacant for many years, begging for rehabilitation and seismic refitting. Unfortunately, this never became financially feasible. In 2009, it was demolished and joined the list of lost historic properties.

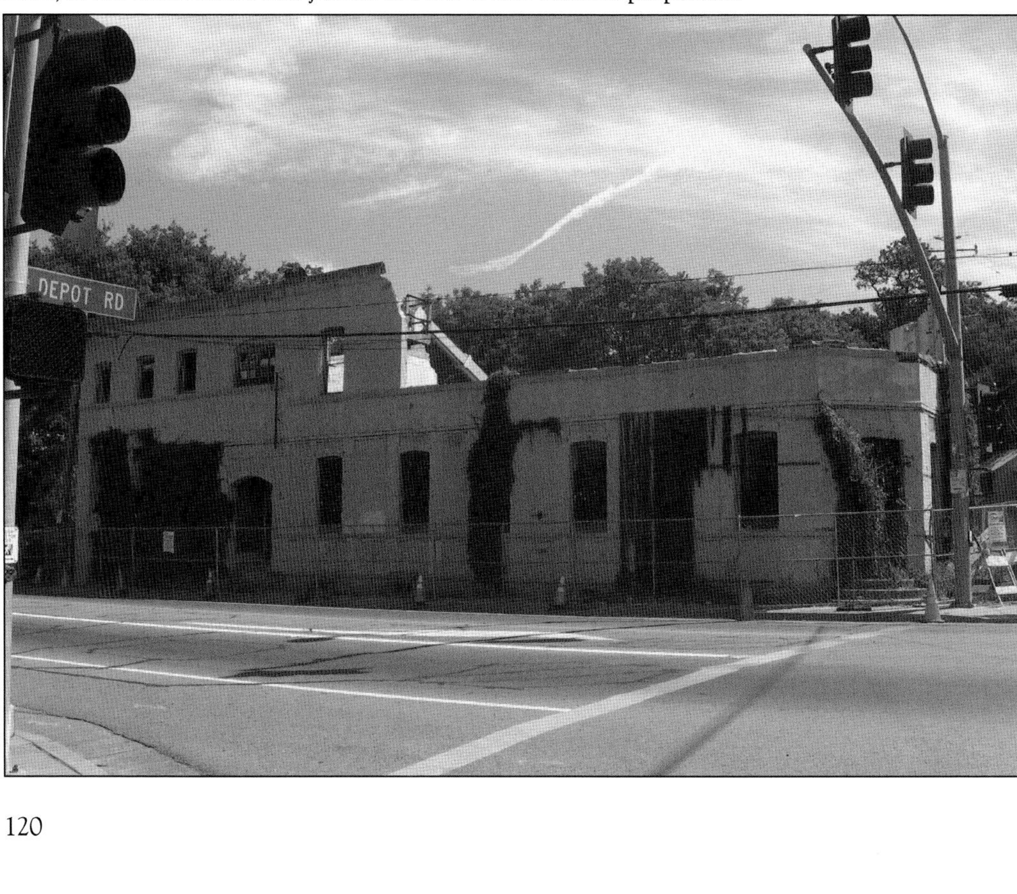

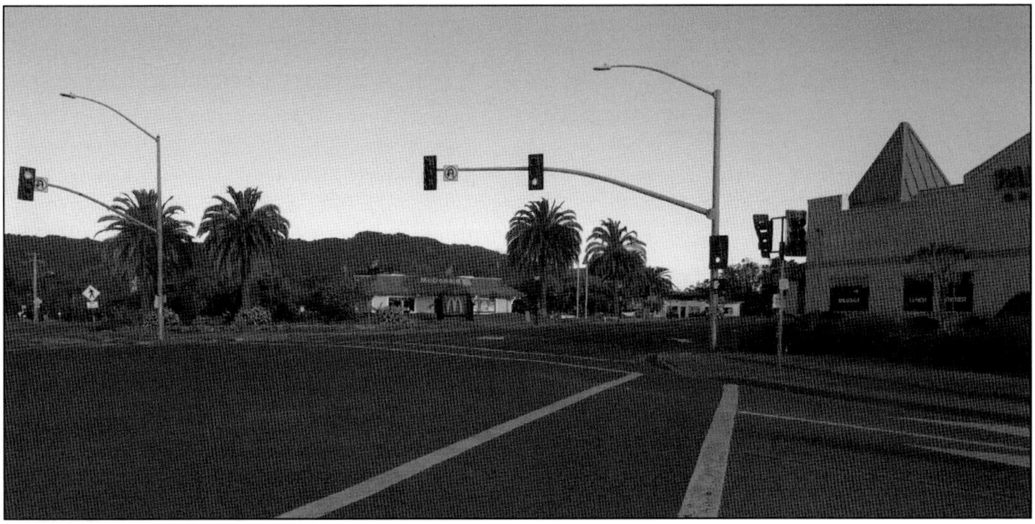

The McDonald's at the corner of Verano Avenue and Highway 12 opened in October 1984. Along with fast food, citizens of the valley got a redesigned intersection that includes traffic lights (see page 104).

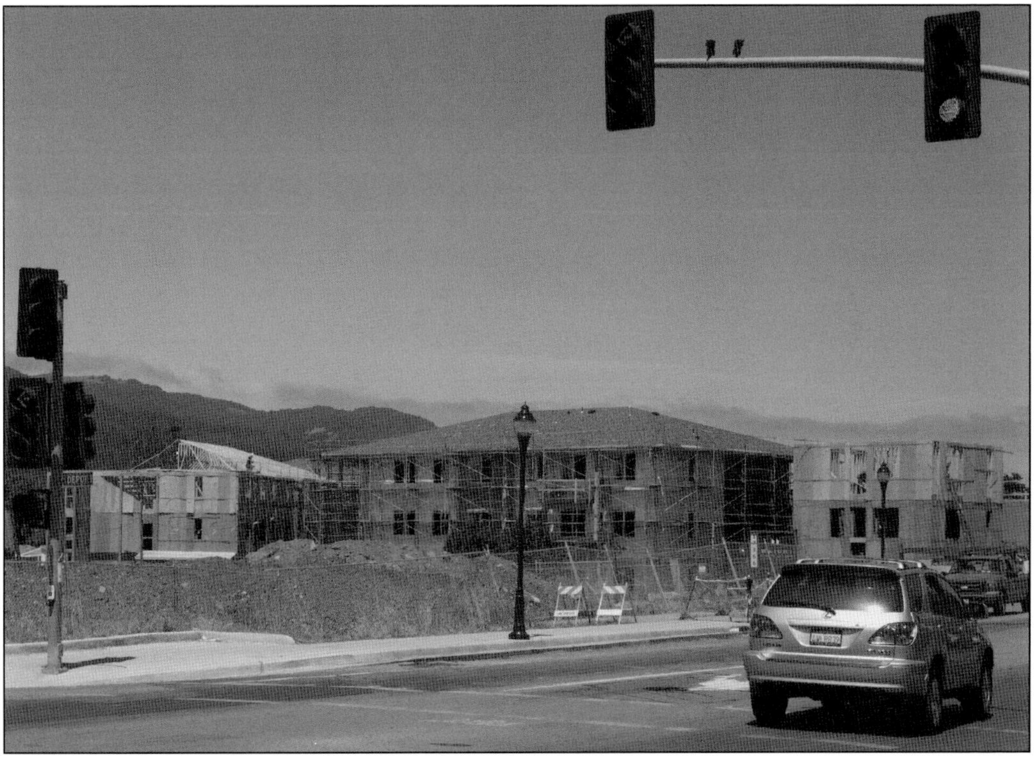

The Fetters resort site was, for many years, a vacant lot still sporting the palms trees of old. In 2016, the site became the scene of major construction when MidPen Housing started building the Fetters Apartments. When finished, the complex of affordable dwellings will include senior apartments, commercial spaces, and a community garden.

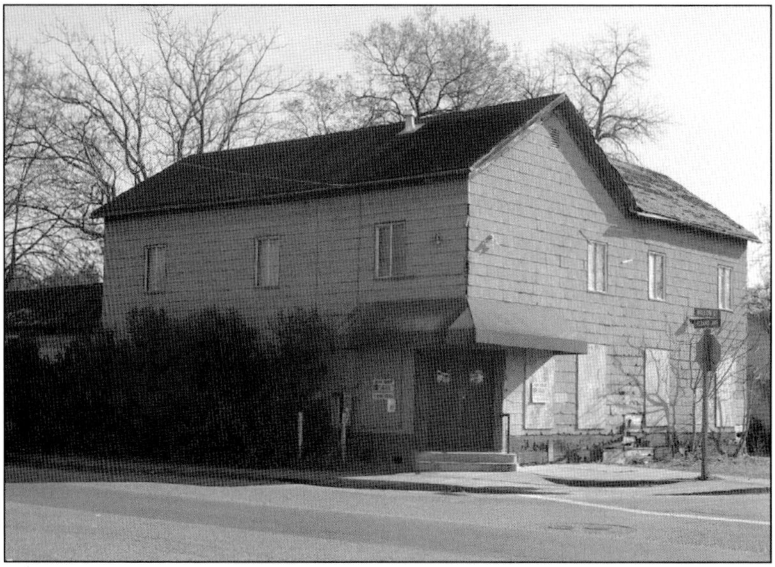

In the early 1900s, the corner of Willow Street and Verano Avenue was the location of an Italian boardinghouse that became Crane's Hotel. In the 1930s, the complex of buildings became Our Resort; later, it was McNeilly's Tavern. In 2016, the structure is being rehabilitated for use as housing. (Photograph by the author.)

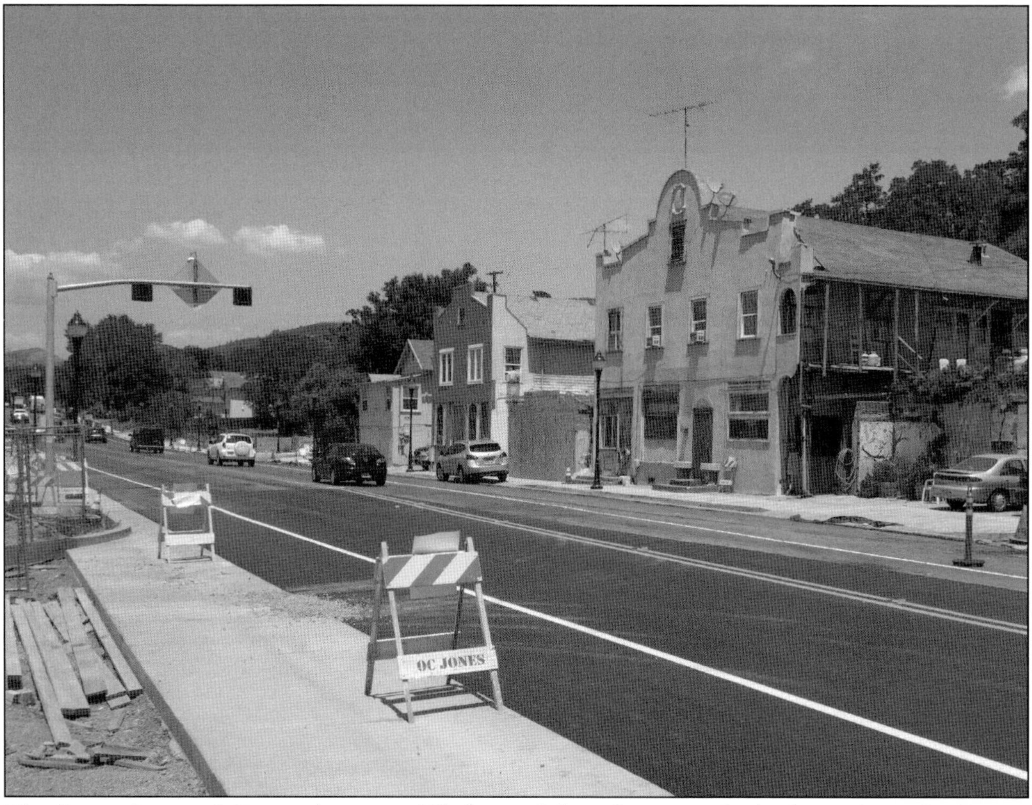

The former Leixner's Resort (see page 58), located directly across the highway from the Fetters resort site, also appears headed for the "lost list." Also known as Nimpfer's, the building has housed many stores and restaurants over the years, including Roy's Grocery, the Oak Tree Cantina, and the Roundup Room and Steak House.

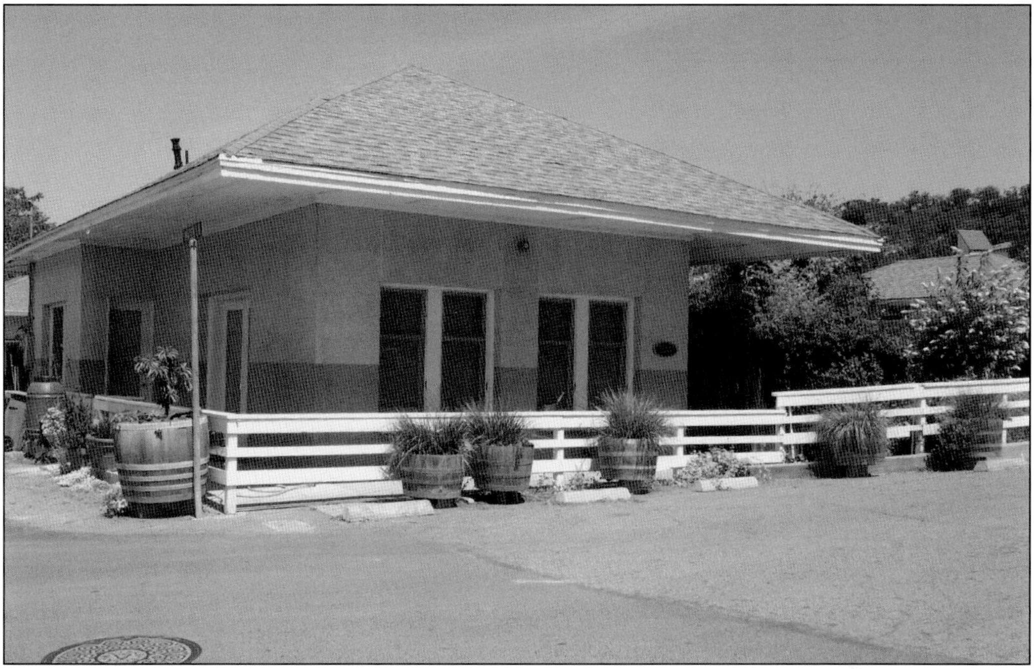

The Northwestern Pacific Railroad depot at Fetters resort (see page 30) was built in 1913. The terrazzo walls, made of cement and marble chips, are an unusual feature of the building. By 1996, the building was so decayed that it was declared a hazard. In 2004, it was completely restored and converted to a single-family residence.

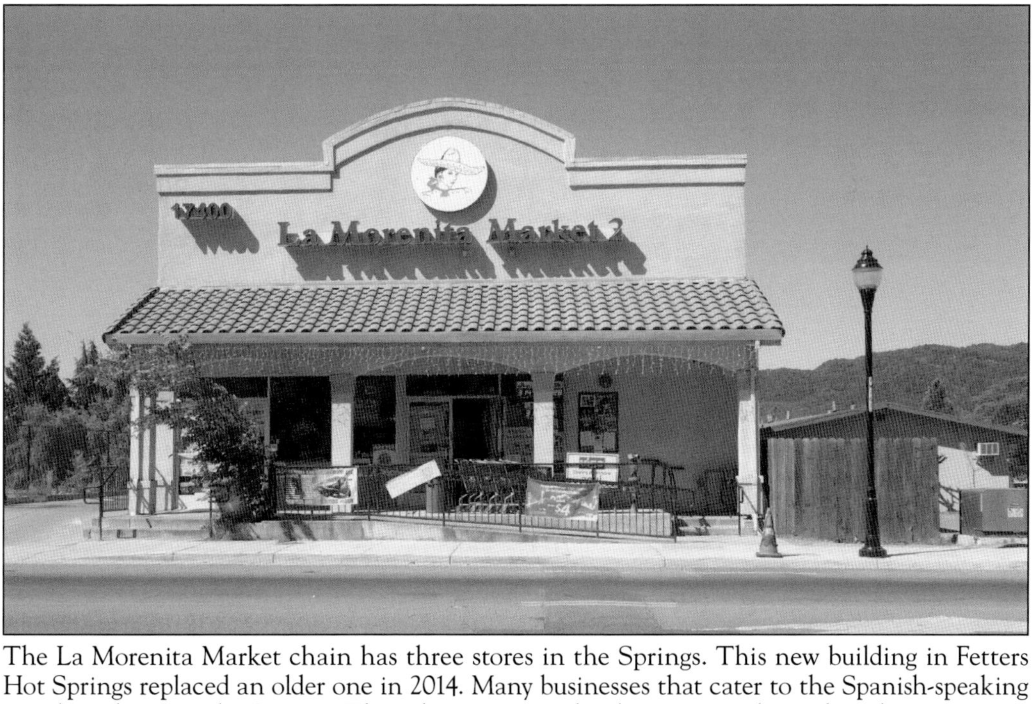

The La Morenita Market chain has three stores in the Springs. This new building in Fetters Hot Springs replaced an older one in 2014. Many businesses that cater to the Spanish-speaking populace thrive in the Springs. They also serve—and welcome—speakers of any language.

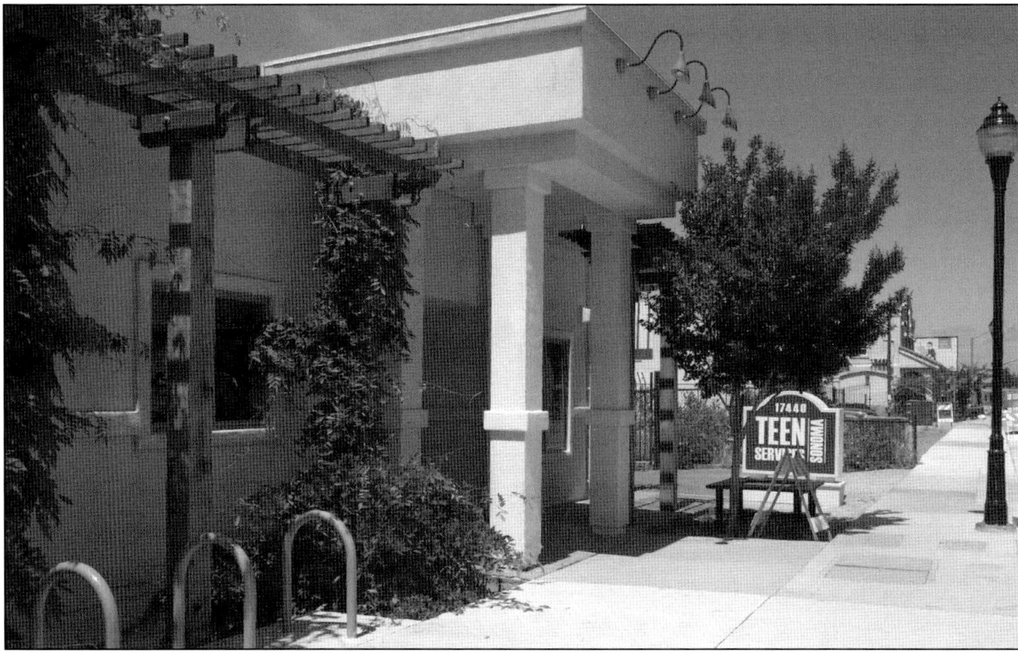

El Nido Teen Center started in 1991 in an old building in Fetters Hot Springs. Along the way, its name was changed to Teen Services Sonoma, which erected a brand-new building in 2008. The mission of Teen Services Sonoma is to support young adults as they prepare for the world of work.

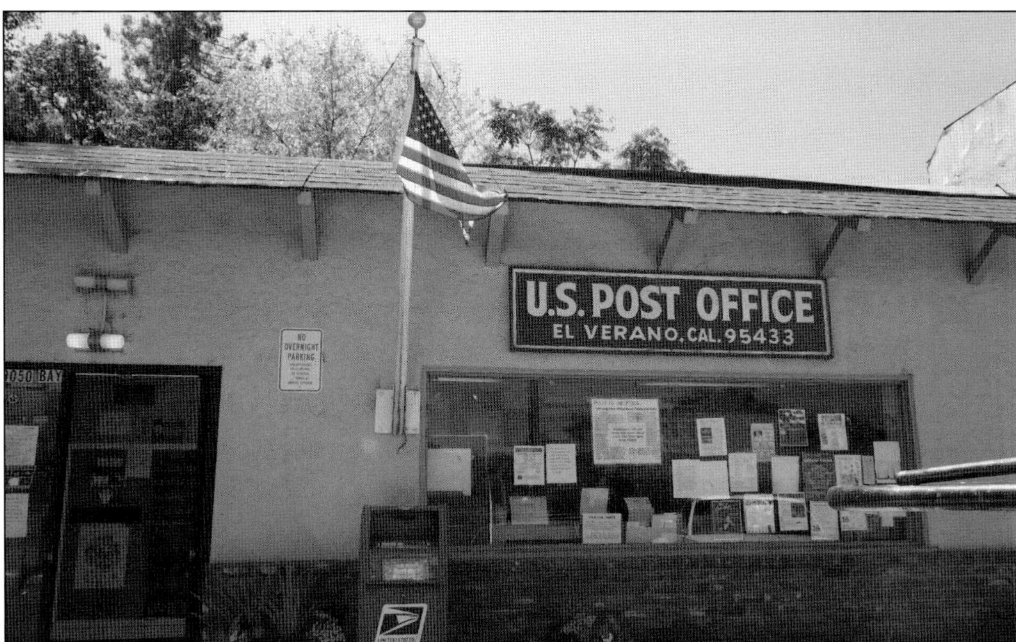

The El Verano Post Office was established in 1889 at Mullen's General Store (see page 95). In 1949, Emmett Mullen retired as postmaster, and Emmett Danieli took over, moving the post office to his new building just across the street. The post office and store continue to be the heart of the El Verano community.

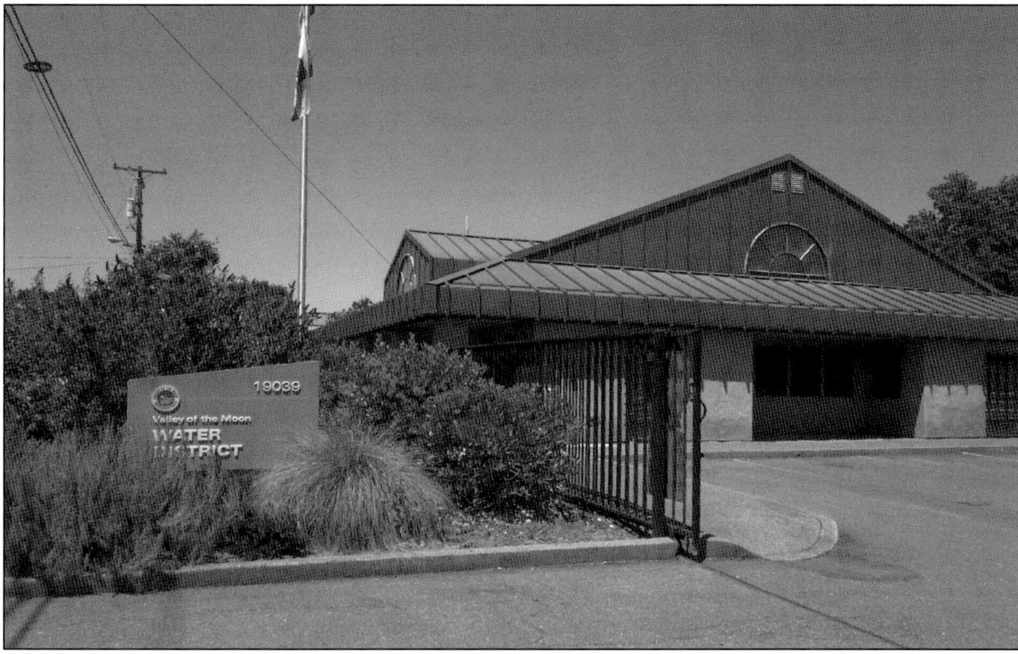

The Valley of the Moon Water District building was constructed in 1986 on the site of the grand El Verano railroad depot, which was demolished in 1984. The water district was formed in 1962 to serve the unincorporated communities of the valley and grew by incorporating some of the many small private water companies in the area. By 1975, the district was serving almost 15,000 residents. In 1994, the district office on Bay Street was adopted by Jerry the cat.

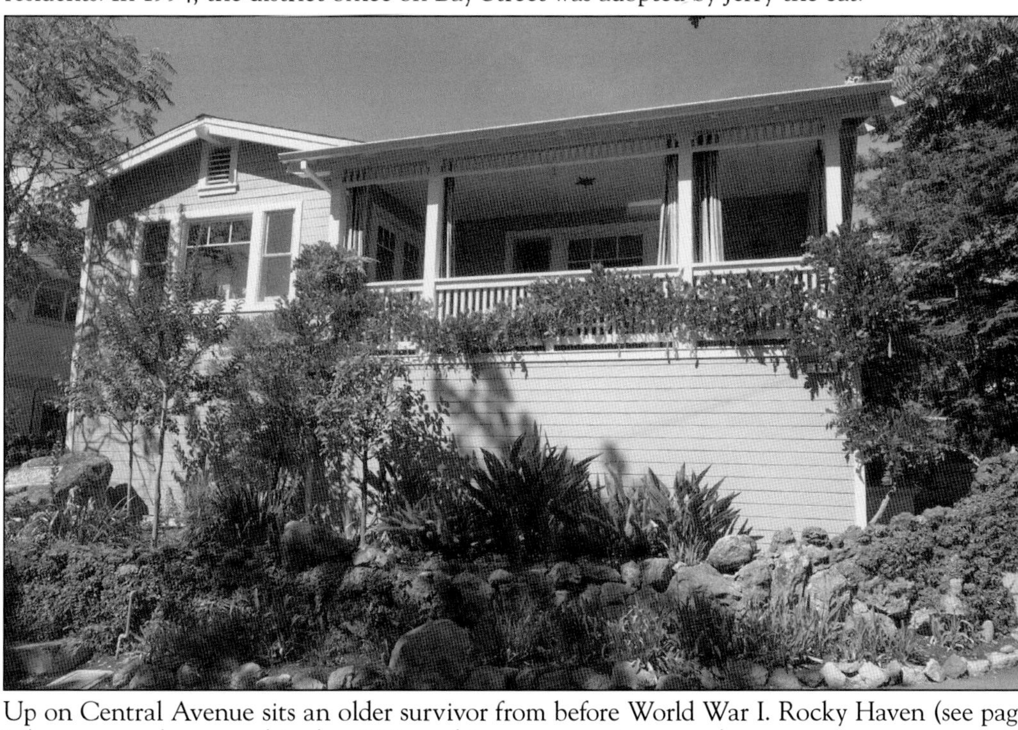

Up on Central Avenue sits an older survivor from before World War I. Rocky Haven (see page 24) was expertly restored in the 2000s and is now a vacation rental property.

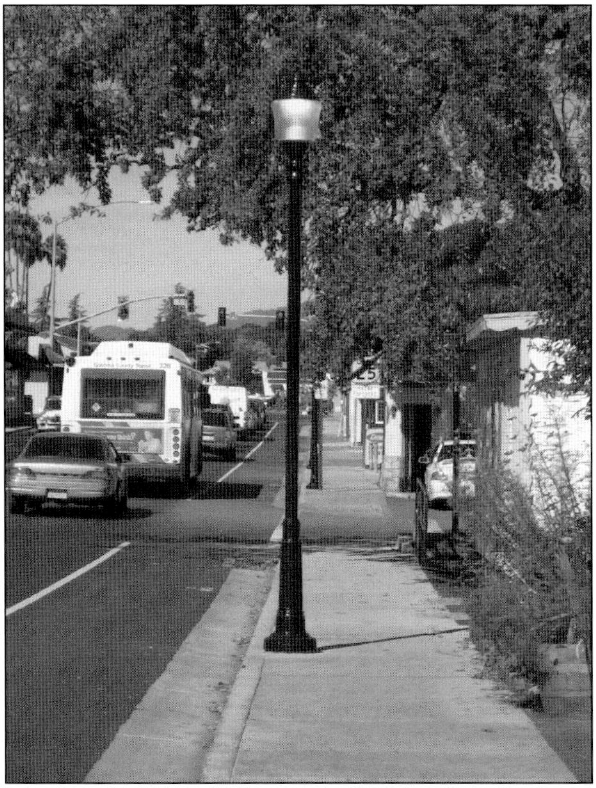

The culmination of planning for over 20 years, the streetlights and sidewalks of Highway 12 in the Springs reflect the citizens' confidence and pride.

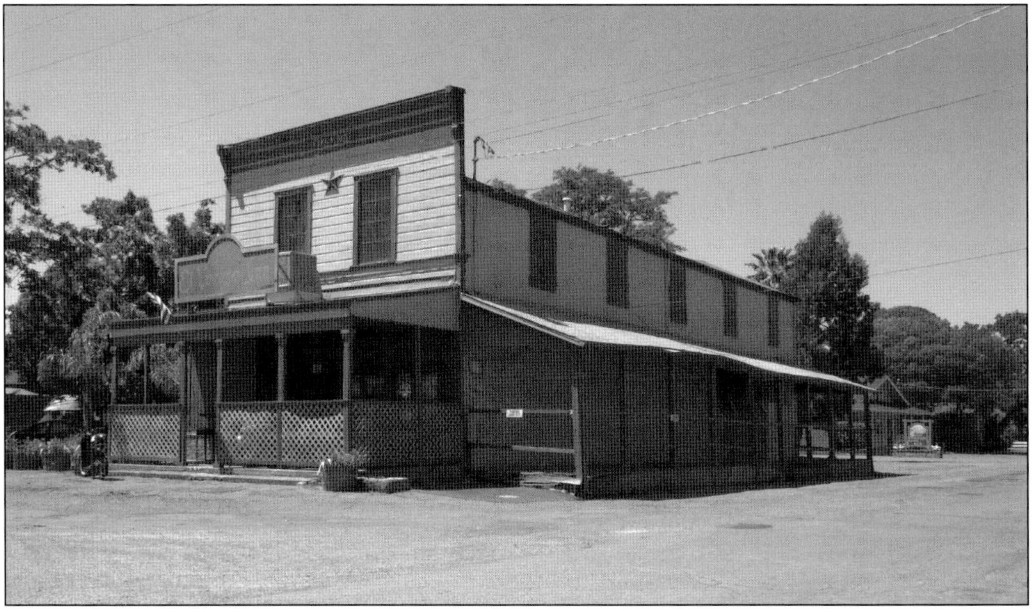

The El Verano Inn, built in 1887, is one of the few 19th-century structures left in "downtown" El Verano. The Mullen family took over the store and post office in 1900 and ran them until the 1950s. After it was Mullen's General Store, the place became Innskeep's Bar. Called the El Verano Inn since 1998, the decaying structure was completely restored in 2010 and may offer another 100 years of service to the community (see pages 33 and 95).

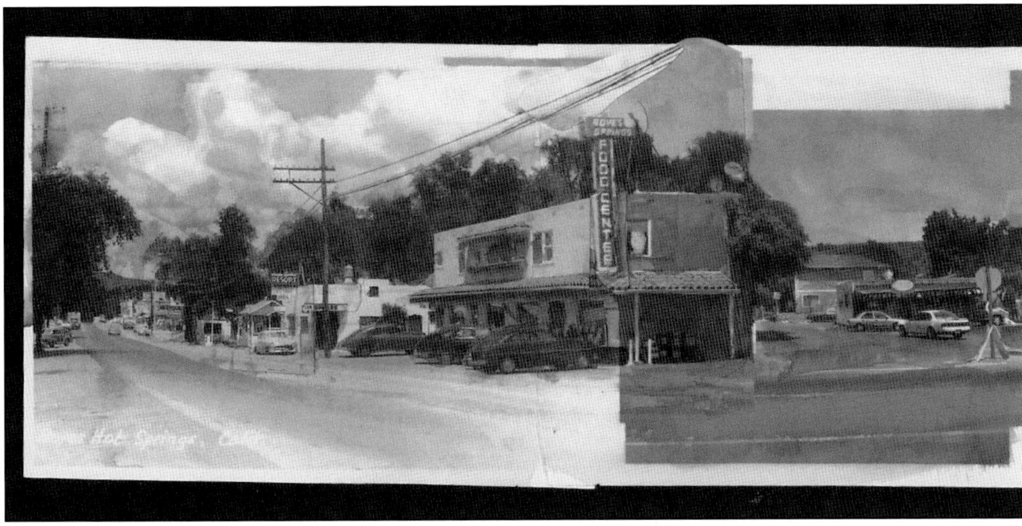

Since 2008, the author has been creating art about the Springs. This collage (split into two images) is part of the Valley of the Moon Main Stem Project, which combines contemporary and historic photographs of both sides of Highway 12 from Verano Avenue to Agua Caliente Boulevard.

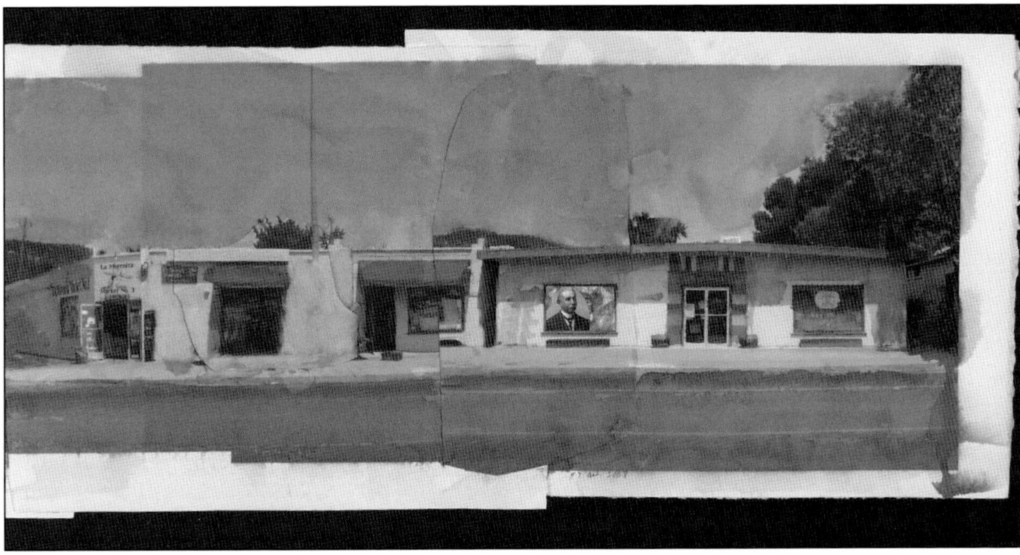

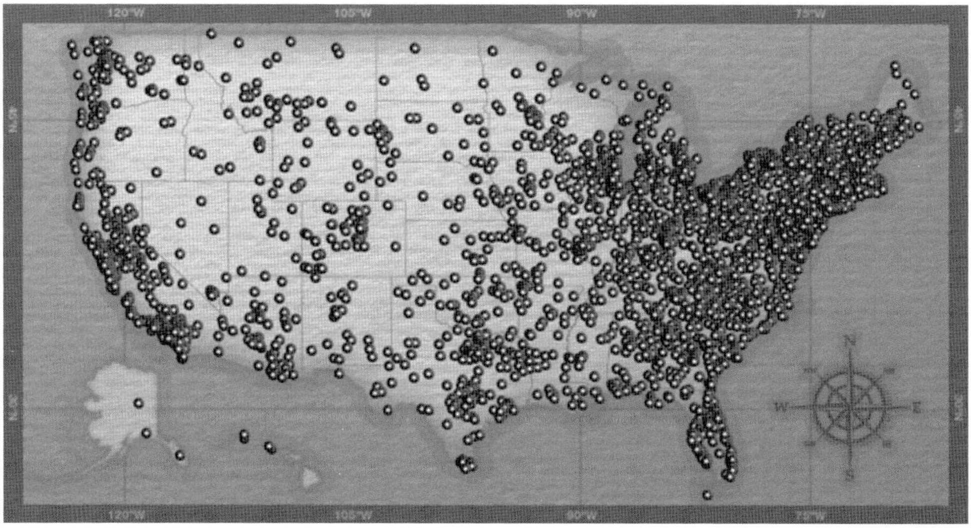